GENE KELLY

GENE KELLY

A biography

Clive Hirschhorn

Henry Regnery Company
Chicago

First published in Great Britain in 1974 by W. H. Allen
Published in the United States in 1975 by Henry Regnery Company
180 North Michigan Avenue, Chicago, Illinois 60601
Manufactured in the United States of America
Library of Congress Catalog Card Number: 74-27811
International Standard Book Number: 0-8092-8260-7

Acknowledgments

(*In alphabetical order*)

Gilbert Adair, Fiona Allan, Rupert Allen, John Altman, Clive Barnes, Ronald Bergen, Betsy Blair, The British Film Institute, Richard Brooks, Saul Chaplin, Miriam Clore, Jack Cole, Betty Comden, Michael Crawford, Irving Davies, Johnny Darrow, Stanley Donen, Racelle Feldman, Harold Feldman, Bob Fosse, Betty Garrett, Adolph Green, John Green, Mrs Anne Greenberg, Paul Helmick, Pauline Kael, Nora Kaye, Fred Kelly, John Kobal, Angela Lansbury, Mrs Fanny Lazaar, Frank Lazarus, Ernest Lehman, Max Loppert, John Mahoney, Walter Matthau, Frank McCarthy, Lois McClelland, Vincente Minnelli, Corin Moore, *New York Daily News*, Kerry Novick, Dale Olsen, Hermes Pan, Marilyn Parker, Joe Pasternak, Walter Plunkett, Dennis Powers, André Previn, Jay Radvansky, Debbie Reynolds, Richard Rodgers, William Saroyan, Dore Schary, Arthur Schwartz, Vivienne Segal, Sue Sharp, Phil Silvers, Jean Simmons, Frank Sinatra, John Springer, Jules Steinberg, *The Sunday Express*, Judy Tarlo, Charles Walters, Igor Youskevitch, and, immeasurably, Gene Kelly.

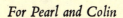

For Pearl and Colin

GENE KELLY

Foreword

The year was 1943, the picture *Anchors Aweigh*, and the producer was saying, 'Gene Kelly, meet your co-star, Frank Sinatra.'

Gene flashed that twinkly Irish smile and said, 'I've got a five-tube radio, so I know you can sing. The important thing is, can you dance?'

I pointed at my feet and issued a pronunciamento: 'These here babies can do anything I tell 'em to do!'

'Good,' said Gene. 'Tell 'em to do this!'

He popped straight up like a champagne cork, did a mid-air somersault, came down in a leg-split, and segued into a tap routine that sounded like a nest of angry machine-guns.

Suffice it to say, I was impressed, and fool that I was, when Gene volunteered to be my dance instructor, I accepted – with humble gratitude yet!

Cut to eight weeks later. I've got seven hundred torn ligaments, compound fractures in every bone in my body, and I've lost vitally needed weight. In fact, I'm down to $116\frac{1}{2}$. (Ounces! In 1943 I used to get weighed at the Parcel Post window.) But my wild Irish slave-driver paid me the ultimate compliment.

'Francis,' he said, 'you've worked your way up from lousy to adequate – I'm ready to dance on camera with you.'

Cut to thirty years later. The Kelly smile lights up a few wrinkles.

The Sinatra lean is well-marbled. Permissiveness in the movies has cut into public demand for our wholesome sailor-boy musicals. Recently, in fact, we've been limiting our terpsichore to an *entrechat* or two when we make a hole in one at Palm Springs. But not even a major sociological earthquake could dislodge me from my position as Gene Kelly's number one fan.

Time, which dulls the lustre of so many of our memories, can never tarnish the brilliance of Gene's achievements in the Hollywood film musical. *Singin' in the Rain*, to name but one. To me, all film musicals before and since look a bit Neanderthal by comparison. Whenever I project my precious print of *Singin' in the Rain*, I still ooh and ahh at his intensity of effort, and the emotional pictures he could paint with his dancing. What an imagination – always at fever pitch. Believe me, you could heat New York City with the fire of his creative candle!

More important to me is the creative warmth which Gene generates in the biggest business of all – daily life.

If Gene was endowed with total talent, so, too, was he endowed with total integrity. His fierce urge for perfection, his almost fanatical need for success, have always been matched by his need for justice for the less gifted, or less advantaged, whose paths crossed his. Gene climbed to the top but he didn't step on any hearts on his way up.

Yes, Mr Publisher, I know, I know! I'm only writing the Foreword, not the book. But let me have one last little paragraph –

If they ever get around to handing out Oscars for outstanding performance as a human being, you'll know where to find Ol' Blue Eyes – on the nominating committee rooting for his old buddy, Gene.

FRANK SINATRA
Hollywood, 1974

Singin' in the Rain

The scene is Grauman's Chinese Theatre, Hollywood, in 1927. Hollywood Boulevard is filled with an excited crowd who have come to see Don Lockwood and Lina Lamont arrive for the première of their latest film, *The Royal Rascal*. At a microphone stands Dora Bailey, a famous film columnist, whose resemblance both in looks and voice to Louella Parsons is unmistakable.

DORA (*highly excited*) This is Dora Bailey, ladies and gentlemen, talking to you from the front of the Chinese Theatre in Hollywood. What a night, ladies and gentlemen, what a night! Every star in Hollywood's heaven is here to make Monumental Pictures' première of *The Royal Rascal* the outstanding event of 1927. Everyone is breathlessly awaiting the arrival of Lina Lamont and Don Lockwood. Oh – look who's arriving now! It's that famous 'Zip Girl' Zelda Zanders – and her new red-hot pash – J. Cumberland Spendrill III, that well-known eligible bachelor.
CROWD (*screaming*) Ohhhhhhh!
DORA Zelda's had so much unhappiness. I hope this time it's really love. And look who's just arrived. It's that exotic star Olga Mara and her new husband, the Baron de la Bouvet de la Toulon.
CROWD Ohhhhhhhhhhh!

DORA They've been married two months already, but still as happy as newlyweds.

(*Another car pulls up*)

Well well well, it's –

(*There is an expectant hush*)

Cosmo Brown.

(*The crowd that has begun to lean forward expectantly is puzzled and disappointed.*)

Cosmo is Don Lockwood's best friend. He plays the piano on the set for Don and Lina to get them in those romantic moods.

(*Suddenly she is terribly excited*)

Oh, oh folks, this is it! This is it!

(*Two motorcycle policemen come roaring past the front of the theatre and stop, followed by a super-limousine that does likewise. A liveried doorman steps forward to open the door as the crowd cheers in expectation, and photographers rush forward to capture the great moment.*)

DORA (*transported*) The stars of tonight's picture, those romantic lovers of the screen – Don Lockwood and Lina Lamont!

(*Policemen are pushing photographers back, and as the blur of bodies clear away, we see Don Lockwood and Lina Lamont standing in front of the limousine door. They are a truly dazzling sight and the crowd goes insane.*)

Ladies and gentlemen, when you look at this gorgeous couple, it's no wonder they're a household name all over the world – like bacon and eggs – Lockwood and Lamont! Don, you can tell me confidentially, are these rumours true that wedding bells are going to ring for you and Lina?

DON Well, Lina and I have no statement to make at the present time. We're just good friends.

DORA You've come a long way together, Don. Won't you tell us how it all happened?

DON Well, Lina and I have made a number of pictures together.

DORA Oh no no, Don. I want your story from the beginning.

DON (*looking around self-effacingly*) Oh Dora, not in front of all these people.

CROWD (*as one*) Yes!

DORA But Don, the story of your success is an inspiration to young people all the world over. Please . . .

Part One

When Harriet Kelly gave birth to her third child, a son she called Eugene Curran – better known as Gene – on August 3rd, 1912, at the Sacred Heart Parish in Pittsburgh's Highland Park district, her husband, James Patrick Joseph Kelly, could not have been more delighted. For, following in the tradition of his Irish ancestors, it was his wish to have a family large enough to be counted in double numbers. His own parents had had eleven. But Harriet's had thirteen, which even James had to admit was a trifle excessive. Harriet's father, however, a wild Irishman called Billy Curran, never did do things by halves. A character peculiar to so much Irish–American fiction, Billy had emigrated to New York from Londonderry in 1845 (on the run, it would appear, from the English authorities) via Dunfermline in Scotland, where a relative helped him raise the fare for the long voyage over.

Once in New York, he took a job sweeping out a general store, which hardly proved to be a challenging or a well-paid occupation. So he decided to seek his fortune in the flourishing coal-mines of Huntington, West Virginia.

But not being an educated man, and totally ignorant of local geography, he stepped out of the train at Huntington, Pennsylvania – and found himself in a strange place, with no job, practically no money in hand and not a coal-mine in sight.

Undaunted, he obtained some temporary work, and soon met and charmed a certain Miss Eckhart who, after a brief courtship, accepted his proposal of marriage.

Though Miss Eckhart – whose family originally came over from Alsace-Lorraine and settled in Maryland – was socially superior to her husband, Billy took it all in his Irish stride – especially as the Eckharts had property on the State Line, and were fairly comfortably off.

So, with a certain amount of finance behind him now, it wasn't long before he moved to the mining town of Houtzdale, Pennsylvania, where, it is said, he put a 'divining stick' to excellent use by discovering a small coal-mine, buying the piece of land on which the mine was situated, and instead of working the mine, opened a general store.

As he began to accumulate money, so he accumulated sons and daughters all of whom helped out, in time, with the family business. Finally, with their purses full, Billy and his offspring moved to Pittsburgh wealthy enough to live in the best part of town, and to open an impressive saloon at the corner of 6th and Wiley Avenue.

One Saturday night after closing time, Billy was walking home with the takings when he was attacked by a couple of thugs who robbed him and left him lying in the gutter. He was only discovered after a couple of hours, and died of pneumonia a few days later, leaving each of his nine remaining children (four having died) $50,000 apiece – which they rapidly blew. Harriet lost hers in the Depression of 1907. At the time she had just married James Kelly who was unable to dissuade her from sinking her entire fortune into real estate.

Three of Harriet's brothers – Frank, Edward and Harry, lost their inheritances through bad clothing-store investments, and her brother John and sister Lillian lost theirs trying to bail them and Harriet out; while Gus, the youngest, the most brilliant and the most colourful of all the Currans, told everyone he was off to Notre-Dame University – then disappeared for a couple of years to see the world. He returned home, a penniless alcoholic and, to the end of his life, a constant source of pain and embarrassment to Harriet, who hated the 'brawling Irish' in him, just as she hated the fact that her father once ran a saloon. If one *had* to be Irish, then rather the lace-curtain variety than the shanty-town type. In her view, Uncle Gus was about as shanty-town in his behaviour as it was possible to be.

Unlike her son Gene (the Eugene was abbreviated as soon as he started high school, initially to his distaste because he considered Gene a girl's name) – who remains intrigued by his heritage and enjoys to the full what he calls the 'ferocious Irishness of the Irish' – his mother, at the time of his birth in 1912, felt a certain shame at being what she was because of America's long history of discrimination against the Irish. The Irish were the labourers and menials who, like the Chinese, were put to back-breaking work such as railroad building. In Boston, there were even signs which warned the Irish to 'keep off the grass'. 'No dogs or Irish' read another. It was a state of affairs which persisted until John F. Fitzgerald (Rose Kennedy's father) became Mayor of Boston in 1906–7 and 1910–14. Before they took over political control in the large cities, the Irish were regarded as scum, and Harriet Kelly who, with relief, could at least claim that her mother's name was Eckhart, did her best to draw a shroud over her husband's antecedents and stubbornly refused to acknowledge that her grandfather was the son of an Irishman.

To Harriet Kelly, being Irish was the same as being an alcoholic – for there was no denying it: the Irish–Americans did drink, if only to drown their sorrows and anaesthetise themselves against the discrimination they encountered.

James Kelly's grandfather, a blacksmith who arrived in America with a few items of clothing and his blacksmith's hammer, had reputedly travelled from Ireland with a man called Lord Peterborough – an absentee landlord from England who, so the story goes, took pity on the Irish potato families, and brought over a boatload of them to Canada with him. They settled in Peterborough, Ontario, a place he modestly named after himself. Whether this is true or not – and no one has been able to authenticate the story – James Patrick Joseph Kelly was born in 1875 in Peterborough, Ontario, among colonies of French, English and Irish loggers who worked various parts of the rivers and lakes in the district and, one might say, were constantly at loggerheads with each other. It was a rough period of American history.

James Kelly claimed that his father was a landscape gardener who owned several acres of land. Again, this has not been verified and could have been a story invented by James to impress Harriet and make her feel that the man she was marrying was a little less 'shanty-town' than she supposed. Honesty, it appears, was always more of a hindrance than a help. For example, Harriet Kelly would never tell the truth about her age. And the reason was simple. Harriet's eldest sister, who was very religious, never married – thus putting Harriet in a most embarrassing position: for she did not want to have people think that she was older than she really was – as in the late nineteenth century it was customary for the eldest sister to marry first. It was also necessary, therefore, for James's age to remain a secret, because Harriet feared that if people knew how old *he* was, they might somehow deduce her age from it. So, whenever his children asked James his age, he would reply, 'sweet sixteen'. It wasn't until his death in 1966 that his true birth date was revealed. Harriet Kelly, who died in 1972, took her secret to the grave with her – and no one quite knows whether she was eighty-five, eighty-seven or eighty-nine.

James Kelly journeyed down from Peterborough, Ontario, as a young man of twenty-eight and, in order to make life easier for himself, became a naturalised American citizen. After spending time in Buffalo, St Louis and Philadelphia as a phonograph salesman, he finally settled in Pittsburgh, working as a shop assistant on salary and commission for the Edison Phonograph Company, and then for the Columbia Phonograph Company. He met Harriet at an amateur concert in which she was appearing and, a year later, in 1906, they married.

Though by no means a wealthy man, James was doing quite well, and on their return from honeymooning in Ontario, where he took his bride against her will to meet his family, they moved into a house on Portland and Bryant Street near Highland Park – where Gene's eldest sister Harriet (called Jay) and elder brother James were born. James and Harriet Kelly were to have two more children – Louise, born in 1914, and Fred, born in 1916 – making a total of five. Not as impressive a number as James had hoped, but times were changing and large families were less fashionable than they used to be.

Shortly after his marriage, James discovered he could make more money as a travelling salesman than serving behind a counter, and he went on the road. Within a year, he was one of Columbia's most successful employees. As he never learned to drive, he took his sample records and phonographs with him by train (using the time between destinations to improve his chess by playing with any stranger who cared to) and spent five out of seven days a week away from home, returning to his family every weekend.

The Kellys lived in Portland Street until 1914, then moved to a modest house in Mellon Street in East Liberty where Louise and Fred were born. Their neighbours were a policeman, a bricklayer, a plumber and a mail carrier. The neighbourhood, Gene recalls, was as nearly a slum as it was possible for a decent neighbourhood to be. But at the time it was all James could comfortably afford. Seven people, he was to discover, could not live as cheaply as two.

The houses in the street were straight out of *The Valley of Decision*, and all looked alike. The Kelly home had a small living-room and dining-room, a tiny room at the back of the house, and three small bedrooms. Gene and his brother Jim shared one of the rooms, Jay and Louise another, while Fred, the baby, slept in a cot in his parents' room.

The neighbourhood in which they lived approximated a slum not only in appearance, but in the behaviour of its inhabitants who were pretty rough as well. Many first-generation immigrant families lived there. They were tough steel-workers who spoke little English – their home tongues being Polish or Slavik – and a man was judged on how much he could drink, or how well he could use his fists. As there were no recreation parks, the children played in the streets and became involved in fights, some of them very serious, with rocks and clubs.

On an average week, James Kelly would earn about seventy-five dollars, and in an exceptional one, a hundred and twenty-five – enough to keep his family well fed and well clothed, and to pay all the bills. Though he was away all week, he was still very much the head of the household, and instilled in his children the good, old-fashioned virtues of honesty and respect. He took great pride in his family, and trusted them. They, in turn, adored and respected him – at the same time fearing his Irish temper (which Gene was to inherit), unleashed only when his authority was questioned, or when it was disobeyed. Otherwise he was relaxed and easygoing, a man of immense personal charm and magnetism, and a favourite with the ladies.

His philosophy was simple: a man must get ahead in life. There could be no finer achievement than to reach the top of one's chosen profession, no matter what it was. And to James Kelly, a prerequisite for success was sartorial elegance and personal cleanliness. Whatever the circumstances, a man's nails, he believed, should always be clean and, regardless of the weather, he should always wear a vest and a tie. Even in his leisure moments, in the privacy of his own home, it was only proper that a man should be fully clothed – just in case some unexpected caller knocked at the door. Years later, Gene was to rebel against this trait in his father's personality by deliberately refusing to wear formal dress except when absolutely unavoidable. His own description of himself as 'a walking slum' is somewhat harsh – though it is true that Gene's nonchalance and indifference when it came to clothing was well known throughout Hollywood.

For James, however, it would have been inconceivable to sit down at the dinner table without a jacket. The same applied to his sons. And if, for any reason, one of his children left the table before the dessert was served, he or she was not allowed to return. He was a man who revered the rituals of domesticity, and did not tolerate change easily.

Each Friday night, the family would dress up, the girls in pretty frocks, the boys in Buster Brown suits and collars – and march off to the station to meet him. Fred recalls that his father was so proper and correct that, walking back from the station, he scrupulously avoided taking a short cut through a well-worn field because of a notice warning that 'trespassers would be prosecuted'. 'The sign,' said Fred, 'was a mere formality. A joke. And everyone ignored it – and had done for years. But not our father. If he was told not to trespass, he didn't – and no arguments.'

He was a religious man who said his prayers twice a day; the nearest he came to having a vice was drink. For, much to the chagrin of his wife, James Patrick Joseph Kelly, Irish to his fingertips, liked to drink. Happily, he did most of his drinking on the road until, of course, prohibition closed the bars and forced America's boozers into speakeasies. As James refused to go to speakeasies, he took to bringing his liquor home – usually a couple of bottles of whisky at a time. His wife was terrified they would be raided by the police and her husband exposed and arrested. But James Kelly drank his way through the Depression without incident.

Once, all three boys, unknown to each other, each brought home three cases of beer as a Christmas gift for their father, which they then carefully hid. Harriet Kelly, however, discovered the cases, and was bitterly disappointed. 'Look Dad,' she said, pointing to the nine cases of beer stacked one on top of the other, '*that's* what your sons think of you!'

But in spite of his predilection for booze, James remained remarkably trim and healthy throughout his life, displaying a passionate interest in sports. Not only was he a fine athlete and boxer, who worked out with dumb-bells and Indian clubs at home, he was also a first-rate ice-skater and hockey player. So was his son Gene, whom he coached and encouraged. 'He had me in double runners when I was four,' Gene said. 'By the time I was six, I could skate like a wizard. The winters in Pittsburgh were very cold, and what he would do was take a hosepipe and freeze over our backyard. Then he'd teach us some fundamentals of ice-skating. After we learned to stay on our feet, we'd all go off to Homewood cemetery, where there was this huge lake which froze over in winter – and we'd skate ourselves into a state of perfection. I was particularly good, and by the time I was eight, there wasn't a kid in the neighbourhood who could outskate me.'

Sunday in the Kelly household was always a family day. It was also considered a holy day. After Mass, for which the family dressed formally, Gene remembers not being allowed to roller skate, play in the back alley, nor make a noise in any way: they were, however, allowed to read the 'funny papers'. Inevitably, Gene began to react against his strict religious upbringing and, already in his junior year at high school, was moving towards atheism. He began to read H. G. Wells's *Outline of History*, and for a year refused to believe in religion as a concept by which to live. In his senior year at high school, he was, he says, well on the way to reform, and once again became a devout Catholic. But in his second year at college, he changed his ideas yet again and was determinedly agnostic. As a young boy, however, he was in no position to rebel against his family's beliefs, and every Sunday, he dutifully accepted the rules laid down by his father.

Five times a year, however, Mr Kelly relaxed his Sunday strictures – for all of his children's birthdays were celebrated on a Sunday so that he could be present. Mrs Kelly did not believe in having organised parties to which other children were invited because the five Kellys, she argued, constituted a self-contained group themselves, and there was no point in going to all that added expense.

As a special treat, the birthday boy or girl could choose whatever menu he or she wanted, regardless of how unbalanced it might be. Gene, who adored cakes, naturally chose an assortment of cakes and cookies. Jim liked pies. Louise fancied breaded veal cutlets. Jay had a passion for raisins, and Fred made himself sick on candy and ice-cream. As no one was invited to these gatherings, the only presents they received came from within the family.

Holidays and occasions such as St Valentine's day were celebrated in the Kelly household in fine style – with each member of the family receiving a Valentine as part of a special St Valentine's day meal – while the table was decorated with St Valentine's day napkins, usually designed by Jay. On St Patrick's day there would once again be the appropriate napkins and decorations – as well as special ice-cream with a shamrock on it or a cake with green frosting.

July 4th was always celebrated with fireworks, which the children were not allowed to light until Mr and Mrs Kelly came home from the traditional Independence Day ball game.

But the biggest, most exciting holiday of all was Christmas. 'We'd all go to bed on Christmas Eve,' Jay recalled, 'and when we came down at five-thirty, on our way to Mass, the living-room would be transformed. From nowhere there would be an enormous tree laden with presents and decorated from top to bottom with tinsel and paper bells. This was always a thrilling moment for us.'

The highlight of the Kellys' year, however, was their annual holiday from June through September. At first, the family rented a place in Ripley, Lake Erie – where the children, having just learned to walk, were already becoming expert swimmers. But after a couple of years, a client of James's told him of a spot on Lake

Conneaut in Western Pennsylvania – in the heart of the territory he served. James investigated it, and there and then decided it should become the family's summer paradise – which it was from 1916 to 1924. Harriet Kelly always took her children out of school two weeks before the term ended and brought them back two weeks after the new term began, knowing that very little work was done during those periods. She was anxious to get her children away from the heat and grime of industrial Pittsburgh and into the country as soon as possible, for as long as possible. She also realised it cost less to live at the lake, and anything that saved money was a prime consideration to Harriet Kelly, whose obsession, next to the success of her children, was thrift.

Gene remembers these summers as the most idyllic of his life. The formal dress his father insisted on at home, and which he hated, no longer applied, and he needn't even wear shoes if he did not want to. A shirt, a pair of shorts and a bathing suit were all that was required.

The family would arrive by train from Pittsburgh via Linesville, Pennsylvania, pile into a taxi, and drive out from the station to the lake and the small double-storeyed cottage they had rented. Then the long, leisurely holiday would begin.

The five Kelly children would wake up at seven each morning, eat a hearty breakfast which Mrs Kelly had started preparing an hour before, then disappear until supper time. There was no fixed pattern to their activities, but they usually swam, played tennis, rode their bikes, went horse-riding, or rented a canoe for a couple of hours.

Each child was given a cash allowance for the summer, which was immediately handed back to Mrs Kelly to bank ; she kept a strict note of everyone's finances, subtracting whatever was spent from the total amount until, inevitably, there was nothing left. The main items of expenditure were rentals for canoes and horses and, in Fred's case, buying as much candy as he could eat. As Gene was physically the most active member of the family, he usually ran out of money first.

They would watch the local farmers milking their cows, go fishing, shoot blackbirds, which Mrs Kelly would bake into a pie, or pick blackberries for the same purpose. On the rare occasions that it rained, the five Kelly children would go indoors and read, or rely on Jay to invent a new game for them – such as the one she called 'Cheese' in which she would place a large piece of cheese with holes in it on the floor and have them aim marbles at the holes.

As he did at home in Pittsburgh, James Kelly would only arrive for the weekends and in those pre-air-conditioned days, the cool of the lakeside was very welcome. He loved the country with a passion, and delighted in being able to ride or swim or fish with his children. He would take them on extensive nature study walks, pointing out along the way winter-green, cabbage and Queen Ann Lace. He would help them pick apples and elderberries, or take them rowing along the lake. As long as it was out of doors, it hardly mattered what they did.

Occasionally the children would put on a show of their own devising for some of the other kids along the lake. Gene would direct it, and Fred, who from the age of four was permanently stage-struck, would be the star turn. They also offered to teach any of the children who might be interested, how to sing, dance and even recite.

One year, as a bonus, Harry Greb, the lightweight champion of the world, was at a training camp near the lake, and offered to give Gene a few boxing lessons. It was just what Gene needed to help him protect himself back home in East Liberty from the thugs who were constantly needling him into fights.

At the time, Gene and his brothers were going to St Raphael's, which was a Catholic school, and almost daily, on their way home, they would be jumped on by kids from the local Protestant school. They generally picked on Gene because, as a child, he was conspicuously undersized and looked utterly defenceless. At ten, when he was in the sixth grade, he was an easy target for the bully boys of the street corners. Not until he turned fifteen did he begin to grow – and even then he was never particularly tall.

As far back as he can remember, Gene was obsessed with sports, and one of the traumas of his young life was the realisation that he wasn't tall enough to be good at certain games that required height – football, and especially basket-ball. But there was no holding him back from gymnastics or ice-hockey, and any team he graced would usually win. Gene was a 'spark plug' on the field, whose speed and

24

energy ignited his team-mates and drew from them play of a breathtaking nature. Immodestly, he describes himself as a 'Mozart of the ice rink' and at twelve years old was playing against adults, and beating them. There was never any doubt that one day he would be playing baseball for the Pittsburgh Pirates.

In his senior year at high school, Gene managed to overcome the problem of his height and captained the second football team, even though, as Fred recalled, his team-mates formed a protective barrier around him whenever he seemed threatened.

Throughout his childhood, Gene revealed an aggressive, competitive streak which he never lost, and the youthful scraps he had with his local neighbourhood louts certainly toughened him up and developed in him his taste for a challenge.

'Because I was so small,' he said, 'I felt that I always had to prove myself, and the best way to do this was with my fists. I wasn't going to be pushed around by anyone. Especially not by the older guys with whom I played football, and whose standards I tried to emulate. Looking back now, I realise I must have annoyed them intensely with my insistence that I was just as good as they were. But I had this obsession to prove to them I was.'

In his early teens, Gene was physically no match for these boys. He became one of Mellon Street's more familiar sights – battered, bruised and bloodied, limping painfully home, determined, in spite of his throbbing wounds, to try harder next time.

Gene's wounds, however, were not confined to the football field or the street corner. As a child he was singularly accident-prone, and at the age of six, while riding a tricycle without handlebars on Mellon Street, he lurched forward on to an exposed piece of cast iron. The metal went through his cheek, causing a deep gash which bled profusely. Mrs Kelly was out at the time, and a neighbour, hearing him cry, rushed him home, and as his wound continued to pour blood into the kitchen sink over which he was perched, she called the family doctor who stitched him up. To this day he carries the evidence of the accident in the shape of a small, half-moon scar on the right side of his face. When he first arrived in Hollywood in 1941, certain studio photographers touched up the scar, but Gene himself never bothered to conceal it in any of his films, and it has become an acceptable part of his appearance.

Another time, while still at grade school, he was driving a home-made sled down a busy street when he was knocked over by a lorry. The sled was a wreck, though Gene escaped injury. He had rolled under the lorry, miraculously escaping its wheels by inches.

Gene was the only member of the five Kellys who ever got sick. His brothers and sisters managed to avoid even the usual childhood diseases. But Gene had them all and, when he was seven, a serious bout of pneumonia nearly killed him. His parents were particularly concerned that his lungs might be permanently damaged, but he recovered completely and, like his adored Uncle Gus, who at sixty could perform tricks on the parallel bars which would have tested much younger men, Gene became a superb gymnast. The combination of Uncle Gus's guidance and inspiration, plus his own determination to excel spectacularly, resulted in his complete mastery of the sport, one more he could add to a list which already included swimming, lacrosse, skating and, of course, ice-hockey. He did not know at the time that his brilliant gymnastic ability was to prove invaluable to him in later years.

All the Kelly children, it turned out, were good at games, exercised regularly and ate healthily. Mrs Kelly believed in a diet which, above all, favoured dairy products, a certain amount of meat (but never on Friday), potatoes, salads, a green vegetable with each meal and, as an indulgence, dessert. (Gene disliked vegetables, and when no one was looking would flick them on to his brother Jim's plate, or whoever happened to be sitting next to him.)

A sound body and a sound mind was Harriet Kelly's simple belief, the one being useless without the other.

If her husband encouraged his children to take part in sports and instilled in them a love of nature, Mrs Kelly was responsible for their interest in the arts. They could not idly sit around doing nothing in her formidable presence. 'If you're bored, I'll find something for you to do,' she told her children – and she usually did.

She was a plump, small woman with brown hair and brown eyes and a determined, dynamic personality characterised by a profound sense of the practical. 'Never talk about politics or religion, and never ask anyone their age,' she used to impress upon them. 'They're sensitive subjects and it only ends up in an argument.' She dreamed the American dream for her family, and had a faith in their combined abilities that would have frightened children less determined to succeed than hers were. Though she herself could neither sing, dance, paint, nor play a musical instrument, there was little, as far as she was concerned, that Jay or Jim, Gene, Louise or Fred could not do. All they needed was encouragement for their talent. She knew it wouldn't be easy, and that she would have to work hard on their behalf. But hard work had never worried her, and like Gene, she never refused a challenge. What she *did* refuse was to fight – and she always made a distinction between working and fighting. For the word 'fight' implied a battle for something which wasn't one's due. Immigrants, for example, fought for some sort of recognition and acceptance. They *had* to fight in order to belong. But Harriet Kelly and her brood were not immigrants. They were red-blooded Americans, born and bred in the 'greatest country in the world and whose birthright it was to succeed.' She was motivated, too, by the contempt she had for her Irish background and wanted her children to be better than she was.

So as soon as they could walk, she saw to it that they took music lessons and attended dancing classes – whether they wanted to or not. From the age of seven Gene remembers being dressed in his neat Buster Brown suit and being taken to a dance school in downtown Pittsburgh by his determined mother. He remembers, too, the taunts and jeers of the rough neighbourhood thugs who would place their hands on their hips effeminately and call him a sissy. As he got older and the derisive comments continued, Gene found that every Saturday when he went to dance school, he became involved in a fight somewhere between school and home. At one stage things got so bad that Mrs Kelly threw thrift to the winds and sent her boys to and from their classes by taxi!

Gene and Jim hated these lessons. Together with Fred they were the only boys in a class full of girls and they felt self-conscious and out of place. Gene would much rather have been playing hockey or football. But his mother insisted that dancing was necessary for poise and posture and there was nothing the two boys could do about it but sulk. They even found themselves part of an act Mrs Kelly was proud to call, quite simply, The Five Kellys, which played amateur nights with great success. They would also split up and dance in pairs: Jim and Gene, Louise and Fred, Jay and Jim. As they grew older they each began to dance separately, except Jim, who dropped out of it completely, adamantly refusing to be drawn into the family's 'amateur theatricals' which he loathed. Fred, on the other hand, was a more than willing customer. He was the 'cutie pie' of the family who took as easily and naturally to tap-dancing as Rogers did to Astaire. From the age of four, show-business had entered his blood and become his way of life. He was a natural performer, and nothing gave him so much pleasure as dancing. Entertaining others became his whole reason for living, so much so Jay recalls, that when they were both older, and she found herself on a 'dumb date' with some guy, she would rope Fred in to amuse her and her beau and brighten up the evening.

After the family's fortunes improved in 1924, they moved out of Mellon Street to a large three-storey house in Kensington Street. Though heavily mortgaged, it was the first house James Kelly had ever bought and one of its features was a spacious basement in which young Fred – aged eight – would stage puppet and magic shows for the other kids in the neighbourhood. Gene, he recalls, had very little to do with these shows. 'He never did like small-time show-biz, though occasionally he would agree to help out with the props. He always believed that if you couldn't do something in a big way, don't do it at all. For example, when Gene and I went out on the road as a dance duo, he hated playing the joints and cloops (a cross between a club and a chicken-coop), as we called them. But not me. The tackier and more down to earth they were, the better I liked them.'

When he was ten, Fred remembers gathering together a handful of the local children to demonstrate a 'great escape' act he had seen Houdini perform at the Stanley Theatre. He asked Gene to tie him in a strait-jacket made from flour sacks, manacle him with a pair of handcuffs from a policeman's toy kit, and chain him with a pair of bicycle chains. He then sat in a high-backed chair, and copying the great Houdini, attempted to rock himself free. But Gene, who rivalled Jay as the most mischievous member of the Kelly family, fixed the chains to the chair in such a way that made it impossible for Fred to free himself, so that when he started to rock to and fro, he fell and hurt his head badly.

Another of Fred's ideas was to stage a dog show in the backyard. Admission was three cents and the star attraction was a long-suffering puppy beset with stage-fright, which would shake uncontrollably whenever there were more than two people in the room with it. It was Gene's idea to put a veil under the terrified dog's chin and place the animal on a rickety wooden box so that the more nervous it became, the more it (and the box) would shake. Fred put a piece of exotic Eastern music on the phonograph, probably 'The Sheik of Araby', introduced 'Little Fatima – the Egyptian Hound' and watched delightedly as the dog shimmied hysterically. At the end of the show, the animals were rewarded with choice bits of dog food, and in the ensuing scramble, chaos reigned. Years later, the film *Summer Stock* had a sequence in which Gene and Phil Silvers are similarly inundated by a pack of over-enthusiastic hounds.

Life in Kensington Street was altogether more comfortable than it had been for the previous ten years in East Liberty. The neighbourhood was middle-class and the family enjoyed a complete sense of belonging. Each of the five children had his or her bedroom, there was a sizeable living-room and dining-room, and a basement, as well as two large porches at the front and back. The outside of the house was covered with climbing roses. Two willow trees, one of which was 'adopted' by Jay, the other by Gene, dominated the smallish garden.

Though today the area has undergone massive development and has grown considerably, in 1924 it was almost like living in the country. The top floors overlooked Frick Park and the Wilkinsberg Hills, and the views were enchanting. All in all, the Kellys could not have been more delighted with their purchase. Arnold Boys' School, a private establishment they did not attend, but whose sports fields and facilities Gene made excellent use of, was a few minutes' walk away, and Peabody High only a short trolley ride.

At school the Kellys were keen, alert pupils whose report cards usually commended them for their vivid imaginations. Gene and Jay, who were very close in temperament, were the brightest academically, as well as the most energetic. Louise, on the other hand, was the serious member of the family. 'Everybody adored her,' said Gene. 'She was well-mannered and lady-like and nothing was too much trouble for her. We all thought of her as the Blessed

Virgin Mary, totally without guile or faults. She was certainly the most loved member of us all.'

Unlike his brothers and sisters, Jim Kelly was never much interested in the family as a unit. At his mother's insistence, he took dancing lessons with the rest of them, but he hated show-business and, as soon as he was old enough to assert himself, he fought for and won his independence. He was a talented painter who became a commercial artist – much to the disappointment of his mother who, in spite of her interest in the arts, felt that he should have become an engineer. The arts, she believed, were fine as hobbies – unless, of course, one was as conspicuously talented as Fred. But Gene and Jim, she felt, were destined for more important things than the stage – especially Gene who, she was sure, had all it took to become a brilliant lawyer. And in the mid-twenties, even a moderately successful lawyer could earn up to five thousand dollars a year.

Meanwhile she was not slow to capitalise on her youngest child's talent and, as soon as she recognised his ability, took him out on jobs in and around Pittsburgh which would pay up to ten dollars a time. It didn't matter whether he was appearing at an amateur night, or at the Golden Rock Showboat whenever it arrived in town. What was important was that her son was using his God-given talent to its best advantage. When he was seven years old, in 1923, she would take him to any little honky-tonk that would have him. By the time he was eight, he did an adagio dance with a six-year-old girl. His little partner would jump off a high piano and into his arms for their 'big finish'.

In a good month, Fred could earn up to fifty dollars in one-night stands, and although the money was not vital to the Kellys in 1924, it was still nice to have. Besides, Mrs Kelly was never one to turn up her nose at ready cash. At the same time, though 'very gentle with a buck' (as Phil Silvers once described Gene), she was never mean. She did not believe in false economies, and bought the best clothes for her children, but always at discount prices – even if it meant walking her feet off to find exactly what she wanted. She hated spending money unnecessarily and could never bring herself to tip: on the rare occasions she and James went out to dinner together, she would take exception to his leaving a quarter behind on the plate, arguing, with a certain amount of logic, that she did three times as much work as any waitress at home without being tipped for it. Anyway, she thought tipping was 'flash' – a cheap way of flaunting one's money. Equally, she never allowed her children to take money from neighbours who sent them on errands.

As a young woman Mrs Kelly had always been keen on the theatre, and if her father had not been so strict with her, she might have tried to make the stage her career – though there is no evidence that she had any genuine talent. But whether she had or not, the professional theatre was no place for a lady at the turn of the century, as she herself was all too well aware; so any yearnings she had for the stage were adequately satisfied by amateur shows in church halls. The very week before Jay was born, she was appearing in a production of *The College Widow*.

Harriet never ever lost her love for show-business, and was delighted to be able to enjoy a vicarious career on the boards first through Fred, and later through Gene. She would accompany her children to all the shows that passed through Pittsburgh – usually at the Nixon Theatre – even if it meant taking them out of school for the day. Jay remembers seeing Billie Burke one afternoon because her mother thought it just as vital to her education as the history class she would be missing. Mary Wigman, a great exponent of modern dance, was another artiste Mrs Kelly insisted they all see. The Kellys also paid regular visits to Pittsburgh's two vaudeville houses, the Davis and the Sheridan – usually after dancing class on Saturday. By the time they were in their teens, there wasn't an act on any of the big touring circuits they hadn't seen – or, when they entered the business themselves, copied.

At home, Mrs Kelly, who was proud of the fact she once took elocution lessons, would attempt to interest her family in the 'legitimate' theatre by declaiming such epic stanzas as Spartacus' 'Address to the Gladiators', while her five kids sat listening to her politely.

She would also insist they each played a musical instrument. After all, she maintained, no self-respecting family could consider itself fully accomplished without this most necessary of skills. Jay, Louise and Jim played the piano, Fred the drums and Gene the violin. When visitors called, they would be asked to perform, and all but Fred hated this. Gene, who was nine years old at the time, was particularly resentful of the time he spent practising when he could be playing ice-hockey. But there was no use complaining. Once again, he and the rest were victims of their mother's stubborn belief that, in addition to everything else, they could all be *virtuosi*.

The violin lessons cost twenty-five cents an hour, and James Kelly provided his son with a quarter-sized violin acquired from a client who owned a music store. A year later, when Gene's regular teacher quit because of lack of pupils, Mrs Kelly, undaunted, found another in Bloomfield and, amid much protestation, packed Gene off to him even though it took two trolley-cars and ninety minutes to get there and back. And until she was confident that Gene could manage the trip on his own, she accompanied him herself.

At St Raphael's school the following year, he continued his lessons with one of the nuns, so that by the time he entered Peabody High School in 1926, he was playing extremely well. All the same, he hated it, and it was not until he broke his arm in a football game and had it in plaster for a couple of weeks, that his mother finally gave in and told him he needn't continue with his lessons if he really did not want to.

To Gene this represented a breakthrough. It meant he was finally growing up, and that his mother was beginning to respect his wishes. In gratitude, he compromised and took up the banjo instead. Not the classiest of instruments; but at least it was better than nothing, and Mrs Kelly never complained.

She also made quite sure her children could read long before they went to school. She believed that as long as a person was illiterate, he might just as well be dead – so, as soon as the children were able to sit up straight and hold a book in their hands, she somehow got them reading. Thus encouraged, the five Kellys grew up with a healthy regard for the written word and, in Gene's case particularly, for games and charades.

At Peabody High, Gene was a good student who could have been even better had his interests been less diversified. Still, he always passed with respectable grades and, at sixteen, shone in a debating society called The Toreadors, which would meet once a week at the local YMCA. He was also keen on journalism, wrote poetry and worked his way on to the staff of the school paper which was called *The Civitan*.

While Gene fancied himself a sportsman whose intellectual life comprised writing and debating – the performer in him was slowly developing as well. And although he hated his dancing lessons as a child – mainly because he did not want to be labelled a sissy – he picked up everything he was taught with incredible ease, and never forgot a step. Early on, the nuns at St Raphael's recognised a talent in him, and much to his distaste put him in school shows, the first of which was a version of Victor Herbert's *Toyland*. He was ten years old, and already found himself cast as the dancer in the show – as he was the only boy at the school who knew how to tap. It was simply a fear of being ridiculed by the other boys which prevented him from actively enjoying these appearances.

'It was all right when I was playing football with them and being one of the gang,' he said. 'But when they saw me all dressed up on the stage – singing and dancing – that was a different story. And being a little guy, you can imagine how self-conscious I was. Fortunately, a lot of the guys who jeered at me were "dragooned" into the school choir themselves – which took the edge off their jeering because they looked just as ridiculous as I did. But the priests, who were all Irish, and the nuns were a pretty tough bunch; they had to be with all the types they had to handle; and if they said you were to sing in the choir, you sang, or else you'd get a kick up the arse. And if you still disobeyed, they'd call your father in, who was usually a first-generation immigrant and superstitious or religious enough to believe that anything the priests said was Gospel. And in those days most parents thought nothing of belting their kids when they were naughty or if the priests or nuns complained about them. So, one way or another, you did what you were told.'

Though Gene complained bitterly about performing in public, it soon became apparent to him that he was rather good at what he did. He discovered too that he had a beautiful high-tenor voice 'like a castrato' – which everyone seemed to like, and at school concerts he was given all the solos and vigorously applauded by parents and teachers; even some of the other boys had to admit he wasn't too bad.

For the first time Gene was receiving compliments for something other than hockey or gymnastics. At the time, though he never openly admitted it, he began to enjoy the praise. Anything that gave him added confidence in himself couldn't be bad; if, for some strange reason, people liked the way he sang and danced, there must be something to it. Mrs Kelly certainly believed that and arranged for them to appear in a local dancing school show at the Nixon Theatre, an excellent showcase for The Five Kellys.

At high school Gene soon found that his ability to entertain was fast making him popular with the girls. And this was extremely important to him. 'Normally those girls wouldn't have given me a second look if I hadn't been such a hit in the school shows,' he said. 'But the fact that I was made all the difference. Most of those girls were head and shoulders taller than me. But it made me popular and I could get almost anyone I wanted to come to the school dances with me. Some of them thought I was bloody marvellous, and pretty soon I began to believe them. The truth is most of the stuff I did in those shows was terrible. But they wrote me up in the high school year books saying I was destined to be a great entertainer – so I guess I must have had *something* at the time. "Chutzpah", probably.'

Once Gene realised his potential as an entertainer, his adolescent problems disappeared and, like Fred, he began to enjoy showing off. Thus liberated, the thing that came most easily and naturally to him was dancing. As was the case with gymnastics, he found that his height was ideal, and soon he began to develop a style which reflected very clearly his love of athletics and his training as a gymnast. At home he would reinterpret the most commonplace incidents in choreographic terms, so that, at the dinner table, for example, dishing out the mashed potatoes became an elaborate ballet as he danced his way around the table handing out the plates – much to the irritation of his mother and father, and the delight of his brothers and sisters.

Jules Steinberg, a boyhood friend of Gene's, remembers occasions they were out walking together when, for no apparent reason, Gene would throw out his arms, swing round on his toes, and do a series of unexpected pirouettes.

'At the time I had no idea Gene was interested in dancing,' he said. 'I was about five years older than he, and hadn't heard how popular an entertainer he had become at school and college. We mainly discussed sport as we were both ice-hockey fanatics. Looking back now, I find it strange that never, in all the time I knew Gene, did he ever mention his interest in show-business to me or his desire to be a dancer. It was something he kept absolutely secret until he graduated from college. At least from me he did. But then there was something very private and secretive about Gene. He didn't have many close friends – only acquaintances. I think I was as close to him as anyone at the time, and I still had no idea what put wind in his sails.'

Towards the end of the twenties, just prior to the Depression, Harriet Kelly, in spite of having her hands full with her family, became interested, through Fred's dancing activities, in the possibility of opening a dance school herself. She gradually became involved, in an administrative capacity, with a man called Lou Bolton, who had a dance school in Pittsburgh (where Fred took lessons), but who was incapable of running it correctly. He was a plump man whose physical appearance hardly suggested his profession. In fact, though he himself could not dance at all, he did have an intuitive feeling for dancing, and hired teachers to put his ideas across. He had flashes of brilliance and, at odd moments, could even be inspired. But he was more suited to running a night-club than a children's dance academy, and Mrs Kelly was quick to realise that the unmethodical Lou Bolton could benefit from her services. They were accepted gratefully, and she found herself in charge of the reception desk. She received no salary as such, but Fred's dancing lessons were given free of charge. It was a satisfactory arrangement all round.

And then, in November 1929, Wall Street struck the blow that winded America.

For James Kelly, the crash was the climax of a period of struggle which began a couple of years before with the advent and growing popularity of the wireless. As more and more people became fascinated by the idea of turning a knob to draw forth an endless outpouring of free entertainment (free, that is, apart from the cost of the machine, which averaged around forty-five dollars, or five dollars down, the rest to be paid in monthly instalments of five dollars), so the popularity of records diminished. James Kelly found, for example, that his numerous Polish customers in the mining districts of Pennsylvania on whom he used to depend to buy his middle-European records, no longer needed them as they were obsessed by the wireless.

Business got worse and, in 1929, after the crash, he lost his job with the Columbia Record Company, an event from which he emerged a broken man. He tried desperately to find other work, in common with so many others at the time; but few jobs were available and with each refusal he became more and more depressed, more and more subdued. It was, said Gene, as if he had had a stroke.

In utter desperation, he took to the road again in an attempt to sell anything – from hammers to cosmetics – but strictly on commission. One day, he went out with an assortment of hats, and arrived back very happy. But a couple of weeks later, the shops returned the hats to him because they weren't able to sell any – and they were despatched back to the factory. Not only did he not get a cent's worth of commission, but he lost out on his train fares and accommodation and everything else the trip had cost him.

After a year or so of this 'abject humiliation', as Fred put it, he gave up life as a travelling salesman, considered his erstwhile profession 'a lost cause', and stayed at home, going out only to drink with a few of his friends who were in a similar position. 'In spite of all the evidence around them,' said Gene, 'both my mother and my sister Jay couldn't quite believe what was happening to the country, and they criticised my father for his inability to cope with the situation like a man. Jay kept saying, "Why can't he go out and get a job like anyone else?" – not realising that there were no jobs to be had. It was the one time in her life she lost respect for him. Though, of course, she later realised how silly she was. As for his drinking, both she and my mother were revolted, and totally unsympathetic.'

At the time, none of the Kelly children realised how serious their situation was. 'There was always enough food,' said Gene, 'and the fact that things were going to get worse was something we never fully appreciated. If we'd gone hungry or hadn't the proper clothes to wear, I suppose we'd have been more aware that something was wrong. I didn't know, until a year later, that my father had to borrow on his insurance to keep up the monthly payments on the house.'

With the money James Kelly had saved, plus the money Fred earned dancing at amateur nights and in shows around Pittsburgh, the family managed to keep going for a while and without interruption to the children's education. In fact, Gene's freshman year at Penn. State College in 1929 was one of the happiest and most important in his life. For during that year he found that his ability to entertain continued to make him popular with the girls, now that he was more of an age to appreciate them. He also grew a couple of inches taller, which worked wonders for his confidence, and gave him an assurance his personality had always lacked.

Gene's interest in dancing began to grow as well, and as his reputation for being the college's number one entertainer spread, so he found the need to learn new and original steps. Expert at the basic tap he had acquired at the dreaded dancing school a few years earlier, he set out with the kind of determination that was later to characterise everything he did, to improve himself and learn from whomever he could.

One of the people who had a tremendous influence on him was a black dancer called Dancing Dotson, whom he saw performing at Loew's Penn. Theatre. What impressed Gene was the originality of the man's dancing, as it was quite unlike anything he'd seen before. The tricks Dotson was doing at the time were absolutely fresh. He went back to see the act a couple of times, and admitted pinching several of the steps for his own use.

Another of his earliest influences was George M. Cohan, whom he saw in *Little Nellie Kelly*. Gene was only seven years old, but that cocky Cohan walk, the vitality of the man, and the almost arrogant way he jutted out his chin when he tapped across the stage impressed him enormously.

Lou Bolton's studio in Pittsburgh also proved extremely useful to Gene, as one of the teachers there was a black from New York called Frank Harrington who, like Dotson, was an exceptionally gifted tap-dancer and taught Gene several new steps and routines. Gene picked them up instantly and absorbed them into his ever-expanding repertoire, in return for which he often helped out at the Bolton studio by giving a few lessons himself. But Harrington left after spending only one season at the studio. Bolton's unprofessional attitude to his work, his unreliability, the disappearing act he performed several times a month, and his failure to pay his staff, disgusted Harrington, as it did the other assistants, and he returned to New York, much to Gene's disappointment.

Just as he had done with Dotson, Gene made up his mind to steal as much as he could from the numerous touring shows that passed through town and played the Stanley or Nixon Theatres. Both he and Fred would look at any act they thought could be of use to them. Then Gene would take down the first eight bars and Fred the second eight. They had their own method of notating a dance which was a kind of choreographic short-hand, and sometimes would copy an entire act. They were absolutely shameless when it came to pilfering, and very good at it.

Even in high school, Gene had no problem learning new steps. Once, while in a school show, he needed a dance routine. So he called on a teacher he'd heard of who charged ten dollars for sixteen bars of steps. She thought Gene would need at least a dozen lessons before he would be able to pick up the whole routine, but he learned it all in two. She was flabbergasted and asked him to join her class permanently as a model to her other pupils. But he reckoned if he could pick up steps so easily by watching, he might just as well watch professional dancers in a theatre – so he said no. Besides, ten dollars for sixteen bars of steps was more than he could afford.

In his first year at college, Gene became friendly with a man called Jim Barry who was a drummer as well as a tap-dancer. They traded routines, and although Jim was five years older than Gene and had played with a big band before quitting to go to college, they entertained at all the college functions together. At this point, Gene began to invent steps of his own for the first time – something which came easily to him, while Jim provided inspiration and ideas by rattling out an assortment of rhythms.

Gene's extracurricular education was not, however, confined to dance steps alone. One of the most significant things he learned in his freshman year at college was the existence of prejudice and bigotry. At high school Gene was friendly with a group of Protestants who didn't give a damn that he was a Catholic. At college he found that he couldn't join the same fraternity as his Protestant friends. There were special fraternities for Catholics,

Jews and Protestants and they were very strict about who joined. Even within the fraternities themselves there was segregation based on status and snobbery. 'I found the whole thing degrading and disgusting,' Gene said, 'including the sadistic initiation ceremonies where a guy would have to drink God knows how many pints of raw peas and water, or suffer the indignity of running around a dormitory naked while being beaten on the back of his legs with a canoe paddle. The prejudice I encountered at college made a terrific impression on me, probably because I'd come from a family where the word prejudice was never mentioned. In fact, I felt so strongly about it that with another fellow called Johnnie Napoleon and a third chap, a Jewish boy called Eddie Malmud, we tried to take a stand against certain of the fraternities, and formed ourselves into a triumvirate of rebel activists in the hope of being able to stop the sort of discrimination that was going on. But we couldn't fight the "establishment" and we lost. None of this had much to do with my career, of course. But it had a lot to do with my thinking and future outlook on life.'

At the end of his freshman year at college, Gene became a counsellor for the summer at the YMCA camp at Lake Erie, for which he was paid one hundred and fifty dollars – enough to cover his college tuition for the next year. His speciality at the camp was staging the Saturday night shows and showing the lads, aged seven to sixteen, that dancing need not be 'sissy'. In addition to staging and choreographing the shows, Gene would appear in them together with several camp counsellors whom he knew to be superb athletes. He found that these athletes were able to pick up the basic steps with a facility similar to his own, proving a lifelong belief of his – that dancing and athletics are inextricably linked, and that the muscular contractions for, say, a dance movement in second position have their athletic equivalent on the gym floor or in other areas of sport. When it finally developed, his own style was based on this observation. He set out, years later, to demonstrate this in a TV programme in the *Omnibus* series called *Dancing: A Man's Game* in which he assembled a handful of the world's greatest sportsmen and athletes, all of whose basic movements he reinterpreted choreographically.

If 1929 was a year of growth (literally) for Gene, in which he

39

found himself, through accident and necessity, becoming more and more involved in show-business, it was a dispiriting one for his father, whose failure to find work humiliated him, it being against the very nature of his philosophy – that a man must constantly improve himself and reach the top of his profession. What was more redundant than a salesman at a time when few people were in a position to buy anything?

Jim Kelly was also out of work, which added to the financial burden of the family so, as a whole, the situation at Kensington Street was serious. What money the Kellys had managed to save was slowly dwindling, and would soon be gone altogether. At one point in the crisis it was doubtful whether there would be enough money to keep the children at school and college. The following summer, therefore, Gene undertook a series of odd jobs to help him pay for his college tuition. He became a labourer on a building site for which he earned twenty-five cents an hour, eight hours a day, six days a week, making a grand weekly total of twelve dollars: hardly enough to buy a half dozen textbooks, let alone pay his college fees. To supplement the twelve dollars, he became a soda jerk three nights a week at Reymers Candy Company, whose soda fountain was the most expensive in town. Consequently he had to be very careful how he made his sodas, for if they were not to the customer's liking, or were clumsily served, he would be fired.

When the college term began in September, he took a part-time job with the Firestone Tyre and Rubber Company, where he learned to roll as many as eight tyres at once. He then became an attendant at a gas station from three o'clock in the afternoon until eleven at night: an ideal situation as he was able to do some studying during the quiet periods. However, a new manager insisted he position himself at the pumps whether there were any cars requiring gas or not, just to show passing motorists how efficient that particular station was. During the Depression years, anything that encouraged business was worth a try.

Gene made twenty dollars a week, including tips, which wasn't too bad, but he found his studies were beginning to suffer and realised that if he teamed up with Fred, who was regularly dancing for money, he could perform at night and have his days free to study.

By now both Gene and Fred were fairly proficient tap-dancers as well as passable acrobats and 'whizzes' on roller skates; and being young, good-looking and clean-cut, they had no difficulty finding work. They bought themselves a portfolio of sheet music which included such current songs as 'Runnin' Wild', 'Has Anybody Seen My Gal', 'Ukelele Lady', 'Sweet Sue', 'Dinah' and 'If You Knew Susie', and pieced together an act for themselves, literally cutting out bars that did not suit their purposes, and gluing on to a piece of paper those that did. As most of the songs they danced to were standards, they had no problems in finding musicians who could provide suitable arrangements.

Initially their 'act' consisted of one or two numbers which they performed at amateur nights. Even before the Depression, vaudeville was dying because of talking pictures, and to give the patient a blood transfusion, theatre managers revived the old custom of amateur night as an added attraction. They were not the most profitable of gigs – but who could be choosey in 1930?

Gradually Gene and Fred became a little more ambitious, appearing in white shoes, white trousers and tuxedos. They developed a routine that ran for about fifteen minutes, which would include gags shamelessly pilfered from Milton Berle or whoever else happened to have passed through town. And if they were asked to 'spread' their act, and do twenty to twenty-five minutes, Fred would indulge in a bit of magic which suited him well enough, for the longer he was on stage, the happier he was. 'Fred,' Gene remarked, 'was like an accordionist. He never knew when to get off.'

Their appearances together would bring them in anything from twelve to fifteen dollars an engagement, which went straight into the family kitty. Many of the theatres they played were silent cinemas that had just been converted to sound, and because of the sound equipment behind the screen which took up a great deal of space, there was very little room for them to move about in, so most of their routines were performed virtually on top of the footlights. Backstage conditions were not much better, and Gene recalls having once had to dress and undress in a flooded theatre basement in a suburb just outside Pittsburgh.

They also played cheap clubs and cloops on the north side for

41

about ten dollars a night, and the first impression of these places was, for Gene, anything but agreeable.

'The audience threw coins on to the stage, which embarrassed me terribly,' he said. 'I felt like I was a prime bull on exhibition. The first time it happened, I looked at the guy who threw the coins, and was ready to punch him on the jaw – then other people started throwing money and as I couldn't go around punching them all, I just had to grin and bear it. Fred, of course, took it all in his stride. He picked up the money, flashed a smile, and just went on dancing. But I was mortified, shocked and ashamed. I realise now it was all good experience, though at the time I was just ready to die of humiliation.'

They played all over Pittsburgh, as well as the outlying parts to the north and south of the city. Occasionally they would even travel a distance of thirty-five miles and back, to Butler, Pennsylvania, for the chance of winning a ten-dollar prize at an amateur night.

At the Butler Theatre one night, Gene learned the difference between being a cheap vaudevillian and a high-class one.

During their act, the young woman at the piano played their piece of music far too fast, and Gene made a snide remark at her. 'I said something like, "Where d'you think you're going? To a fire?" Well, it made no difference. She just looked up at me and went on playing as before – and the audience, who'd heard the remark, began to hate both me and the act. The result was that we lost the ten bucks, which we should have won because we were the best turn on the bill. But everyone resented my behaviour so much, we didn't stand a chance. What I should have done, of course, was stop the music politely, and graciously ask her to play a little slower please. I should have blown her a kiss or something and started all over again. That would have been classy. Anyway, all we finished up with that night was a dollar "insurance" money which the theatre paid us for our efforts. But one way and another, we kept the money coming in, which was the main thing.'

Then one day, Harriet Kelly had an idea. If Fred and Gene were managing to make a profit out of something they did better than any of their contemporaries, why shouldn't she do the same? The business side of the Lou Bolton studio was running efficiently, thanks to her, so why not open a studio herself?

The challenge was both practical and appealing. At the time, Mrs Kelly's brother Gus was living in a suburb of Johnstown, sixty-five miles from Pittsburgh and suggested that she should try opening a dance school there.

It was not a bad idea, for Johnstown, with its emphasis almost exclusively on steel mining, was virtually bereft of culture, and Harriet Kelly was sure that a school such as the one she had in mind would succeed. But a certain amount of capital would be needed, and while she had the drive and the enthusiasm, capital was the one thing she did not have. So she asked Lou Bolton whether he would come in with her on a partnership basis. At first he was sceptical about travelling all that way for what would obviously amount to no more than pocket-money as far as profit was concerned, but she convinced him it was an idea with possibilities, and finally he agreed to give it a try.

They hired the American Legion Hall, which could just about accommodate a dozen pupils, bought a second-hand piano, and engaged a lady who lived in Johnstown to play for them, although she couldn't read a note of music, and banged everything out by ear. Then they declared Lou Bolton's School of Dancing officially open for business, their first pupils being the children of friends and relatives who had promised to support the venture as soon as they heard about it.

Initially, the classes (every Saturday morning) were given by Lou Bolton himself, and one of Bolton's assistants from Pittsburgh. They would travel the sixty-five miles, across mountains and over hazardous roads, sometimes in appalling conditions of ice and snow.

Occasionally, when Lou Bolton failed to appear, Gene would step in and take over. But in 1930 his connection with the school was still negligible, and he spent most of his spare time taking rudimentary ballet lessons from a teacher in Pittsburgh.

In 1931, Lou Bolton began to feel that the dancing school in Johnstown was too 'small time' to make it really worth his while and, as a result, he became increasingly more unreliable. He would have no scruples about not turning up to take his classes, or squandering the profits – such as they were – by throwing a party for a visiting dancer or anyone else he considered celebrity enough to impress.

Each time Bolton failed to appear, Gene would deputise for him, and within a few months, he became an extremely adept teacher, and even began to enjoy his trips to Johnstown. What started out as a favour to his mother, was to become an immensely important part of his life in the next few years.

As Lou Bolton's interest in the Johnstown school continued to dwindle, Mrs Kelly realised she would just have to make a go of it on her own. And the only possible way for her to do so was to involve her children in the business. With the exception of Jim, they all knew how to dance, and with some effort and much hard work, there was no reason at all why the school shouldn't continue to function as a family concern. Bolstered by sheer necessity, and motivated by the Kelly determination to succeed, the family officially entered the dance school business in 1931. 'If someone had left us a grocery store, we would probably have all become grocers,' Gene said, 'that's how desperate things had become.'

The initial problem was finding enough pupils to make it financially viable. The handful of children who had enrolled before Lou Bolton opted out remained, but they hardly provided enough money to support a family of seven. There was also competition from the local opposition, a dance school Gene remembers being run by a 'schmuck' who did his best to oppose the Kellys' presence in Johnstown by claiming that they weren't members of the dancing teachers' union, and as such had no business teaching. Gene was so incensed by the man's petty efforts to keep him out of town, that he made up his mind to run the school so well, that his opposition would be forced to close rather than compete with him.

In those early days, when newspaper advertising was still beyond their financial means, the Kellys relied on word of mouth for their business and gradually things did begin to improve, although they still only travelled out once a week – on Saturday, which suited Gene fine as he had his studies to think about as well.

'Unlike the "schmuck" down the road who gave his pupils a little heel-and-toe, and after one lesson convinced their parents their little geniuses were dancing, we taught them properly. We taught our kids to dance like professionals. We got them working at the barre, and though it could take a month before they mastered a step, it remained with them for the rest of their lives.' At first the parents complained. Everyone wanted instant results. After a while even

Mrs Kelly thought the 'schmuck' might be right after all, and that they too should give the impression their pupils were dancing after only a couple of lessons – if that's what the parents wanted. But Gene was adamant. If they were going to make a name for themselves, they were going to do things properly, even if it took a little longer.

The lessons cost fifty cents each, and if, for some reason, the mothers were unable to pay, Mrs Kelly would 'carry' them for a while, which was appreciated, and helped build goodwill. Later, when the school was actually showing a profit, some of the better students, who had been with the studio from the beginning, but whose parents were unable to continue paying for their lessons, would be taken on for free – but only if they had the necessary talent to justify so generous a gesture. One woman who had three children at the school, agreed to clean the studio each week in lieu of payment, while there were others who paid Mrs Kelly in sacks of potatoes, or bread, or vegetables.

In the first two years of its life, whatever money the school made went on the Kelly children's education, the upkeep of the studio, and, of course, the running of the house in Pittsburgh. Needless to say, there was very little change left for the luxuries of life.

Though Gene had made up his mind that teaching was merely a temporary means to an end, and that the profession he really wanted to pursue was law, his reputation both as a teacher and a dancer was beginning to spread. One day he received an offer from the Sisterhood of the Beth Shalom Synagogue in Pittsburgh to take over from Lou Bolton and stage its annual show, or Kermess – the idea being to raise money for the synagogue. At the time, the Sisterhood of the Beth Shalom was having difficulty raising funds to pay its rabbi and, speculating on Lou Bolton and his ability to stage a money-making revue, they had hoped to earn enough to cover its financial obligations. But Lou Bolton skipped town, and at Harriet Kelly's suggestion, Gene was asked to replace him for fifteen dollars a week.

The main problem was whether or not Gene had the ability to stage a full-length show. Naturally, he said – and thought – he could. Not as well as Bolton, perhaps, but at least he would not let them down.

45

Having himself been forced to go to dancing school at the age of seven, the way he persuaded the youngsters at the synagogue to take part in the shows, and make them feel that what they were doing wasn't effeminate, was to give them some basketball training before the classes, or football, or gymnastics – and show them that it wasn't all that different from dancing. It worked, and boys who, like himself at that age, hated the very idea of performing, found it wasn't too bad after all.

Gene started at the Beth Shalom in September 1931, and in a few months proved so popular with his young pupils, that his classes, which were held between 2 and 4 pm every Sunday, became well-known throughout Pittsburgh. His first Kermess, a show called *Revue of Revues*, which at the age of nineteen he directed, choreographed and appeared in with Fred, was an enormous success. Tickets cost seventy-five cents for children and a dollar fifty for adults. Expenses were kept to a minimum: the children's clothes were made by their parents, and the scenery was confined to a single back-drop. If any other items were needed for the show, Mrs Kelly would scour the discount stores until she had found what she wanted.

In all, the Sisterhood made eleven hundred dollars with the show, and was able to retain the services of the rabbi. Gene, too, was retained, and found himself working for the Beth Shalom until his departure for New York seven years later. His fee remained fixed at fifteen dollars a week.

Soon, Gene had more pupils on Sunday afternoons than he could cope with. 'He worked so fantastically well with children,' said Mrs Anne Greenberg, who was on the committee of the Beth Shalom at the time, 'that practically every child in the Squirrel Hill neighbourhood wanted to attend his classes. You could tell at a glance he was a star. He had this incredible magnetism, and he could somehow get children to do anything he wanted them to do. And the Kermesses he staged were fantastic. Children who didn't really have much talent would shine under his guidance, and do steps which I think even surprised their adoring mothers. And whenever Gene himself was dancing, our audience would just break out into applause. He was that good.'

Gene's popularity with the Beth Shalom gave him an idea. If

46

children were flocking to his Sunday classes, why didn't he start giving some private lessons to kids whose parents could afford it? So, through the kindness of the synagogue's shamus (caretaker) who allowed him to use one of the basement classrooms, Gene began to teach private pupils, passing on to them everything he himself had picked up or filched over the past couple of years.

When he had collected enough pupils, he and his mother rented the ballroom of a Pittsburgh Hotel, which, he remembers, had a marble floor that was murder on the feet, hired a pianist, and managed to get a small but regular class going. For a while, though, there was too much competition from the numerous other dance schools in downtown Pittsburgh, and business was disappointing.

Still, the fifteen dollars a week he picked up from the Beth Shalom plus the little that came from the Johnstown school made it possible for him to put a down-payment on a Chevrolet which transported him and his family to Johnstown and back each week. As he wanted to arrive in Johnstown fully rested and relaxed, he hired a man for two dollars a week to act as the family's 'chauffeur'. They would leave Pittsburgh on Friday afternoon and, in order to save money on hotel bills, would spend the night in an inexpensive boarding-house run by friends of Mrs Kelly.

Classes would begin on Saturday morning, and continue until 10 pm that night, when they'd all pile back into the car and return to Pittsburgh in time for morning Mass, and the Beth Shalom class on Sunday afternoon.

Though teaching had now become an integral part of his life, he still found the time to play various night-clubs in and around Pittsburgh with Fred. Financially, the family were better off than they were in 1929 and 1930, but they were still far from rich, and badly needed every cent they earned.

On very rare occasions, and if there was enough money to tempt them, Gene and Jay (who had received her master's degree at twenty and, by 1931, had become a schoolteacher), would fulfil a gig together. Once Gene received a call from an agent who asked him if he knew of an act which would be suitable for a rather chic country club near Johnstown. Gene said he had just the thing, and told Jay to get out her dancing shoes and go through a few steps because they were going to pair up that night and earn some money.

They arrived at the country club in a place called Jennerstown, introduced themselves as Joe and Kay, and did a couple of numbers. 'One was the obligatory ballroom bit – because ballroom dancing, like that of the de Marcos, was very much à *la mode* at the time, and a must at any posh supper club – and the other was a kind of jazz ballet item, which, when I think about it, was pretty awful. But we did it with aplomb and we got by. Naturally everyone was curious to know whether we were brother and sister. Well, we told them we most certainly weren't, and that we were a professional dance act who toured the country together. I don't know whether we fooled them or not, but we did make a hundred and fifty dollars that night, which was more than anything Fred and I had ever made together. It was the only time I'd had that sort of windfall. I know I couldn't have done it with Louise because she wasn't that good a dancer yet, and she didn't have the necessary "chutzpah". Because, apart from talent, "chutzpah" is the other important commodity you need in this business.'

By mid-1932, Gene was managing to juggle his numerous activities in a remarkably efficient way. Though he certainly regretted not being able to devote as much time to his sporting interests at college as he would have liked, he kept himself 'honed' by working out at the gym whenever he could. He also managed to keep ahead of his studies and was pretty proficient in French and Italian. 'Italian was particularly easy for me,' he said, 'because of all the time my friend Doc Steinberg and I spent in Bakey's speakeasy late at night, where a lot of Italian was spoken. I know the last place a guy goes to learn Italian is a speakeasy, but that's the way it was.'

One of the things Gene enjoyed about the speakeasy was observing the people who frequented it. 'He seemed to find it more entertaining than going to a movie,' Doc Steinberg recalled, 'or flirting with the girls at his college. He'd spend hours drinking the owner's home brew bath-tub liquor at twenty-five cents a bottle, and watch the passing parade. He claimed he was an agnostic, but on some nights, he'd leave Bakey's at 3 am to go to Mass, then come back and drive me home. He could also be pretty irreverent when he wanted to, and once told me his father could play a song through his rear end – that it was the only musical instrument he could play. He still refused to discuss his ambitions with me, and I never knew why he always kept in training. He seemed, almost, to revere his body, and there were times when I thought he was a bit of an exhibitionist. But he was pretty even-tempered, and the only time I ever recall seeing Gene lose his temper was late one night when a newspaperman who was drinking with us, said that priests were just like other men, and that, deep down, underneath their religion, all they wanted to do was have a good time like anyone else. Well, for some reason, Gene couldn't listen to another word, and got up to leave. But the guy pulled him back and said that he had been a devout Catholic once, who used to go to Mass. But after living in Italy as a correspondent, most of the priests he met spent all their time in brothels. Gene was furious, called the man a "goddam liar", and would have laid into him if he wasn't stopped. For a guy so full of confidence, and who claimed no longer to be religious – it was very strange behaviour. There was something very unworldly about Gene. White was white and black was black. If he had an idea in his head about something, he wasn't going to let anything come between it and him.'

One of the ideas Gene had in 1932 was to leave the American Legion Hall in Johnstown and hire a larger place on Main Street – something that looked more like a dance studio and less like a rabbit hutch. Naturally it was a risk because the financial outlay involved was considerable. But business was steadily improving, and the risk, he felt sure, was a calculated one. Mrs Kelly agreed that if they really wanted to establish themselves and improve their image, larger, more imposing premises were a necessity.

They planned a gala opening party with lots of food and drink, and sent out invitations to all their old students and, they hoped, some new ones whose names they got from a mailing list.

On the day of the opening, the entire Kelly family, including James, assembled in the new hall and proudly awaited the arrival of their guests. It was a big moment for them, and the culmination of a year of struggle, hard work and an unfaltering belief in their abilities. The tables groaned under cookies, fizzy drinks and candy – and the room looked fresh and inviting. Harriet Kelly could barely contain herself with excitement.

But no one arrived.

An hour ticked by, and still no guests. Suddenly the door opened, and a pair of twins who had been at the school since its inception, and who were being 'carried' because their mother was unable to afford the fifty cents a lesson, entered the room holding hands. They looked around nervously, wondering if there had been some mistake, and whether they had come on the wrong day. For, apart from the Kellys standing forlornly at the end of the hall, the place was utterly deserted.

For the first time in her life, Mrs Kelly weakened, and wept uncontrollably. The rest of the family were heartbroken, confused and bitterly disappointed.

At the end of the day, when it was clear that no one else was going to arrive, Harriet Kelly was convinced the only thing to do would be to forget about the school and return to Pittsburgh for good.

But Gene had other ideas. Whatever had gone wrong (and to this day, he cannot imagine what it was) he was not going to be defeated, and there and then decided to take over the new school himself. Before that, he had merely been helping his mother. Now it was going to be his. It was almost, he said, like his *barmitzvah* – because he suddenly became a man. Gene was twenty years old, and more than ever he was determined to succeed. It was one more challenge which had to be met, regardless of how much hard work was involved. So he changed the name of the school to The Gene Kelly Studio of the Dance, and waited to see what happened.

In only a couple of weeks, Gene's faith was rewarded. All his old pupils returned (without any explanation of why they did not attend the fateful opening party) plus quite a few new ones as well. By the end of the year he had more pupils than even he had thought possible.

One of Gene's main problems now was to find teachers he considered good enough to take the more advanced classes for, at twenty, he, too, still had a great deal to learn. He scanned the dance and theatre magazines, spoke to local acts, and would even travel as far as Cleveland, Ohio, if he heard of the existence of a new teacher who might help out both in Johnstown and in Pittsburgh – where business had also improved.

Though the school was now in his name, and he was virtually in charge of all 'artistic' decisions, his mother, characteristically, took over the financial side of things, gathered in the takings, and still gave Gene, Fred and Louise only just what they needed to live on. Jay and Jim were both over twenty-one and would have to earn their own living.

One of the highlights of the year, and a reason for the studio's popularity, was the annual summer show Gene and his pupils staged in Johnstown. 'Mr Kelly's work with children,' said a reviewer in a local paper in June 1932, 'speaks for itself. He has presented clearly and thoughtfully every type of dancing in a manner that cannot be surpassed on the Keith circuit. The production was staged magnificently with ten brilliant, special drops and gay lighting effects. It is the best entertainment offered here in a long while . . . full of beautiful and luxurious reds . . . black and bronze backgrounds . . . attractive side effects . . . the only kiddies show to hold an engagement a full week on any legitimate stage in the United States.'

The revues, which were staged each year for the next five years, had titles such as *Johnstown on Parade, Gene Kelly's Kiddie's Vodvil* and *The Talk of the Town Revue*; they always employed a full orchestra, and did much to entice new pupils to the school, for their presence at the studio more or less guaranteed an appearance on stage in what invariably became one of Johnstown's most popular annual attractions. Several of the girls who started out with Gene in Johnstown went on to make show-business their career. 'They could dance like devils, those girls,' Gene said. 'Some of them were absolutely sensational. Even at thirteen, fourteen or fifteen they were knockouts and certainly the best advertisement for the school we ever had.'

The shows Gene presented were, in the main, designed to accommodate all his pupils (by 1933 there were a hundred and fifty of them in Johnstown alone), from four to eighteen, and would consist of a medley of items ranging from simple little ballets to military tap routines. There were acrobatic solos, apache dances – even *The Dying Swan* and Chaminade's *Scarf Dance*. Precision hoofing (in the style of the Rockettes) was always popular, as were the toe solos danced by the more advanced pupils. But the real crowd-pleaser was the spot in which the youngest members in the cast warbled out an arrangement of popular songs before going into a 'point-your-toe and away we go' dance, which raised the rafters.

Singing played an important part in the school, and although many of Gene's pupils were more interested in learning how to sing than dance, one of the conditions of their acceptance was that they had to take dance lessons as well. In fact, anything that might be the fad or hit of the year was taught, and if the pupil wanted to learn the Black Bottom or the Turkey Trot or the Big Apple – that was okay as well.

In 1932 Gene finally became a member of the Chicago National Association of Dancing Masters. He had applied for membership a year earlier, but was opposed by his competitor down the road who insisted that Gene wasn't eligible and sent off a letter to the Association saying so. The following year, after he had lost most of his pupils to Gene Kelly's Studio of the Dance, he left town.

1932 was also the year James Kelly became part of the school. Since the crash in 1929, he had opted out completely, but when the school in Johnstown began to grow as fast as it did, Gene persuaded him to come in and help out with the accounting, because the work was getting too much for his mother, who was coping with the business side of the Pittsburgh school as well.

At first James was reluctant to be drawn into the affairs of the studio, feeling that his pride and dignity would suffer – and that he was better off doing nothing at all instead of compromising his authority by working for his son. But as soon as he realised he was genuinely required to help keep the books in order, and his 'employ-ment' was not a matter of mere charity, his sense of inadequacy passed and he was happy to be of use again.

Whenever Gene or Fred were doing a show, James Kelly would take charge of the desk and handle the business side of the studio completely, because his wife would invariably accompany her sons whenever they were performing. It would be unthinkable of her not to be present. In fact, she considered herself a very necessary part of their shows – almost as if she were the producer. 'It was just one more way she could enjoy the show-business career she had never had for herself,' Gene said. 'And as we did more and more shows, my father found himself with a full-time job on his hands, for which I think he was very grateful, particularly as he had given up drinking and needed something to take its place.'

One of the features of Gene Kelly's Studio of the Dance in Johnstown was its talented line of young girls. Unlike the Pittsburgh pupils, most of whom became housewives, the Johnstown girls took the business seriously, and were an additional source of revenue for the Kellys for, together with Gene, they played various dates in small iron towns around Johnstown, such as Nanty-Glo and Cresson or Portage and Ebensburg where, once a year, volunteer firemen, or the VFW (Veterans of Foreign Wars) would put on a little show for their hard-drinking members in the local American Legion Hall or the Moose Club.

Gene's fee for such a show was thirty-five dollars, out of which he would pay his eight or ten girls a dollar apiece, and his pianist five dollars, leaving him with approximately twenty dollars clear profit: not a fortune, but a profit. And invaluable in terms of the experience he was gaining. Later, as his popularity increased, the shows became more ambitious, and instead of making do with a pianist, Gene assembled a small orchestra formed from local high school talent, and his fee shot up to seventy-five dollars a performance. One of the most successful of these shows, called *Hits and Bits of 1932*, was in a town called Lilly, Pennsylvania. But it started disastrously. When Gene and Fred (who was on the bill as well) plus their ten most attractive, most talented Johnstown girls arrived, no seats had been sold. The show was a midnight matinée at the Liberty Theatre – and at six-thirty that evening, the theatre plan was still empty. It was a hot summer's night, and the volunteer firemen, for whose benefit the show was being held, were snugly ensconced in their local bar. 'They were smashed out of their minds,' Gene recalled. 'So what we did was borrow a fire engine, pile our girls on to it, and drive through the town ringing bells like crazy, and holding up a sign which advertised our show, and which we'd taken off the theatre marquee. We got hold of a megaphone from somewhere and just shouted promises that if they came to the theatre later on, they'd see the best girlie show of their lives, which wasn't true, of course. But the girls were wearing their stage costumes, which were very sexy, and we thought it was the only way to get the men interested. Well, pretty soon we attracted a crowd – but what we didn't realise was that the guy driving the fire engine was just as drunk as everyone else that night, and he refused to stop because he was having so much fun. And the more we asked him to slow down, the faster he drove, and the more frightened our girls became. The whole thing must have looked like something out of a Mack Sennett comedy.'

At last the driver stopped, and Gene mingled with a few of the locals who'd stepped out to see what all the noise was about, and had a couple of drinks with them. By eleven o'clock, people gradually began to file into the theatre – and when the performance finally began, they had a full house.

Their act relied on broad and corny sight gags. Subtlety was a dirty word. When the show started, Gene was convinced they would all want their money back as soon as they realised they had been hoodwinked into believing they were going to see a girlie show. Fred was so nervous of the deception, and its possible repercussions if the audience turned violent, that during his magic act, he dropped a bowl of goldfish which shattered across the stage, frying the poor fish on the footlights. For the rest of the evening, he recalled, the theatre smelled like a fish shop. But happily the audience seemed to forget about the girls and were so drunk, that they laughed and applauded everything that was offered.

'All our stuff was lifted straight out of vaudeville,' Gene said, 'and of course, it couldn't really miss with that crowd. For example, I'd run across the stage with a fire extinguisher and Fred would say to me: "Say feller, where are you going with that?" And I'd reply: "I've got a hot date." Well, the firemen broke up laughing at that one. Then I'd run on with a second extinguisher and Fred would say: "*Now* what?" To which I'd reply: "I've just met her sister." And believe me, it got worse! We had one of our Johnstown girls walk across the stage saying to Fred: "Yoo hoo, why does the chicken cross the road?" And Fred would say: "To get to the other side. Everybody knows that." "Wrong," she'd say. "To get some ice-cream." "That's ridiculous," said Fred. "Chickens don't eat ice-cream." Then the blonde would put her finger into her mouth and

54

coyly say: "This chicken does." Believe it or not, I actually wrote that.'

The show in Lilly, Pennsylvania, brought two important changes: Fred dropped the magic from his act, and Gene dropped the comedy. Yet in spite of the cornball quality of their scripts, the dancing and dancers they featured were excellent and in a town called Ebensburg, the manager of the local theatre was so impressed with what he saw, that he invited Gene to open a branch of the school right there. Gene was enthusiastic about the idea, visualising a chain of Gene Kelly schools across the country. The thought appealed to his ego and to his mother's sense of commerce.

Initial reaction to the idea was excellent. He and Mrs Kelly hired a hall, and the cream of Ebensburg's talent enrolled. But two months later Gene had only three students left. 'I never ever discovered what went wrong,' he said. 'They were so enthusiastic to start with and welcomed us with open arms. We were almost treated like Hollywood stars. So I went to the guy who first suggested it and told him we had to face facts: we were a big flop there. It was a little town that should have been proud and honoured to have us, but after two months they didn't want to know. By the time we packed it in, it was costing *us* money in gasoline. Still, it was probably all for the best, because it gave us an extra day in Pittsburgh which we needed, because our school there was finally beginning to take off as well.'

During part of the summer of 1932, when both the Pittsburgh and Johnstown schools were in recess, Gene and Fred took the Chevrolet to Chicago and performed at the World's Fair. The idea was to earn money and, at the same time, to gain experience. They worked under several names, often doing six or ten shows on the same day. Because they were so alike in appearance (though according to Phil Silvers, Fred had 'more blood'), they would often stand in for one another, and Fred remembered playing many of Gene's dates for him if Gene received a better offer elsewhere.

During the day Fred, who was sixteen, and a girl called Elizabeth Morgan, did adagio dancing at the Fair's Isle of Enchantment for children, while at night he and Gene played separately or together – depending on the booking – the tough, drinking men's cloops!

'In one show I'd be a smash, in the next a flop,' Gene remembers. 'The trouble was, my dancing was just too classy for those guys. They'd come to see some down-to-earth hoofing, and I was giving them a bit more than that. The main thing about playing a cloop is you have to judge your audience, and I was too inexperienced and too "grand" to adjust my act to that particular sort of clientele. The last thing those guys wanted was a sophisticated dancer. What they wanted was someone to come out and tell them half a dozen dirty jokes and sing a song, because during the songs they could look away without missing a thing. But with dancing, unless they paid attention, they weren't getting their money's worth. What would happen is they'd watch me for a few minutes, then turn around to talk to their friends and miss some of my best steps. A few years later, when I went into pictures, I thought back to my club days, and realised how important it is for a dance number to be edited correctly, because otherwise you lose continuity – which is the equivalent of having someone turn his back on you at the wrong moment – and so destroy the rhythm of what you're trying to do.

'The other thing I had to put up with playing the cloops , was verbal insults. It's bad enough when people look away, but when they shout out names at you, that's something else. You can do two things: shout back at them, which is undignified, and not particularly satisfying, or you can belt them, which isn't very dignified either, but *very* satisfying. Sometimes I belted them. One night a guy called me a fag, and I jumped off the stage and hit him. But I had to make a run for it, because the owner of the place and his brother took after me with a couple of baseball bats.

'But the thing I remember most about those cloops ,' he said, 'was just being ignored. That was the usual reaction. And the hardest for my pride to take. I usually followed some broad who did a strip-tease or a bubble dancer whom they wanted back because she bared her breasts. That's what they wanted. And a "classy" male dancer (at least *I* thought I was "classy") was no substitute, believe me.'

In 1933, Gene graduated from college as an economics major. The dance schools were flourishing and made a decent profit for the first time. Mrs Kelly still controlled the finances, although James was in charge of the book-keeping. Gene, who did most of the teaching and whose personality was largely responsible for the popularity of the studios, was still being given pocket-money rather than a regular salary, although he had turned twenty-one. His mother refused to tell him how much the two schools were making each week, as she did not think this was any of his business. It was quite a considerable amount though – for, without making financial sacrifices elsewhere, she employed a full-time maid to look after the house in Kensington Street.

In the summer of that year, prior to Gene's enrolment as a law student at the University of Pittsburgh (in spite of the success he had made of the two schools and the work he was doing for the Beth Shalom, he was still intent on becoming a lawyer), he returned to Chicago, not to give lessons, but to take them. For in the mid-1930s Chicago was the dance centre of America. Dancers such as Kotchetovsky, who had arrived in America after fleeing the Russian Revolution, fanned out to various parts of the country rather than saturate New York with ballet schools. Several of them settled in Chicago, where their schools and academies were well supported by the uncultured millionaire meat barons whose wives (in much the same way that Mrs Kelly sought refuge from her shanty-town relatives by feeding culture to her children), became patrons of the arts to 'better themselves' and escape the origins of their husbands' wealth.

Every year, for two weeks, the Chicago Association of Dancing Masters, who numbered among their members some of America's finest teachers, met and held master classes, which Gene found invaluable. For there was a limit to what he could learn from the acts that passed through Pittsburgh. And if he wanted to advance, he needed the expert guidance the Association provided.

Each summer he would check into an inexpensive hotel, and for a fee of a few dollars was allowed to attend as many classes as he wished. Many of the teachers were specialists – such as Snr. Gambelli, the eighty-year-old master who taught only the Cecchetti method, and it was left entirely up to the individual to choose the class from which he thought he would derive the maximum benefit.

Gene found that his own tap-dancing, with its strong athletic

57

emphasis, was admired by many of the professional dancers in Chicago, and it wasn't long before he was asked to give a few classes himself – a considerable compliment for a young man of twenty-one. It also boosted his own reputation, and that, of course, was excellent for business.

'I got to know several of my teachers extremely well,' he said. 'A lot of them, like Kotchetovsky and Rita Hayworth's uncle, Angel Cansino, who taught me Spanish dancing, were real down-to-earth, even tough guys. There was nothing effeminate about them. Cansino was a little fellow, but strong as a bull. He could walk into a moving train and come away unscathed. The same for Kotchetovsky. We used to go out and drink together in Chicago and have a ball. They were terrific men, and at the same time their whole life was the dance. They taught me a lot.'

After his Chicago stint, Gene motored to Lake Erie for a couple of weeks' holiday not unlike those at Lake Conneaut. It was a welcome rest, and always well earned.

In the autumn of 1933, Gene returned to Pittsburgh ready to enter law school and begin a new phase of his life. He bought several of his prescribed textbooks and found a lawyer called Louis Little to endorse him. His dancing activities during his three years at college had certainly been important to him, and had provided his family with a good living. But his mother wanted him to have a 'proper' profession, and he agreed with her. As for the two schools, they were running quite efficiently. Gene had employed several capable teachers, and as long as he maintained a part-time, weekend interest in what was happening, there was no reason at all why they shouldn't continue to do well.

For several weeks Gene attended his law classes. But, somehow, his enthusiasm for the legal profession had already begun to evaporate. While lecturers droned on about the difference between corporate law and mercantile law, he found himself in quite another world, as new dance steps pirouetted through his imagination. In the background, he was vaguely aware of the lecturer rambling on about a book on torts, and how they would all be using that book for the rest of their lives.

For the rest of their lives! The phrase reverberated through his soul.

Suddenly a cold sweat dampened his forehead as he realised, with frightening clarity, that something he had always taken for granted and never questioned – his commitment to law – was a dreadful mistake. The words being spoken by the man in front of the class were no longer vague, unrelated half-digested sentences, but a warning which tattooed itself onto his brain. The writing on the blackboard was also the writing on the wall as far as he was concerned.

By the time the lecture was over, he knew he'd 'gotta sing and gotta dance'. He quickly sold most of his brand new textbooks – at a loss, which did not bother him for he considered himself lucky to have escaped from a world where his impatient feet did not belong.

At first his mother was disappointed at his decision but knew, in this instance, there was little she could do about it. So she consoled herself by believing that if it was her son's wish to teach for the rest of his life – at least he would be the best teacher in America.

Now that Gene was free of his academic obligations, he became increasingly involved with his two schools, and devoted more time to his annual shows which he continued to direct and choreograph. He also slaved away at his ballet dancing, realising that he had started too late in life to become another Nijinsky, but determined none the less, to overcome the deficiencies in his technique.

There was something about ballet dancing which really excited him. As a child he used to run for miles through parks and streets and woods – anywhere, just as long as he could feel the wind against his body and through his hair. Ballet gave him the same feeling of exhilaration, and in 1933 he was convinced it was the most satisfying form of self-expression.

Late at night, after all his pupils had gone home, he would spend an extra hour at the studio in downtown Pittsburgh, practising his ballet steps in front of a long mirror. It was well after midnight before he locked up. But instead of going home to bed – for his energy was inexhaustible and he rarely felt tired – he would wander over to Bakey's speakeasy for a nightcap with Doc Steinberg.

Shortly after he had decided not to do law, the Ballet Russe de Monte Carlo came to Pittsburgh and one night after a performance Gene went backstage, and asked the company's star dancer, David Lichine, whether he could audition the following morning. Gene was wearing a formal smoking-jacket, and was uncharacteristically dressed up for the occasion, in the hope that his appearance would impress Lichine.

But Lichine was not impressed. 'How can I see whether you have the right sort of body for a dancer underneath all those fancy clothes?' he said in his broken English. 'Come to the rehearsal tomorrow morning wearing something more simple.'

So the following morning Gene arrived at the rehearsal hall, and auditioned for the ballet master who was impressed with the way he moved. (Lichine was nowhere to be seen.) He told Gene he could probably use him in the male ensemble once they got to Chicago, which would be in two weeks' time.

Gene discussed the possibility of joining the ballet with his mother, and tried to decide whether he was prepared to live off 'two dollars a week and a doughnut', far less even than he could earn playing a local nightspot. It was a difficult decision to make. Finally he rejected it.

'As much as I loved classical ballet,' he said, 'I had to face the fact that my style of dancing was more modern. I really couldn't see myself doing *Swan Lake* and *The Sleeping Beauty* for the next twenty years of my life. So, after much soul-searching, I decided not to go with them. I think it was probably the right decision.'

By 1934, Gene Kelly's Studio of the Dance was well known, not just throughout Pennsylvania, but among professional dancers in New York, many of whom would stop over at Pittsburgh while on tour and visit the studio for a workout, or to pick up some new steps themselves. Often they would ask Gene to provide them with a 'big finish' to their act; or they might simply dance out their routines and wait for a reaction. Gradually, he began to make show-biz contacts himself, including the Broadway choreographer Robert Alton, who invited Gene to look him up if ever he decided to try his luck in New York.

At the same time, he kept watching as many dancers as he could, and voraciously absorbed the steps he thought would be of use to him.

'Like a boxer, I felt I had to keep honing my body finer and finer. A lot of dance teachers – Lou Bolton, for example – wouldn't dance a step. They'd just tap their cane and tell their pupils what to do with their left foot and their right arm, and so on. But I'd get up in front of my kids and dance – all day if necessary, improving the skills I already had, and learning all the time.'

During the next few years, Gene was invited to choreograph and direct several big shows at the Pittsburgh Playhouse (at a hundred and fifty dollars a show), using amateurs and professionals, and in which he himself appeared.

He also staged and appeared in several Cap and Gown shows for the University of Pittsburgh (for a fee of three hundred and fifty dollars), which usually engaged professional directors from New York, but saw no need to continue doing so once Gene had proved himself at the Playhouse. He presented the Junior League shows as well, and found time between his numerous commitments to stage his annual school revue, both in Johnstown and in Pittsburgh, not to mention the Beth Shalom Kermess.

Louise and Fred, who had both graduated from college as Bachelors of Arts, worked on the school shows and, like Gene, appeared in them as well. Jay would help out occasionally if she were needed, but apart from a single flutter into professional show-business, when she toured the RKO Circuit as a chorus girl with an Earl Lindsey revue in the mid-thirties, her interests remained in education. Jim broke away from the family and became a commercial artist.

In general, life was pretty good to the Kellys. Time had straightened out the dent imprinted by the Depression on the family's fortunes, and on James Kelly's pride; and as Gene's reputation continued to grow, so did the schools. The Hollywood movie musical, with its constellation of stars, reached a peak of popularity in the thirties, and directly helped the dance business: for young girls everywhere identified with the touchingly innocent Ruby Keeler in *42nd Street*, who went out an unknown kid and came back a star. Astaire and Rogers had just flown down to Rio; and, in the process, made their dancing appear so effortless that aspiring young hopefuls throughout the country thought there was nothing to it, and paid dance schools hard-earned money to prove how wrong they were. Ballroom dancing was all the rage as well; and as teams such as Velo and Yolanda and the de Marco's tangoed and fox-trotted their way across the forty-eight states, couples everywhere demanded to be taught how to do the same. Gene himself disliked this form of dancing, but its popularity prevented him from ignoring it at his schools, and as it made easy money, the Carioca, the Continental and the Yam were there for the asking.

Another factor that boosted business was the arrival of the Hollywood child star. Mothers everywhere thought their daughters were just as gifted as Shirley Temple or Mitzi Green or Jane Withers, and invested millions of dollars in dance schools through-out America speculating on their progeny's undiscovered talents.

By 1935 the Kellys had bought and sold several cars, graduating from their second-hand Chevrolet to a Chevrolet convertible, which Gene would thoughtlessly insist on driving from Pittsburgh to Johnstown in the middle of winter, with the roof down, while his mother, wrapped in a blanket, shivered as they ploughed through snow and ice.

In 1935 they had three hundred and fifty pupils, and money was no longer the prime consideration. Business was so good, particu-larly in Johnstown where there was less competition than in Pitts-burgh, that Gene added an extra day to his schedule, and moved the studio to a two-storey building to accommodate all the pupils. The new premises comprised a large office in which James Kelly worked, and a dressing-room, both of which were on the first floor; and an enormous hall which took up the entire second floor.

Even at this stage Gene was not aware of how much money the schools were making though, at a conservative estimate, the amount was probably in the region of between eight and ten thousand dollars a year.

Whatever it was, none of the Kellys complained.

In the summer of 1935, after attending master classes in Chicago, the Kelly family took a trip to California to see some relatives. While in

Los Angeles, Gene did a screen test for a Mr Willey, an executive at RKO Pictures who, while passing through Pittsburgh earlier that year, had popped into the dance school to see him at work.

Gene thought it all a big joke, but his mother relished the idea of her son becoming a movie-star, and packed him off to the studio convinced they'd take one look at him and put him straight into a picture.

Mr Willey was very charming when Gene arrived, and introduced him to a director whom he had not heard of before (or since), then sent him off to the make-up department where he was 'given the works'. 'I remember thinking,' Gene said, 'that I looked like a raving fag by the time they put the cameras on me. Anyway nothing came of the test, though I wish I had a copy of it as a memento. I'm sure they just took one look at it and laughed. The only good thing about the test as far as I'm concerned, was that I was introduced to Fredric March at the studio, which was quite a thrill for me.'

Apart from the Johnstown flood, which temporarily suspended classes and turned the Kelly house in Kensington Street into a hostel of sorts when Mrs Kelly accommodated several of her pupils whose homes had been washed away, 1936 was not all that different from 1935. Gene continued to 'hone' his skills by directing and appearing in Cap and Gown shows, and his work for the Pittsburgh Playhouse was distinguished by a professionalism which, in the years to come, characterised everything he did.

The following year, with the two schools securely established as part of Pennsylvania's cultural life and making a great deal of money, Gene felt he had gone as far as he could, or wanted to go, as a teacher. He realised that, if he wanted to expand as a dancer and choreographer, he would have to go to Broadway. At last he felt he was ready to take on 'the big time'. His work with the Pittsburgh Playhouse; the Beth Shalom; the Junior League and Cap and Gown shows; the cloops even, as well as the annual school productions he had been presenting since 1932 – all of these had given him the sort of grounding in the business which normally takes a lifetime on the boards to acquire. He was attractive and talented. Fame, as his mother had always believed, was his birthright. And he had all the confidence he needed to succeed.

Fortunately, the two schools were so well established by now, that they could sustain themselves without Gene. Though they would still bear his name, and though he was the focal-point of their activities, they had started off as a family concern with Mrs Kelly in charge and, in many ways, remained that way. Ostensibly Fred and Louise were, in a way, 'glorified employees' of Gene and his mother. But they were never made to feel subordinate, and when Mrs Kelly called on them to take over, they did so willingly and with complete confidence.

Mrs Kelly did not dissuade Gene from trying his luck in New York. If, for some reason, the schools were ever in trouble, she knew she could rely on him to return and put them right. In the summer of 1937, Gene received an offer from a producer to choreograph one number in a new Broadway show. He should have been excited with the offer, but wasn't. Had he been invited to stage the *entire* show – well, that would have been a different story. But he did realise that if the single number he was asked to do turned out to be the best thing in the show, it would only be a matter of time before other producers made him offers. And Broadway *was* Broadway!

Encouraged by his mother, who saw this as her son's big break, Gene finally decided to take the job, and a couple of weeks later he arrived in New York.

But the big city, he discovered, wasn't exactly waiting for him, and on his first day there he was informed that he would not, after all, be choreographing the number in the show, but would merely be required to appear in it. Understandably, Gene's pride was hurt, and he now had to decide whether he wanted to remain on in New York and appear in the one number, or return to better and more lucrative things in Pittsburgh. He decided to return to Pittsburgh, and four days later he was home again.

A full year was to pass before he realised that provincial success meant absolutely nothing, and that if he wanted to make a name for himself on Broadway, as he had done in Pittsburgh, he would have to start at the bottom. It was one of the facts of life he just had to accept. He also knew that if he delayed his departure any longer, he might never make it. As it was, at twenty-six he was several years older than the average juvenile or Broadway chorus boy. This time he would not return home unsuccessful. That much he promised himself. Where there was doubt a year ago, now there was only determination.

On August 5th, 1938, Gene, accompanied by his mother, left his house in Kensington Street and, once again, made his way to Pittsburgh station, where he bought a one-way ticket to New York. All he had with him was a small suitcase and a couple of hundred dollars. And, of course, a characteristic will to succeed.

If Mrs Kelly felt like shedding a tear or two – for she knew just as well as Gene did that this time he would not be returning four days later, she hid it well. She had never been sentimental where her family was concerned, and was not going to start now. Besides, there was an inevitability about the moment, as if it had all been planned years ago, which disarmed emotion completely.

As the train began to pull out of the station, she kissed Gene lightly on the cheek, never doubting for a moment that the next time she saw her son, he would be a star.

Part Two

In August the official theatre season on Broadway is over; the flops have been siphoned off and, as the temperature soars into the nineties, the activity around Times Square winds down conspicuously. The sidewalks burn through the soles of the tourists' shoes, and those New Yorkers who aren't already on vacation, are cooling off indoors. Enervating August is Broadway's least favourite month, and only the established hits are able to compete with the heat. In 1938 such hits were Robert Sherwood's *Abe Lincoln in Illinois* at the Plymouth Theatre, the long-running *Helzapoppin* at the Winter Garden, and Walter Huston in Maxwell Anderson and Kurt Weill's *Knickerbocker Holiday* at the Ethel Barrymore.

Apart from the intrepid actors and actresses who sweat six nights a week – and twice on Wednesdays and Saturdays – producers and directors preparing productions for the following season are also kept busy in August holding auditions and searching for 'angels', without whom Broadway would fold on Saturday night.

Gene planned his arrival in New York to coincide with these summer auditions and, after finding cheap accommodation at the 44th Street Hotel, on West 44th Street between 6th and 7th Avenue, he bought a copy of *Variety* and ticked off the shows he thought might have something in them for him.

One of the announcements that caught his eye was a new revue

67

which Max Gordon, George S. Kaufman and Moss Hart were planning for a September opening called *Sing Out the News*. It was to be directed by Charles Friedman and the dances were to be staged by Dave Gould, who in 1933 had created the elaborate musical numbers for the film *Flying Down to Rio*. The music and lyrics were by Harold Rome, whose left-wing revue *Pins and Needles* had brought him fame the previous season. Everyone's credits (and politics) were good, and as Gene had limited his finances to two hundred dollars, he wasted no time at all in auditioning for the show.

The audition was held the Saturday morning after he arrived. As soon as he got to the theatre and watched a few hopefuls going through their routines, he realised there was no one who was as good as he was. The producer realised this too and offered him a feature spot in the show. Gene was thrilled. Then the stage manager told him his salary would be thirty-five dollars a week – which was the going chorus rate. Gene took a deep breath, coughed and said no. If he was going to be given a spot he said, the very least he was prepared to accept was seventy dollars a week. So he asked for seventy-five, thinking they would eventually compromise on seventy. But they turned him down. Once again he was to discover that Broadway was not exactly at his feet.

It wasn't that the money was too low. It was, he insisted, the principle of the thing. 'I wasn't going to accept the same salary a chorus girl was getting for wriggling her arse when I was doing a helluva lot more in the show. They wanted to exploit me, but I wasn't going to have it. I had to begin this game as I intended finishing it, so I walked out of the theatre without a job.'

This time, however, he did not return to Pennsylvania. The following Monday, he went to see Robert Alton, the choreographer whom he had met in Pittsburgh. Alton was rehearsing a new musical comedy by Cole Porter called *Leave It to Me* when Gene called on him at the Imperial Theatre on 45th Street. They chatted for a while, then Alton suddenly excused himself to call his agent and manager, Johnny Darrow, and ask him to come over to the theatre.

'When I arrived at the Imperial,' Darrow said, 'Alton called me up on to the stage and introduced this good-looking guy to me. "This is Johnny Darrow," he said to Gene. "He's going to look after you. Do as he tells you. He's a good guy." Well, we shook hands and that was that. Anyone recommended to me by Alton had to have something.'

The first thing Darrow did was to try and change Gene's name to Frank Black. But Gene was having none of that. He insisted his own name was good enough, and Darrow did not pursue the matter further.

Next, he arranged an audition with the Shubert Brothers, who liked what they saw, and offered Gene a hundred and fifty dollars a week to appear in one of their shows. Darrow, however, feigned indignation at so 'paltry' a sum and, without telling Gene, asked for three hundred dollars a week minimum – which the Shuberts flatly refused.

'I knew Gene didn't have much money with him in New York,' Darrow said, 'and that he was pretty anxious to get a job. So, after holding out for a couple of days, I finally decided to go back to the Shuberts and accept their offer. I saw J. J. Shubert personally and said, "Now, about Kelly . . ." "What about him?" Shubert said. "I'll tell you what, let's make a compromise," I said. But before I could say another thing, Shubert assured me he didn't need him any more. And that was that. Well, I had to go to Gene and tell him – which was one of the hardest things I've ever had to do in my life. Fortunately Gene took it amazingly well. He was behind me all the way. Instead of throwing his hands up and saying "For Christ's sake, what the hell d'you think you're doing!", which would have been the natural reaction under the circumstances, and for which I couldn't have blamed him, he was very nice about it and said, "Well, I guess you're holding out in my best interests, so what the hell." From that moment on, Gene could do no wrong as far as I was concerned.'

When Alton heard about Darrow's goof, he offered Gene a small part as a speciality dancer in *Leave It to Me*, not at three hundred dollars a week, or even a hundred and fifty, but seventy-five. Darrow accepted on Gene's behalf.

As soon as he began work on *Leave It to Me*, Gene checked out of the 44th Street Hotel and moved into a small apartment with a fellow dancer in the show. He also looked up a young Jewish girl called Helene Marlowe, a dancer whom he had met during one of his Pittsburgh Playhouse shows the previous year, and a romance developed between them.

As rehearsals for *Leave It to Me* progressed, he saw more and more of Helene, who became a sort of oracle to him, and whom he consulted about his future and ear-bashed about his dancing and choreography. He discussed the work of Martha Graham, Doris Humphrey and Charles Weidman with her, and explained that as much as he admired them, they were the antithesis of what he wanted to do. He was just a Pittsburgh kid, he said, who wanted to dance to Cole Porter and Gershwin and Jerome Kern, because their music had the kind of beat that excited him, and although the strange cacophony that Martha Graham used moved him tremendously, it did not make him want to dance.

Helene would spend hours listening patiently to him talk, or watching him practice his routines. What he *really* wanted, he told her, was to evolve a form of modern dancing which would combine straight tap with ballet in a new, exciting way, but which was not as recherché or as inaccessible to the general public as so much contemporary dance seemed to be. She tried to understand his ideas and share his enthusiasms – even when the ideas he was formulating meant absolutely nothing to her. But she was in love with him, and that was all that mattered.

Gene's involvement with *Leave It to Me* was perfunctory, to say the least, and Johnny Darrow promised to find something which made more demands on his talents. Gene did, however, meet Cole Porter while doing *Leave It to Me*, and although they were not to work together until 1949, in the film *The Pirate*, they became good friends.

'I was sitting alone in a corner of the theatre during rehearsals one morning,' Gene said, 'when Cole spotted me and asked Bob Alton who that "unusual" man was – and what was I doing reading instead of "making time" with the girls like the other guys. Alton asked him whether he'd like to meet me, and Cole said yes, he would. He was curious to know what I was reading. So Alton introduced Cole, who was still in a wheelchair as a result of his riding accident, and we shook hands. I told him I was reading *Point Counterpoint*, and he asked me what I thought about Huxley. Then he wanted to know if I'd been to college and what, ultimately,

I wanted to do in show-business. I told him, and he promised to help if he could. He was very charming and very polite. We talked together often during the show, and though he never actually gave me any advice about my career, he seemed to take an interest in the little I had to do.'

On a couple of occasions Cole Porter invited him to luxurious parties in his town house. For the first time Gene was given a peep into the sophisticated delights of New York high-life. The elegant milieu in which Porter moved, the dazzle of his friends, whom Gene met as equals over champagne cocktails, the opulence of the surroundings, the sparkle of the conversation, and the sheer brilliance of the wit, as generously in supply as the caviar, represented a kind of glamour beyond his wildest imagination, and he was greatly impressed. Which was more than he could say for the parties thrown by the elderly 'angels' who had sunk money into *Leave It to Me*, and whose policy was to invite only chorus girls. 'They treated the young men in the show like second-class citizens,' he said. 'And this brought out my resentment of the establishment – the same resentment I had against the fraternities at college. Anything that had to do with inequality upset me, and if someone was throwing a party for the kids in the show, I naïvely believed everyone should be invited. Looking back, I understand now that those sugar daddies didn't want youngsters in their twenties hanging around because of the competition. Though, in 1938, they needn't have worried. A lot of the chorus girls *were* gold-diggers who went after money. And how many chorus boys had money?'

On November 9th, 1938 – a couple of months after Hitler had convinced Neville Chamberlain that there would be 'peace in our time' and that all he really wanted was the Sudetenland – *Leave It to Me* opened at the Imperial Theatre. It was a spoof of the Soviet Union in which Victor Moore starred as Alonzo P. Goodhue, a woefully confused American Ambassador who believed the only reason he was sent to Russia was because nobody in Washington liked him.

Though the show also starred William Gaxton, Sophie Tucker and Tamara, the performer who attracted the most attention was a newcomer from Weatherford, Texas, called Mary Martin, who sang a song called 'My Heart Belongs to Daddy', and overnight

71

became the most luminous star in New York. Her début was one of the most sensational in Broadway history, and 'My Heart Belongs to Daddy' with its *double entendre* , became the hit of the season. Thirty-five years later, the song is still closely identified with her. Another memorable number to come from the show was 'Most Gentlemen Don't Like Love', written for Sophie Tucker.

Gene had very little to do and considers his contribution no more than 'set dressing'. He and four other dancers appeared as eskimos feeding grimaces to Mary Martin in her big number, and indulging in a few innocuous motions as they lifted her off the set and then put her back on it.

After *Leave It to Me* opened, Gene hired a dingy rehearsal hall for fifty cents an hour, plus fifty cents an hour for a rehearsal pianist. Not a fortune, but when added to the rest of his expenses, such as food and rent, it left him with very little over. He realised, of course, that with the money the schools were making in Pennsylvania he need not go short of anything, but it had always been his intention to start from scratch and 'rough it' for as long as it took. The dance schools were one thing; his career on Broadway another.

He also continued to see Helene Marlowe who was now trying to nudge him into marriage, although he strongly resisted these nudges – much to the delight and relief of her parents, who were Russian Jews. They disliked Gene intensely and could not accept the thought of an Irish Catholic as a son-in-law.

Leave It to Me closed in July the following year, and after a brief summer recess, opened again in September. As World War Two had begun, and Stalin and Hitler were allies, the political content was drastically changed and the programme carried a note assuring audiences that the musical was in no way meant to be taken as a satirical comment on contemporary world events.

Gene, however, left three months after the show opened. Vinton Freedley, the producer, threatened never to use him in another of his shows if he quit, but Darrow saw a chance for Gene to make more of an impression in a new revue called *One for the Money*, for which he managed to boost Gene's salary to a hundred and fifteen dollars a week. As Gene did not have a run-of-the-play contract in *Leave It to Me*, he was able to leave the show as soon as rehearsals for the revue began.

One for the Money, which opened at the Booth Theatre on February 4th, 1939, was presented by Gertrude Macy and Stanley Gilkey, who were associated with Guthrie McClintic and Katherine Cornell, but whose first independent venture this was. Their idea was to stage three revues, with *Two to Get Ready* and *Three for the Show* still to come.

Apart from Gene, Johnny Darrow placed Robert Alton in the show as choreographer, and Raoul Pene du Bois, another of Darrow's clients, as set designer.

If Harold Rome's *Sing Out the News* and his earlier success *Pins and Needles* were angled very much to the Left, *One for the Money* was quintessentially an establishment revue, whose opening line was: 'We think that right is right and wrong is left' and, as its title suggests, was aimed at the country's élite 400. The sketches and lyrics were by Nancy Hamilton, and were written to give the Park Avenue penthouse brigade the thrill of seeing themselves mirrored on stage in instantly recognisable situations; and the subjects under revue ranged from parlour games to unravelling the plots of Wagnerian operas. It closed after a disappointing run of a hundred and thirty-two performances.

Writing in the *New York Journal*, John Anderson (not to be confused with the show's eminent director, John Murray Anderson) described *One for the Money* as one of the 'glossiest vacuums of the season ... an intimate revue that is smartly, prettily and disastrously empty.'

Gene, whose political sympathies were certainly out of line with the right-wing sentiments expressed in *One for the Money*, did some excellent work in the show (dressed mainly in white tie and tails) and made the most of the sketches and songs he was given. He did not exactly burst onto Broadway in the way Mary Martin did, but it was definitely a 'leg up' for him, as he puts it. He had a carousel number with a couple of the girls, and began the finale to the first half with a song called 'Teeter Totter Tessie' before being joined by the rest of the company for the 'finaletto'. 'I suppose I was the juvenile lead in *One for the Money*,' he said, 'except that there weren't any leads. It was an ensemble revue of six performers without stars as such, and where everybody was equally important.'

One of the six performers was William Archibald, who later

successfully adapted Henry James's *Turn of the Screw* for Broadway. He and Gene became friendly and moved into an apartment together in the Village.

If *One for the Money* hardly rocketed him to stardom it did, at least, bring him into contact with Guthrie McClintic and Katherine Cornell, whom he met in Chicago when the show went on the road during the summer.

McClintic, who with his wife did much to improve the general standard of Broadway production and acting, was tremendously impressed with Gene and his capacity for hard work. So many actors, he remarked to Gene, spent their leisure time drinking, that if actors were acrobats, they'd all be killed. It was an observation Gene never forgot for it applied equally to dancers, who were 'dead' if they did not stay in shape.

Katherine Cornell was also taken with Gene and his engaging personality, but so appalled by his diction, that when he returned to New York at the end of the year, she packed him off to an elderly elocution teacher of immense experience who lived on 57th Street, and whom Miss Cornell herself frequently visited.

'I've never had a good speaking voice,' Gene admitted, 'but in 1939, my flat Pittsburgh accent must have sounded really terrible. I remember this speech teacher would ask me to say "water" and I'd say "wadder". Or she'd ask me to say "orange" and I'd say "ooringe" – just like the Jean Hagen character in *Singin' in the Rain*. Anyway, the main thing was that my diction did improve, and after a few months of hard work, I felt I was ready to play Shakespeare.'

After *One for the Money* took to the road several people dropped out of it, and Gene was given the opportunity to coach the replacements. Bob Alton was committed to another show and couldn't devote the time to do so himself, so the director, John Murray Anderson, trusted Gene with the assignment, which involved more than simply recreating Alton's original choreography. Several of the road replacements were basically actors who had to dance as well – 'doubling in brass', as it were – so that Gene had virtually to work out a set of more simple routines. His years of experience in Johnstown and Pittsburgh now paid off, and he quickly completed the job to everyone's satisfaction, without compromising Alton's

74

original work, or in any way changing the intrinsic personality of the Broadway show.

During their Chicago season at the Selwyn Theatre, Gene, William Archibald and an actor called Robert Smith took a suite in the expensive Ambassador East Hotel, and generally had themselves a ball. One of the highlights of the six weeks Gene spent in Chicago, was his meeting with the legendary John Barrymore, who was playing the Harris Theatre next door to the Selwyn and whom he would see each night in a local bar after the performance, though by 11 pm Barrymore was usually so drunk that it was possible only to respond to the great man's 'aura' rather than anything he actually said.

Orson Welles was also in Chicago at the time, doing a magic act and appearing in excerpts from the George Arliss piece, *The Green Goddess*. But the dramatic highlight of the season was a production of *Romeo and Juliet* with Laurence Olivier and Vivien Leigh. Gene would regularly meet with his fellow actors for a green room session in what he considers to have been his true initiation into the theatre of heavyweights.

No one, however, impressed Gene more than his director, John Murray Anderson. 'I learned more about staging a show from Murray than anyone else in the business,' he said. 'During rehearsals for *One for the Money*, I never took my eyes off him. His timing was superb. He could create any mood he wanted through his brilliant use of lighting. He'd watch a song, then make one simple suggestion that would turn a good number into a hit. He had that sort of ability. Quite a few directors, like Vincente Minnelli, Charles Walters and Bob Alton learned a great deal from Murray. And although he wasn't a choreographer as such, he understood about dancing and often he'd look at a routine Bob Alton might have done and say "Throw it out Fleming, throw it out." He always called people nicknames and Fleming was the name he'd given Bob after a group of famous circus acrobats. He said he couldn't find an appropriate nickname for me, so he just called me Kelly in that marvellously resonant mid-Atlantic accent of his.

'The thing about John Murray Anderson was that you'd be aware of a particular mood, but you wouldn't know how it was achieved. Which couldn't be said for men like Alton, or even

George Abbott. Both were great directors who certainly knew how to construct a scene. But the difference was their work had a tangible quality to it. You could see the seams. You could *see* how Abbott got his laughs or Alton his effects. But with Murray, all you saw was the magic and wonderment of the effect. The cause was his own personal secret. When I went into pictures, I tried to adopt his approach to colour by insisting on certain tints and washes for many of the numbers – that's why, when I see some of those pictures on TV today, either in black and white or in a bad colour print, I can't watch them because the whole mood on which the dance was constructed has disappeared, and all you get in its place are a series of dead images. I would say no one has had as great an influence on my work as John Murray Anderson. The biggest compliment I ever had, certainly up to then, was his approval of my work on *One for the Money*. I didn't know it at the time, but it was to lead directly to my first solo credit on Broadway as a dance director.'

When *One for the Money* closed in Chicago in June 1939, Gene and Bill Archibald motored to Orr's Island in Maine, and hired an old broken-down cottage by the sea, which he and Bill worked over and used for about six weeks. They lived off the land paying no more than a few dollars a week; after receiving their bill from the Ambassador East Hotel, they had little choice in the matter.

Their cottage was roughly a mile off the coast and was connected by a beach-head. It overlooked the Atlantic and the Casco Bay Islands which were especially favoured by writers.

Food, Gene remembered, was never any problem. They made friends with the local lobster fishermen's daughters, so every night it was lobster for dinner. And when they tired of lobster, they ate mackerel bought from the fisherman for a nickel a pound. The mackerel was accompanied by potatoes, which they 'found' all over the place and, occasionally, by adding milk to the mixture, they'd make a fish stew of sorts, which Gene even now recalls with a certain pleasure. They lived luxuriously on practically nothing, their main expenditure being gasoline for the car.

It was an entirely healthy vacation, with nothing to do but loaf around, lie in the sun, or dive off the rocky cliffs into the icy salt water below.

Having recently met so many people who were involved with the 'legitimate' theatre, Gene decided that summer to try his hand at writing a play. Ever since high school and college he had fancied the idea of doing some writing on the side and now, with nothing on his mind but fresh air and sunshine, he thought it a perfect time to make a start. He was inspired, too, by Bill Archibald, who took his own writing seriously and devoted several hours a day to it.

So Gene began to draft out a three-act drama – about a young man who arrives in New York from out of town and finds himself in serious trouble. 'I wrote an act and a half,' Gene said. 'And then I got stuck. It was a pretty frustrating business, but I didn't despair. I just put it aside and started a comedy which I thought would be easier. It was a very sophisticated S. N. Behrman sort of thing – but again, after completing two acts, I was stuck for a third. It just wouldn't come to me, and I experienced the writer's nightmare of facing a blank piece of paper which remained blank two hours later. And I realised, that summer, that writing was definitely out. I had to move about, run into the wind, swim – anything, in fact, that kept me active and burned up my energy. Writing was too sedentary for me. And far too lonely an existence.'

After about six months' friendship, Gene and Bill Archibald found themselves arguing about too many issues, some petty – some serious, and an irrevocable friction developed between them. So, after they arrived back in New York from Maine, they decided to go their separate ways.

Gene motored down to Pittsburgh to visit his family – and although he wasn't exactly returning as Broadway's conquering hero, he had at least appeared in two Broadway shows, and the local publicity carried by the Pittsburgh press was, naturally, flattering. To the folks back home, he was more of a celebrity now than he had been when he left.

'So much so,' Doc Steinberg said, 'that Louis Little (the same man who endorsed Gene to study law in 1933), decided to throw a party for Gene and some of his pals. He had a beautiful home in Pittsburgh, and when Louis suggested the party to Gene, he agreed. So, when the big night came, Gene arrived dressed in his usual sneakers and white socks and I came in a pair of slacks and an open-neck shirt. Very casual, for Gene had told Louis Little not to go to any trouble. We were the first to arrive, and about ten minutes later the door opened, and about a dozen or so players from the Pittsburgh Symphony Orchestra appeared – all formally dressed. Five minutes later, the mayor of the city arrived and after him a few more prominent citizens. Well, Gene's face dropped. He got up from the floor (Gene always sat on the floor), and said: "Well, I think I gotta go now." And he left. The next day when I asked him why, he said that Louis Little was exploiting him, and he didn't want to be exploited. The party was to be for him and some of his pals. If he'd known strangers were going to be invited – he wouldn't have accepted, he said.'

While in Pittsburgh Gene naturally visited the two dance schools, which were continuing to do well under Louise and Fred. Mrs Kelly was still the overall boss and James Kelly the accountant. By now, the schools had well over five hundred pupils, and the annual income was about ten to twelve thousand dollars. Jay, who had married a schoolteacher, was teaching at a public school, and had virtually dissociated herself from the studio. Jim Kelly had left the family completely and was living in Cleveland.

In the summer of 1939, Gene was hired by Johnny Haggott, the stage manager of the Theatre Guild, to choreograph a season of three shows for the Westport Country Playhouse. Haggott had seen Gene in One for the Money, and was impressed. Although he couldn't offer him more than a nominal salary, he persuaded the young dancer that the experience would be compensation enough. The Playhouse itself, like the Theatre Guild's winter activities in New York, carried considerable prestige, and Gene took the job.

His first assignment was to put some appropriate choreography to the organ accompaniment that composer Paul Bowles had written for a production of Eugene O'Neill's The Emperor Jones starring Paul Robeson. The cast was an all-black company from Harlem, and Gene devised a series of dramatic dances which added enormously to the play's highly-charged atmosphere.

Next, he was to choreograph a musical version of Lynn Riggs' *Green Grow the Lilacs*. Johnny Haggott suggested they do it as a folk musical, using such traditional American folk-songs as 'Blood on the Saddle', 'Come Along Little Dogies' and, of course, 'Green Grow the Lilacs'.

The production was a great success, and was held over for a second week. Teresa Helburn who, with Lawrence Langner, ran the Guild, recognised its possibilities for a full-scale Broadway musical and in the next few years her obsession with the project came to be known to everyone at the Guild as 'Terry's Folly'. 'Terry's Folly' materialised into *Oklahoma!* and had a Broadway run of 2,248 performances.

Gene's final show of the season had him appearing as Master of Ceremonies in an intimate revue featuring two New Yorkers called Betty Comden and Adolph Green who had an act called 'The Revuers'.

'The show was called *The Magazine Page*,' Betty Comden said, 'the idea being that each section of it would be represented by a page in a magazine, and as the show progressed the pages kept turning. Gene came into the show at the last minute, and I remember thinking how attractive and how full of vitality he was.'

Adolph Green recalled that his first impression of Gene was more of the 'salt-of-the-earth, all-American boy type' – rather than the deep-thinking intellectual, which was a later impression he had of Gene. 'To me, he was just an energetic young man who looked much younger than his twenty-seven years. He was a hoofer with something extra hidden away. He had this terrific outgoing quality combined with a street-boy earthiness which was extremely appealing. You just knew he was going places. I hadn't seen either of his shows on Broadway, and when I saw his act in Westport, I was knocked out immediately.'

The highlight of Gene's performance was an item in which he did a series of satirical take-offs on how various types of dancers would negotiate a tap routine. He demonstrated how, for example, a ballet dancer might approach some basic hoofing; or how a 'flash' dancer might cope with an elementary time step; or how the 'personality' girl would handle a simple tap-dance – all of which he had observed back home in his two dancing schools. The 'big finish' to his act was a highly effective combination of dance and acrobatics as he sprang across the floor bouncing on the palms of his hands, with his legs stretched out behind him.

'Everything that Gene was, or was later to become, was already there in a nugget in that act,' Adolph Green said. 'His qualities were immediately apparent, and the surprising thing was, when you first looked at him, what struck you most was his charm and his clean-cut good looks. You didn't think of him as a dancer at all. But the minute he took off, it was a different story. He was full of grace and vitality, and what I remember most of all, was the effect he had on an audience. They just loved him. He could do no wrong. There was this magic – this "star quality" he exuded. His dancing was very athletic and he had the wonderful ability to make the most complicated things look ridiculously simple.'

The morning after *The Magazine Page* opened, the *Bridgeport Post* noted that 'Gene Kelly, an added starter not listed on the programme, was probably the individual hit of the show' – a view endorsed by another reviewer who commented that 'the dancing of Gene Kelly, especially his demonstration of the various types of tap-dancers, was the evening's high spot.'

Though the season at Westport made him very little money, it did make him several good friends, not least of whom were Lawrence Langner, his wife Armina, and Teresa Helburn – three of the most influential people in the American theatre at the time. It also introduced him to Comden and Green who, ten years later, were to begin their Hollywood association with him on *Take Me Out to the Ball Game* for which they wrote the lyrics.

In September 1939, after his season at Westport, Gene took a trip to Mexico with his father via the Great Smokeys, Laredo, Texas, the Mississippi, Louisiana and New Orleans. The poverty he encountered among the Mexican peasants distressed him a great deal, particularly as the churches he visited were overflowing with objects whose monetary value was incalculable. What he saw shocked him, for it was totally against the socialist principles he had been developing since his college days. He could not reconcile the starvation and deprivation he saw all around with the bounty inside those churches, and returned to New York disturbed by what he had seen, and doubting the worth of a religion which valued material objects more than the physical and spiritual well-being of its adherents. His Mexican trip opened his eyes to the hypocrisy of what he called 'organised religion' and by 1940 his agnosticism was complete.

After returning to New York, Gene lived on social security (at fifteen dollars a week) and, in the autumn of 1939, continued to do the rounds of auditions. He moved out of the Village and shared a 'cubby hole' apartment on West 55th Street, between 5th and 6th Avenue, with a friend called Dick Dwenger. If anything, Dwenger was even more hard up than Gene so, in lieu of his share of the rent, he played an out-of-tune rehearsal piano for Gene in a squalid, depressing and rat-infested Masonic Hall in the West fifties between 9th and 10th Avenue, which Gene rented for twenty-five cents an hour. Its only good point was that it was large enough for him to leap around in.

In spite of these penurious circumstances, Gene enjoyed his life in New York, and made friends with people like Lloyd Gough and Francis Cheyney, whose politics, like his own, were decidely to the left. They would meet every night at Louie Bergen's bar on 45th Street, talking and drinking until 'Broadway babies said goodnight, early in the morning.'

Then one day he received a call from his agent, Johnny Darrow, to tell him that Eddie Dowling, who was presenting William Saroyan's play *The Time of Your Life* in conjunction with the Theatre Guild, was having problems and needed to recast the role of Harry the Hoofer. In the play, Harry is described as a 'dumb young fellow' whose simple philosophy is that the world is full of sorrow and needs laughter. Martin Ritt (now a successful film director), who was originally cast as Harry, was failing to make people laugh, and Saroyan, who took over the direction of the play from Dowling in New Haven, wanted him replaced. Initially the Guild suggested that Charles Walters, then one of Broadway's leading young dancers, might be suitable. Walters, who was also one of Darrow's clients, read for the role, which was offered to him.

But when he learned that the salary would only be a hundred and seventy-five dollars a week, he turned it down, and suggested they try 'that new kid Kelly'. Darrow thought it an excellent idea, and asked Gene what he felt about it.

Gene was delighted with the suggestion. But Lawrence Langner, who had seen him work at Westport, felt he couldn't possibly be right, and didn't think there was any point even in seeing Gene. The impression Langner had was of a clean-cut youngster whose face shone and who wore tuxedos. And his 'accent' (which Gene had been working on steadily) was too 'posh' for the role. In the end, he and Dowling did audition Gene, and both thought him wrong. A couple of days later, however, Saroyan himself saw Gene, and liked what he saw; for this time Gene had come prepared. He had let his beard grow, and the clothes he wore corresponded exactly to Saroyan's description of the character. 'His pants were too long, his coat too large and too loose, and nothing matched.'

'After Ritt had been given his notice,' William Saroyan remembered, 'I was seriously considering casting a young fellow named Ray Middleton. In fact, Middleton would probably have got the part if he had been able to shout. But he couldn't. At least not well enough. Suddenly, from deep in the shadows of the Guild Theatre on 52nd Street, a voice boomed out saying: "I can shout." Lawrence Langner, who was attending the audition, was most indignant and wanted to put the upstart, whose name was Gene Kelly, back in his place among the other waiting aspirants. But I said no, and I asked the man, who certainly *looked* right for Harry, to step forward and to shout out the monologue about who's behind the 8-ball, and so on. He then did some tap and other dancing, and I said okay, you'll go up with us to Boston, where I was putting the play into some kind of approximation of what I had originally intended it to be, instead of the absurdity the arty boys at the Guild had made of it while I had been in San Francisco writing a new play.'

The following day Gene saw the play in New Haven, and a week later took over from Martin Ritt in Boston. He had Saroyan's approval to work out his own choreography, and when the play opened in New York on October 25th, at the Booth Theatre, Gene's characterisation of Harry the Hoofer was one of the highlights of the evening.

'Gene Kelly helped me get the play in its true dimension of theatre, along with several other replacements for ridiculously miscast people,' Saroyan said. 'In the same visit from Boston to New York, I hired William Bendix and Celeste Holm, for instance. Well, Gene was inventive and full of useful ideas which I instantly was sensible enough to seize upon and put into the play; and his ballet leaps near the end of Act Two were especially effective when Kitty Duval, played by Julie Hayden, is studying the carousel Joe (Eddie Dowling) had had Tom (Edward Andrews) go out and buy for her. Gene Kelly helped both the playwright and the other players by doing his part magnificently. Before we actually opened in New York, the theory held by the residue of the original cast was that I was wrecking the play, and that my working methods were decidedly unorthodox. Yet they couldn't explain why, for the first time, audiences were now finding the piece deeply satisfying. Gene Kelly was a very significant part of that about face. His tap-dancing, moving in and out of the action, made a kind of new Greek chorus comment on what was going on – somewhat along the lines of the end of one order of reality in the West. I don't mean this to be too big in significance,' he said, 'I mean simply to report what came across to me from what I saw and heard, and what seemed to come across for others too. The tapping of his feet was not unlike a drum roll at a funeral; an end that was both a loss and a welcome beginning of something else – almost anything else. Gene Kelly is a great man of the theatre.'

Set in a San Francisco water-front saloon, and peopled by a rag-bag collection of sailors, cops, bums, prostitutes, drunks and young men in love, *The Time of Your Life*, which Saroyan wrote in six days, and which has been described by critic Louis Kronenberger as 'a chant of love for the scared and the rejected', ran for twenty-two weeks. Though possibly too whimsical a piece to satisfy the flinty audiences of today, in 1939, exactly ten years after the Stock Market crashed, and two months after World War Two had been declared, its geniality and warm-hearted faith in mankind had a reassuring effect on American audiences, whose values during the past decade had been changing as fast as the world, and whose beliefs in America as a great political and economic power were seriously being questioned. Saroyan's play with its dream-like quality, stubbornly refused to acknowledge reality and bathed the world in a roseate glow. Its childlike insistence on the essential goodness of people made an appealing change from much that was brittle, sophisticated and world-weary on Broadway at the time, and the author's simple philosophy – that we're all mad but beautiful – was a timely and refreshing affirmation of life in a world once again plunged into the misery of war. Saroyan's view of the world was the same as Chaplin's in the mid-twenties – the nostalgia the play evoked for America's lost innocence won for it both the Pulitzer Prize and the Drama Critics' Award.

Any doubts that Messrs Langner and Dowling may have entertained about Gene's ability to breathe life into Harry the Hoofer disappeared on the opening night on Broadway, when his performance stopped the show. 'I knew,' said Gene, 'if I didn't make it that night I might as well pack up and go home. But by some miracle, it all worked.'

During the run of *The Time of Your Life* Gene discovered, while playing Harry the Hoofer, that the style of his dancing in the play was dictated solely by the part. For the first time he was actually required to characterise a role through movement and to *act* a dance. 'I realised,' he said, 'that there was no character – whether a sailor or a truck driver or a gangster – that couldn't be interpreted through dancing, if one found the correct choreographic language. What you can't have is a truck driver coming on stage and doing an *entrechat*. Because that would be incongruous – like a lady opening her mouth and singing bass. But there was a way of getting that truck driver to dance that would *not* be incongruous – just as there was a way of making Harry the Hoofer, a saloon bum, look convincing. It may seem obvious now, but at the time, it was an important discovery for me.'

While *The Time of Your Life* continued to play to audiences appreciative of its charm and innocence, the diminutive showman, Billy

Rose, whose mammoth extravaganzas more than compensated for his physical stature, was preparing another show for his *Diamond Horseshoe* club. The director was to be John Murray Anderson, who had recently staged Rose's spectacular *Aquacade* at the New York World's Fair, as well as the previous *Diamond Horseshoe* show. Rose wanted Bob Alton to do the choreography, but Alton being committed elsewhere, John Murray Anderson suggested Gene who, he assured Rose, was as good as, if not better than Alton. For Rose that was recommendation enough; he called Gene and offered him the dance direction on his forthcoming *Diamond Horseshoe*. 'Murray Anderson tells me you can handle it,' Rose said to him on the 'phone. 'But of course, he could be wrong. *Can* you handle it?'

Gene assured him he could. This was no time for modesty.

'All right then. This is what I have in mind for the show,' he said. And he gave Gene a breakdown of his ideas. 'Now give me a mental audition of how you see it all.'

Gene paused at the other end of the 'phone for a moment, then proceeded to dazzle Rose by outlining exactly what he would do with each part of the show.

'I talked for an hour or more,' Gene said, 'and after I was through there was a silence. I thought he'd fainted or something. Or just tiptoed quietly out of the room. Then he said: "Great. That's exactly what I want." And he offered me a hundred dollars a week. I told him he was out of his mind. Then he got tough with me, and I got tough back. I told him I had been getting more than that in both my last shows. He was unimpressed. He offered me a hundred and twenty-five. I said no. Nothing doing. He said, "I'll give you a hundred and thirty dollars a week and not a cent more." I said forget it. After all, there was a lot of work to be done, and I knew how much Alton was getting. I told him he was a bastard to take advantage of me. By this time we were both slanging away at each other, and I don't think he could believe his ears – a young guy turning down an opportunity to do a show for the great Billy Rose.

'Suddenly, in the middle of shouting at each other, he burst out laughing. "Okay," he said. "I'll give you a hundred and thirty-five dollars a week – and that's my final offer. Take it or leave it." "Okay, I'll take it," I said. And the following day I went to work.'

At about the same time as Billy Rose's *Diamond Horseshoe* went into rehearsal, the International Casino Supper Club, which boasted the youngest and prettiest show girls in New York, closed when the manager made off with the profits. Billy Rose heard about this, and sent all the girls in the show a postcard inviting them to audition for his *Horseshoe* show in the ballroom of the Capitol Hotel. One of the girls was a sixteen-year-old dancer from New Jersey called Betsy Blair. Her mother was a teacher, and her father an insurance clerk. Average parents, from an average home. Too average, in fact, for Betsy, whose real name was Betsy Boger – and who sought the glamour and the excitement of show-business. Betsy was particularly thrilled at the prospect of working for the important Billy Rose. So she borrowed a cousin's inherited fur jacket plus a pill-box hat with protruding violets and, looking like Ann Sheridan, made her way to the Capitol Hotel.

When she arrived, the ballroom was deserted. A single light cast gloomy shadows across the room and the chairs were piled high on the tables. There wasn't a soul in sight. Suddenly, a voice called out: 'Can I help you?' She looked around and saw Gene. 'I have a call from Mr Rose,' she said. 'He's auditioning for dancers, I believe.' 'That's not until tomorrow,' Gene said. 'You've made a mistake.' Then he said: 'Are you a good dancer?' Betsy looked at this total stranger, and wondered what business of his it was whether she was or wasn't. 'Actually,' she said, 'I happen to be a *very* good dancer.' 'In that case,' said Gene, 'I'll see you tomorrow.' And he smiled at her. She looked at him for a moment, registered that whoever or whatever he was, he was really rather attractive, and left. It wasn't until she returned the next morning that she realised he was the choreographer.

'There was John Murray Anderson, Billy Rose and Gene,' Betsy said. 'And it seemed to me they were in the process of eliminating girls rather than employing them. John Murray Anderson who, I later heard, described me as a "knobbly filly", was just about to eliminate me because I was too skinny and had a flat chest. Naturally, I was desperately disappointed, and must have looked as though I was about to burst into tears, because Gene suddenly turned to John and said: "I hear she's a very good dancer, and I need some talent in this show." So they kept me,' Betsy said. 'And after that, I developed such a crush on Gene that John used to call me "teacher's pet". I changed my rehearsal clothes twice a day, and couldn't have been cleaner, fresher or more hard-working. I wanted Gene to like me, and I wanted him to like my work.'

One morning Dick Dwenger, who continued as rehearsal pianist, and who had noticed the king-sized crush Betsy had on Gene, asked her whether she wanted to join them for lunch. Betsy was over-joyed, and the three of them went out together and continued to do so over the next few weeks. Finally Gene asked her out by himself, not as part of a threesome, and she was ecstatic.

A couple of nights after the show opened, Gene slipped into the club and stood at the back to see how things were going. 'I noticed him immediately,' Betsy said. 'And I could see that he was with a dark-haired woman, who I later learned was Helene Marlowe. Suddenly I began to cry uncontrollably, and finished the rest of the routine with tears pouring down my cheeks. I was that smitten. What the people in the first couple of rows must have thought I'll never know.'

When the Broadway run of *The Time of Your Life* ended, Gene decided not to go on the road with it, and Eddie Dowling began to look around for a replacement. He saw no one who satisfied him and asked Gene if he had any ideas. Gene did. 'You're not going to believe it,' he told Dowling, 'but there's only one person who can do it, and that's my brother Fred. We look alike, we dance alike, and he'll be just great.'

So Dowling brought Fred to New York, and auditioned him. They agreed he was fine, and Gene took a couple of days off to go through the routine with him. 'Naturally there were certain divergences in style,' Gene said. 'But basically the steps were the same and Fred picked them up without trouble. After all, he'd been a pro since he was five!'

While Fred was on the road with *The Time of Your Life*, Mrs Kelly and Louise ran the two studios with the help of assistants, and both schools continued to run profitably.

Though Gene was still seeing Helene Marlowe, he and Betsy went out with each other a couple of times a week, and a genuine relationship developed. 'There was definitely something going between us,' she said. 'He treated me like an angel, almost. Very gently – as if I were someone to be taken care of and educated. His friends were all left-wing intellectuals, and would hang around Louie Bergen's, talking about Ibsen or the Spanish Civil War and other subjects of which I had never even been aware. I'd never met such stimulating people before. Their views made quite an impression on a girl of sixteen – as Gene hoped they would. They all agreed on one thing though; if I wanted to make it in show-business, I'd better get out of night-clubs and into musical comedy.'

So she auditioned for *Louisiana Purchase*, a musical about crooked politicians by Morrie Ryskind and Irving Berlin, but was turned down on the last day of auditions, whereupon she burst into tears. Next, she auditioned for Cole Porter's *Panama Hattie*, with Ethel Merman, Rags Ragland, Betty Hutton and Arthur Treacher. The choreographer, once again, was the ubiquitous Robert Alton, who asked Betsy whether she would burst into tears again if he turned her down. She said she would. So Alton gave her a part in the chorus which she gladly accepted, for 'Alton's girls' were well known to be the best in the business, and included June Allyson, Vera-Ellen, Adele Jergens, Miriam Franklin and Bonnie Green.

Gene released her from the *Diamond Horseshoe* contract and she, June Allyson and a secretary called Claire Moynihan moved into the Henry Hudson Hotel – an all-girl establishment which did not allow men to get any further than the lobby.

June Allyson, the most ambitious of the Alton girls, got her big chance in *Panama Hattie* one night when she stood in for Betty Hutton, who had gone down with the measles. 'We all knew it would only be a matter of time before June made it,' Betsy said. 'If, for example, she knew Charles Boyer, or Ty Power or someone equally famous was out front, she would deliberately fall down in order to attract attention. She was the smallest girl and the last in the line – and on our exit, she would pretend to trip. When she picked herself up, everyone would applaud out of sympathy, which was just what she wanted. Not the most subtle way of getting noticed – but it seemed to work.'

Panama Hattie opened to generally favourable reviews, with raves for Ethel Merman and the Porter score and lyrics, and settled down for a run of five hundred and one performances: Porter's biggest success to date.

Early in 1940, George Abbott and Rodgers and Hart were planning to stage a musical adaptation of John O'Hara's *New Yorker* short stories *Pal Joey*. Bob Alton, fresh from his stint on *Panama Hattie*, was engaged as dance director; O'Hara himself agreed to do the book, and Vivienne Segal was chosen to play Vera Simpson, the society lady who befriends Joey Evans, the owner of a sleazy night-club.

The question around Broadway was – who was going to play Joey?

One morning, Johnny Darrow, who was in California, received a 'phone call from Richard Rodgers who wanted to know 'whether that guy Kelly', whom he had seen in *The Time of Your Life*, could sing as well as dance. Sure, Darrow said, and asked Rodgers what he had in mind. 'Something,' said Rodgers and volunteered no more information. 'Give me a ring in three weeks' time and we'll talk about it.'

Immediately Darrow called Gene and told him about his conversation with Rodgers. Obviously, Darrow said, Rodgers had Gene in mind for *Pal Joey*, and suggested to Gene that he find himself a singing coach as soon as possible, and learn as much as he could about how to project a song.

Three weeks later, Darrow returned to New York and called Rodgers, who told him he'd like to hear Gene sing. They arranged to meet the following Saturday morning at the Century Theatre at ten o'clock.

The atmosphere at the Century Theatre was polite but formal. Gene was introduced to the creative team all of whom, except Alton of course, were strangers to him. Then he and his singing teacher – a middle-aged woman whom he had asked to play the piano for him that morning – positioned themselves on stage. Abbott took a seat half-way down the stalls and signalled that he was ready. Gene cleared his throat and began with one of Rodgers' own compositions – a ballad called 'I Didn't Know What Time It Was'.

'I thought,' said Gene, 'that if I sang one of his own songs, it would impress him, little knowing that there's an unwritten law that says *never* sing a song back to a composer at an audition, unless of course he specifically asks you to do so. But there I was, singing one of Rodgers' most beautiful – and difficult – numbers, and not singing it very well because I couldn't sing then – and I still can't. Well he didn't bat an eyelid. Though years later, when I was directing *Flower Drum Song* on Broadway, if any of the kids came to an audition and sang one of his numbers, he'd blandly tell them that flattery would get them no place at all. On this occasion though, he said nothing, and when the song came to an end, there was no reaction at all. I was convinced I'd blown it. All he did was ask me to sing something else – a bit faster. So I went straight into a lively ditty I used to do in the cloops called "It's the Irish In Me", which had a lot of pep and dash to it, and which I knew how to put across.

'After I was through, O'Hara, who hadn't said a word throughout the audition called out from the back of the theatre: "That's it. Take him."'

Abbott and Rodgers, however, were in no hurry to make a decision. New York was full of talented young men, and they wanted to exhaust all possibilities before committing the taxing role of Joey Evans to a relative newcomer. So, while they continued to hold auditions and make up their minds, Gene returned to Maine for a rest, and Johnny Darrow returned to California. Weeks went by and neither heard a word. Rumours via the grapevine had every leading man in New York already signed up, and Gene was sure he wasn't going to get it.

Then Abbott arrived in California and took an office at the RKO studios. He called Darrow as soon as he arrived and said, 'Where's Kelly?'

Darrow told him Gene was in Maine. 'Well, we're seriously thinking about him for *Pal Joey*,' Abbott said. Darrow played it cool and said that if they could come to a favourable decision moneywise, he would be glad to negotiate a contract. The next few days passed agonisingly slowly as both Gene and Darrow waited to hear from Abbott.

A week later Abbott called Darrow and told him they'd finally settled for Gene, and asked him to draw up an equity contract for three hundred and fifty dollars a week.

'It was far less than such a role deserved,' Darrow said. 'But I'd loused up one chance for Gene, and I certainly wasn't going to do so again. As far as I was concerned, he could have played *Pal Joey* for nothing. It was that important a show.'

Rehearsals began in the autumn. Apart from Vivienne Segal, there was Leila Ernst as Joey's girlfriend, and the relatively small part of Gladys was taken by June Havoc, making her Broadway début. Van Johnson was in the show as well – so was a sixteen-year-old youth from South Carolina called Stanley Donen.

'I was nothing at the time,' Donen said. 'A *shlepper*. A real zero. And I remember being impressed by Gene as soon as I saw him on the stage. He had a cockiness, a confidence in himself, and a ruthlessness in the way he went about things that, to someone as young and green as myself, was astonishing. I also found him cold, egotistical and very rough. And, of course, wildly talented. He was the only song and dance man to come out of that period who had balls. There were good dancers around, like Don Loper, Jack Cole, Gower Champion, Charles Walters, Dan Dailey – even Van Johnson. But they somehow weren't as dynamic as Gene. No one was. That's why he was such an explosion on the scene. It was the athlete in him that gave him his uniqueness.'

George Kaufman, the celebrated humorist, once remarked that plays are not written, they're rewritten, and so it was with *Pal Joey*, where George Abbott's main concern was to present a show which in no way under-played the intrinsic cynicism of the original stories but, equally, would not keep the public away from the theatre. It was not easy; for Joey is basically an unlovable heel – a hoofer who will stop at nothing to get what he wants, regardless of who gets hurt in the process. His pretty girlfriend Linda becomes the first victim of his ruthlessness when she is thrown over for Vera Simpson, a wealthy society woman who has her sights set on Joey and is prepared to pay anything to get him – even when the cost is an expensive night-club in Chicago's south side. But Joey is no more faithful to Vera than he was to Linda or all the other 'chicks' – and wanders off in search of fresh sexual encounters. For all his bravado, however, he is really rather gullible and is soon blackmailed out of his club and left penniless. Even Vera and Linda refuse to comfort him, and the musical ends as Joey realises he is answerable only to himself for the lonely future which awaits him.

O'Hara, Rodgers and Hart continued to work on the show until they thought they'd got it absolutely right. Hart was particularly skilful at playing the Genie to Abbott's Aladdin, and would conjure up new lyrics with amazing speed whenever they were required.

'He was so witty, it was unbelievable, not in an extrovert way like Oscar Levant,' Gene said, 'but quietly, subtly. Like Lincoln scribbling down the Gettysburg address he'd jot down lyrics on anything that came to hand – a brown paper bag or a cigarette box. He'd call these jottings his "dummy run", and shove in a whole lot of four letter words or abusive expressions to help him get the right rhythm. Then he'd disappear for fifteen minutes, and return with the most polished stylish lyric you've ever seen.'

Gene remembers that Hart was a sentimental, pleasant, highly emotional little man. 'He was tortured by his small physical stature, and by his homosexuality. For all his wit, he was one of the saddest, loneliest people I ever knew, and like O'Hara, also drank a great deal and had a reputation for disappearing suddenly without trace. But he was very dear to all the people in the show.'

Before going to Philadelphia, *Pal Joey* was seen by an invited show-biz audience in New York. The reaction was excellent, but Abbott knew this response was not to be regarded as typical. He would have to wait until the Philadelphia try-out for a more reliable barometer.

Philadelphia, however, was beset with the usual out-of-town problems. The book wasn't quite right yet, and Gene felt nervous and unready. His voice was strained and overworked, and he was convinced that any freshness he may originally have brought to the role was no longer there. The whole thing had become a burden – a heavy job of acting, singing and dancing, the scope of which he felt was beyond him. And he continued to feel this way right until the opening night in Philadelphia.

After the curtain came down on Act One, Johnny Darrow went backstage to see him. When he came into his dressing-room, Gene looked up from his make-up mirror. 'I know. I know exactly what you're thinking,' he said. To which Darrow replied: 'I only have one thing to say to you. Your Joey is already so fantastic that by the time you get to New York you'll be knocking the shit out of the part.' 'And,' said Darrow, some thirty-three years later, 'I meant every word of it. He was incredible.'

But the show still had problems. The first act went well, but the second act 'needed work', and Abbott decided to cut one of Gene's numbers because it slowed down the finale. To aggravate matters, John O'Hara chose Philadelphia in which to disappear just when he was most needed, leaving Abbott to doctor the invalid second act himself. And although Abbott had written (with Philip Dunning) the successful comedy *Broadway*, O'Hara's style eluded him. 'I write what I *think* O'Hara would have written,' he told Gene, 'but somehow it never sounds the same. It comes out dead and lifeless. Something is missing.' Fortunately, O'Hara returned from his hiding-place in time to work on the act. After the company's initial three-week engagement in Philadelphia, *Pal Joey* was finally ready for Broadway.

But was Broadway ready for *Pal Joey*?

At about six o'clock on Christmas Eve, 1940 – Gene, who was now staying at the Hotel Woodward on 55th Street and Broadway, left his room and checked into the Ethel Barrymore Theatre. Earlier, he had spent some time with his mother and Louise, who had come from Pittsburgh to be with him. He felt nervous, but not nearly as nervous as he had felt in Philadelphia. He was encouraged by the stage manager of the Ethel Barrymore Theatre who, in a lifetime of seeing at least a thousand shows come and go, told Gene that rarely had a performance in a musical impressed him as much as his. In five hours' time, he predicted, Gene would walk out into Times Square a star.

To the boys and girls who crowded into the communal dressing-rooms *Pal Joey* was just one more show. But to its principal players and creators, it was the culmination of months of hard work in preparation for judgement night, and an important step forward (or backward) in their respective careers. Everyone was anxious in case the critics might react unfavourably to the show's hard-boiled, down-beat theme; the usual feeling of excitement and expectation which accompanies most first-nights was especially tinged with tensions.

Fifteen minutes before curtain-up, Gene was about to embark on the most exciting adventure of his life, still uncertain whether he would return victorious or vanquished. Vivienne Segal popped into his dressing-room to wish him good luck, and Johnny Darrow gave him the few obligatory words of encouragement.

Then suddenly Gene was all alone. In five minutes' time though, he would be joined by a thousand expectant people, including his anxious mother and New York's major theatre critics. He dared not think what was at stake. His job now was to get out there and give the performance everything he had. He checked his make-up in the mirror, combed back his hair and made his way from the dressing-room to the side of the stage.

After what seemed an eternity, the stage manager gave the musical director, Harry Levant, the go-ahead, and suddenly Richard Rodgers' lushly scored overture filled the Ethel Barrymore Theatre.

During the overture, Gene positioned himself on stage. The setting was a cheap cloop of the sort he and his brother Fred had often played in Chicago together – and he felt at home in it.

When the overture ended, and the applause subsided, the curtain rose. This was it. Harry Levant cued him in and he began to sing what was a deliberately corny number called 'Chicago'. 'There's a great big town, by a great big lake called Chicago . . .' For about thirty seconds he sang on his own, then the orchestra suddenly sneaked in, and took the number to its finish.

Act One went like a dream, with the New York first-nighters accepting Hart's risqué lyrics in their sophisticated stride. Rodgers' music, with numbers such as 'I Could Write A Book' and 'Bewitched, Bothered and Bewildered', were immediately accessible and, judging from the atmosphere in the theatre, no one seemed offended by the show's morals or lack of them.

The second act went just as well. O'Hara's book, Hart's lyrics, Rodgers' music and Abbott's direction continued to weld themselves into a satisfying dramatic entity and the ovation that greeted the show at the end seemed to indicate that it would have a long and profitable run.

For Gene the evening was especially memorable. Just as Mary

Martin had caused a sensation a couple of seasons back in *Leave It to Me*, so he captivated audiences at the Ethel Barrymore that night. From his unaccompanied opening to his unsentimental portrayal of spiritual bankruptcy at the end, Gene's performance was a revelation, as strong dramatically as it was musically. That compulsive star quality hinted at in *The Time of Your Life* was now on the loose. His ability to capture and hold an audience was complete.

His mother rushed backstage after the performance. Gene had never before seen her choked with joy, for she had always expected more from her children and was never satisfied with what they gave. But that night there was no way in which she was able to control her happiness and pride. Gene had justified her belief in him beyond her most extravagant dreams. She *knew* she had been right in insisting, from the age of seven, that he attend dancing classes. Without her none of this would have happened. In a way, therefore, the evening was as much a triumph for her as it was for Gene – a vindication of her beliefs and the fulfilment of his promise.

Betsy Blair, who could not be at the opening night because she was still appearing in *Panama Hattie*, rushed over to the theatre as soon as she could, and spent the rest of the night with Gene at a party given by Lorenz Hart in his apartment – jointly to celebrate Christmas Eve and what they all assumed to be the show's success.

It wasn't until December 26th, however, that the reviews finally appeared. Gene and the cast were again at Lorenz Hart's apartment when, just after midnight, they received Burns Mantle's notice in the *New York Daily News*. It was an enthusiastic review which praised everything and everyone, not least of all Gene, of whom Mantle generously wrote: 'Mr Kelly is able to give the part personal attractions that justify the O'Hara picture. He is likeable as an individual and gifted as a dancer. Technically his range,' Mr Mantle went on, 'is wide without including any impulse toward the eccentric, which makes for an agreeable artistic balance. It was a fortunate day for him, and for us I think, when Mr O'Hara and Mr Abbott picked him out of the group that helped to make *The Time of Your Life* a prize-winning play.

'*Pal Joey*,' he concluded, 'adds definitely to the current competition in musical entertainment, and this is cheering.'

Next came Richard Watts Junior's rave review in the *Herald*

Tribune. 'The quality that has made Mr O'Hara's writing so robust, salty and realistic has been captured with fine gusto, and combined with one of Richard Rodgers' most winning scores, some of Lorenz Hart's finest lyrics, the brilliant staging of dances that Robert Alton always provides, an utterly satisfying cast and George Abbott's most expert manipulation; the result is a delight. Put *Pal Joey* down as an outstanding triumph of a suddenly awakened theatrical season.'

And of Gene he said: 'It was a happy stroke of casting that placed Mr Kelly in the title-role. This young man is genuinely life-saving to *Pal Joey* for, if the chief part were not properly cast, the new musical show might have been too merciless for comfort. Mr Kelly does nothing obvious about softening his characterisation, but he does manage to combine a certain amount of straightforward personal charm with the realism of his portrait, so that Joey actually achieves the feat of being at once a heel and a hero. *Pal Joey*,' he concluded, 'is a hard-boiled delight.'

Then came the most important notice of all: Brooks Atkinson's in the *New York Times*. For the power jointly invested in Atkinson, New York's most influential theatre critic, and the *Times*, New York's most influential paper, could make or break a show.

Atkinson, alas, did not rave about *Pal Joey* and grudgingly commented that 'if it is possible to make an entertaining musical comedy out of an odious story, *Pal Joey* is it.' And although he acknowledged that it was 'expertly done', he ended the notice with the observation that it was not possible to draw sweet water from a foul well. Atkinson's review put a decided damper on the evening. Lorenz Hart, who had tremendous respect for Atkinson's opinions, burst into tears after the notice was read to him and went sobbing to his room.

The rest of the reviews were mixed, and it was doubtful now whether *Pal Joey* would succeed at the box-office.

The matinées were half empty and were attended by suburban ladies in suburban hats who hated every second of it, and thought it tawdry and pornographic. But the weekend audiences loved and cheered it. Opinion was sharply divided. There were those who appreciated the show for its fresh, honest, unsentimental approach – and those who hated it for its fresh, honest, unsentimental approach –

96

arguing that the kind of realism portrayed on the stage of the Ethel Barrymore Theatre had no place in musical comedy. *Pal Joey* ran for two hundred and fifty performances in its first season and returned the following year for a run of a further hundred and four. On neither occasion could it be called a popular success.

All the same, following the 'tough' tradition of musical 'low life' comedy – which goes back to John Gay's *The Beggar's Opera* – *Pal Joey* was an epoch-making Broadway event. Contemporary musicals such as *Panama Hattie* and *Dubarry was a Lady* were tough, brash shows. But they had an aorta of sentimentality coursing through them which guaranteed the sort of public approval *Pal Joey* was not to enjoy until it was seen ten years later, in a diluted, less hard-hitting revival starring Harold Lang as Joey.

But at its inception, even Broadway's jaded audiences were unprepared for the mixture of sex and blackmail that underlined the evening. Nor could they accept the fact that although the show bristled with carnality, it was uniquely bereft of romance. In the original production Vivienne Segal and Gene did not once make physical contact, in spite of the overtly sexual nature of their relationship. As a result, there is only one love-song, the very beautiful 'I Could Write A Book', and even then it is difficult to believe that Joey actually means what he is singing. (Years later, in the musical *How to Succeed in Business Without Really Trying*, also about an unscrupulous young man on the make, Frank Loesser, who wrote both music and lyrics, solved the problem of the obligatory love-song by making the hero sing one to himself as he sees his reflection in the mirror while shaving.)

Pal Joey was also the first Broadway musical to open on an empty stage without the traditional chorus. It was no coincidence that *Oklahoma!* – another work by Richard Rodgers – had a similarly quiet opening as Curly, alone on stage, goes straight into 'Oh What a Beautiful Mornin' '.

In an era when most musicals were little more than an excuse for a series of galvanic speciality numbers whose relevance to a plot was, to say the least, tenuous, the unrespectable *Pal Joey*, with its tightly integrated, skilfully incorporated book, music, lyrics and dancing (especially dancing) did more than any other show before it to make the musical respectable. Even the night-club numbers were integrated into the plot of the musical, providing a show within a show, as the musical *Cabaret* was to do twenty-five years later. Certainly no musical before *Pal Joey* presented audiences with so complex a character study as Joey Evans.

Gene's main concern was to keep O'Hara's intentions intact without alienating the audience, and decided the best way to do this was to play him as an amoral rather than immoral character. He had to get across the idea that Joey simply had no idea what was right or wrong.

'For example,' said Gene, 'he would accept his promiscuity as a matter of course, completely unaware of the hurt he was causing, and just when he was being especially offensive, I'd look at the audience, smile at them, and go into a song and dance, turning the character round, almost.

'I instinctively felt that this was the right approach and when George Abbott did nothing to stop me from pursuing it, I stuck to it. But I was worried as hell at first. I said to O'Hara, "Jesus, they're going to hate me so much, I'll never get through the first act." And he said, "No, they're going to hate Joey, but they're going to like *you*." And I think, unconsciously, I got the clue to my interpretation from that remark. But I did worry, of course. In O'Hara's stories, you hate the guy. And I knew it would be fatal if the same applied to the stage version.'

In *Pal Joey* Gene learned, for the first time, how to manipulate an audience while playing a dramatic role, how to make them respond to him in just the way he wanted – mesmerise them, almost. He was assisted a great deal, not only by George Abbott, who taught him some fundamentals of timing and helped him structure his performance (until then he had never played a role as long as this); but also by Robert Alton, who saw what Gene was trying to achieve in his dances and encouraged him. It was an extension of what he was doing in *The Time of Your Life* – interpreting the character through dance. Slowly he was beginning to develop a style which had nothing to do with the work he did in Pittsburgh, or even in *One for the Money*. What was coming across was absolutely new, and audiences liked it.

'They couldn't quite pigeon-hole it,' Gene said, 'but they responded favourably and that was all that mattered. At the end of

Act One, for example, I'd do some ballet, and it was straight classical ballet, but without the tights. Then I did a Spanish type tap-dance in a tango rhythm, so my work in *Pal Joey* was really a combination of all sorts of things which the public found unusual. Anything that cannot be instantly categorised is exciting. Whereas in *The Time of Your Life* I played a simple, down-and-out hoofer whose obsession was to make people laugh, in *Pal Joey* the character was less clear-cut. Joey had several sides to his personality, and several dance styles were needed to reflect this. It was a way of overcoming the problem of characterisation through dance.'

Gene also overcame the problem of convincing the audience that Joey wasn't a particularly good dancer, just as in the movie *Cabaret*, Liza Minnelli sang brilliantly in a role that, realistically, would call for her to be mediocre. In each case their ability to act helped disguise the fact that they were much more talented than the people they portrayed.

As John Martin, then dance critic of the *New York Times* put it: 'Gene Kelly is not only glib-footed, but he has a feeling for comment that both gives his dancing personal distinction and raises it several notches as a theatre art.'

Regardless of the reservations people may have had about *Pal Joey*, Gene's success in it was total and unqualified. He was Broadway's newest star. Though underpaid, as his agent was well aware, three hundred and fifty dollars a week was more than he had earned in his life, and he made up his mind to save as much of it as possible. This season's hit could be next season's flop and he was too practical not to have noticed how ephemeral success can be. Besides, he would be failing his mother and the thrifty example she set if he suddenly decided to live it up and go grand. He did, however, allow himself the luxury of a room with private bath at the Hotel Woodward. Otherwise, his life-style remained the same. Occasionally he would accept an invitation to spend a weekend in the country with Jack Ray, or Richard Rodgers, or Helen Hayes, but his favourite haunt was still Louie Bergen's, where he and Betsy Blair continued to go each night after their respective shows were over. Louie Bergen himself was a burly, bald-headed Runyonesque New Yorker (although German by birth), whose formidable, bull-like appearance intimidated all but his friends, most of whom were actors.

By midnight the club was so crowded that he would lock the doors and only admit the people he liked. To Gene, Louie Bergen's bar was a way of life.

Shortly after *Pal Joey* opened, Johnny Darrow managed to arrange an audition for Gene at the Rainbow Room – New York's most chic night spot. Gene was to make an unscheduled appearance for one performance in the existing show, in order to give the owners of the room an opportunity to see how he worked in cabaret.

The audition, however, was a disaster, one of the worst in Gene's career, and as such is worth noting. In spite of his recent success in *Pal Joey* and the rave reviews he had received, the orchestra leader introduced him as George Murphy and, having thus made one *faux pas*, went on to conduct in a manner impossible for Gene to follow. The management took one look at the result and said no. He was, in his own words, 'a miserable flop'.

Jack Cole, who was the choreographer of the show at that particular time, said that 'He didn't get the job not because he was bad, but because he just wasn't suited for so sophisticated a room and would have been more at home in the Latin Quarter.

'He was a nice-looking man, but not a beauty – and he didn't have the kind of false, idiot social bit that people like Charles Walters, or Don Loper, or Fred Keating had – which was essential to Rainbow Room audiences. He was a perfectly nice American, ideal for musical comedy who, at that stage of his career, rattled his feet quite competently.'

During the run of *Pal Joey* Gene saw more of Betsy and less of Helene Marlowe, and continued to educate his seventeen-year-old protégée. In the daytime, he took her to the Museum of Modern Art, the Metropolitan or the Museum of Natural History, while at night he surrounded her with his socialist friends in an earnest attempt to steer her towards his own political beliefs. 'Most of New York's intellectuals were committed left-wingers,' Betsy said, 'and before I knew it, I'd become interested in socialism myself – so much so, in fact, that I even attended some Marxist lectures, which

Gene didn't. In that area of my life, it was really a case of the pupil overtaking the master.'

At Louie Bergen's, she also met William Saroyan who took a tremendous liking to her and later directed her in his play *The Beautiful People*, a typically Saroyanesque flight of fancy dedicated to showing how easy it is to rise above the simple, everyday practicalities of life.

By now her relationship with Gene was becoming serious, but remained 'pure'.

'I was doing everything in my power for it to be a bit less pure, but until Gene considered it was "serious" enough, he didn't touch me. His *not* making love to me was his way of showing me that he *did* love me, though at the time I didn't understand that and wondered what the hell was wrong with him – or me for that matter. I wasn't used to being treated with such consideration by men – particularly not men in the theatre. So I just had to be patient and wait.'

Gene's performance in *Pal Joey* continued to attract attention, and one night a writer from MGM, called Fred Finklehoffe, saw his performance and told Arthur Freed, a producer at MGM, about him. Freed, who had admired Gene in *The Time of Your Life*, having gone backstage to congratulate him after the performance, saw *Pal Joey* and, more than ever, was convinced that Gene was a young man to watch. He even persuaded Louis B. Mayer to see the show. Mayer did not go backstage after the performance, but the following day contacted Gene through Johnny Darrow and invited him to his New York office for a chat.

Several movie companies were interested in securing Gene's services, but he turned them down, insisting that he was not yet ready to take on Hollywood. Louis B. Mayer, however, could not be ignored.

Gene arrived at the MGM offices as arranged, and was ushered into a large and imposing office, at the end of which sat Mayer behind a large and imposing desk. Mayer congratulated him on his performance in *Pal Joey* and without wasting words, asked him whether he would like to work for MGM. Mayer told him he was so impressed by what he saw on the stage of the Ethel Barrymore Theatre that there would even be no need for a screen test.

Gene was stunned. He could not believe his good fortune. Every actor in America longed for an offer from MGM, the greatest, most powerful studio in the world. The two men shook hands and Gene, still unable to believe his luck, left Mayer's office in a daze.

A few days later, however, he was approached by one of MGM's New York representatives, who had been instructed, the man said, to arrange a screen test. Gene assured him there must be some mistake. Mr Mayer had clearly said no test would be necessary. The man then produced a memo from Louis B. Mayer which distinctly stated that a test *had* to be made. Gene was astounded at Mayer's deception – not that he would have minded making a test; it was just the principle of the thing – and immediately wrote Mayer a vehement letter accusing him of lying, and informing him, furthermore, that he was no longer interested in the offer.

When Johnny Darrow heard what Gene had done, he almost had a heart-attack. But Gene was quite adamant. As far as he was concerned, Louis B. Mayer was a right-wing establishment punk who had lied to him. And that was that. Pictures were definitely out!

A couple of months later, however, David O. Selznick, the producer of *Gone With the Wind* and *Rebecca*, who was also Louis B. Mayer's son-in-law, saw *Pal Joey*, was as taken with Gene as everyone else, and invited him to come to his office to discuss the possibility of his going to the coast with a Selznick contract in his pocket. If only to appease his agent, who had still not quite recovered from the Mayer incident, Gene agreed to talk to Selznick, whom he warmed to on sight. Like Mayer, Selznick wasted no time in offering Gene a contract. This time, however, Gene was hesitant. He was aware, of course, that Selznick was the hottest producer in America – but he was wary of film folk and their devious ways.

'What about a screen test?' Gene asked cagily.

'Who said anything about a screen test?' Selznick replied. 'Just send your agent over and we'll draw up a contract.' Gene was not convinced. 'You sons of bitches are all alike,' he said. Selznick asked him what exactly he meant by that remark, and Gene began to tell him the story about his father-in-law. When he was through,

Selznick threw his head back and roared with laughter. 'Well *he* might do that,' he said. 'But I won't. I give you my word.'

Gene believed him, and Johnny Darrow was brought in to negotiate terms. But as Darrow did not have a licence to deal on the coast (and the Actors' Equity and Screen Actors' Guild for Motion Pictures would come down heavily on him if he did), he offered to split his commission with Leyland Hayward, an agent who was later to become a successful Broadway producer. Together, they drew up a seven-year contract for Gene with a starting salary of seven hundred and fifty dollars a week. Leyland Hayward also agreed to take on several of Darrow's other clients – such as Charles Walters, Bob Alton, June Havoc and Van Johnson, and represent them for motion pictures, splitting the profits fifty-fifty.

Gene's contract with Selznick would begin, officially, in November of 1941 – about three months from then.

Pal Joey, meantime, had played two hundred and seventy performances and was 'laying off' with a possibility of reopening in September. During the summer hiatus, George Abbott began work on a new musical by John Cecil Holm called *Best Foot Forward*, with words and music by Ralph Blaine and Hugh Martin. The show was a youth-orientated romp, not unlike contemporary Judy Garland–Mickey Rooney musicals such as *Babes in Arms* and *Strike Up the Band*. Its setting was a high school, and its story concerned a famous film-star who receives an invitation from an undergraduate to attend a school prom. It was the sort of light-hearted nonsense both Hollywood and Broadway churned out with ceaseless regularity, and a few weeks after rehearsals began, Abbott who had struck a bad patch with it, asked Gene if he would like to 'doctor' the show and take over the dance direction. As it would provide him with his first choreographic credit on a Broadway show, he accepted.

The musical starred Nancy Walker and June Allyson; and apart from a fit of temperament thrown by Miss Allyson who threatened to leave if Martin and Blaine added a couple of extra verses to a number Miss Walker was singing particularly well, all went smoothly. Gene kept the show bouncing amiably along, and as the accent was on youth, it gave him an opportunity to use several of the more talented dancers from Johnstown, which did the dance school no harm at all. The Misses Walker and Allyson received excellent reviews when the show opened and the inconsequential *Best Foot Forward* ran for three hundred and twenty-six performances, fifty-six more than *Pal Joey*.

While *Best Foot Forward* was being rehearsed, Abbott decided he would definitely bring back *Pal Joey*. As *Best Foot Forward* was scheduled for the Ethel Barrymore, *Pal Joey* was booked into the Shubert. Gene was approached to repeat his performance, this time at a salary of five hundred dollars a week, and with his name in lights above the title. But because of his forthcoming commitment to Selznick, he had to decline. Abbott then asked him whether, as a special favour to him, he would agree to play two weeks after their September opening, during which time his replacement, Georgie Tapps, would have a chance to watch Gene work. Gene agreed. Those two weeks, in which he worked on *Pal Joey* by night and *Best Foot Forward* by day, were the most back-breaking of his life.

After leaving the cast of *Pal Joey* and finishing his work on *Best Foot Forward*, Gene decided that he was definitely 'serious' about Betsy and proposed to her. He said he couldn't go off to California without her and that, with a movie contract all signed and sealed, the time was at last right for him to marry and settle down. So, at 5 am one morning, outside the all-girls hotel she was still staying at, he proposed to her.

Betsy accepted without hesitation, and they planned to elope to Philadelphia where *Best Foot Forward* was playing a trial run. But because she was only seventeen, elopement was out of the question: they would never have been granted a licence without her parents' consent. There was no way but for Gene to pluck up his courage, call Betsy's father and humbly ask permission to marry his daughter.

Permission, happily, was granted, and on 24th September, he and Betsy were married in Philadelphia.

Though Betsy was not Catholic, the wedding took place in St John's Church at a side altar for the sake of Mr and Mrs Kelly, who had come to Philadelphia for the ceremony, and would never have forgiven Gene if he had done otherwise.

No woman of Gene's choice could ever have his mother's unqualified approval – and Betsy was no exception. But at least Betsy spoke well and her parents were decent, average, middle-class people who would in no way prove to be a liability; so Mrs Kelly accepted her new daughter-in-law, with as much enthusiasm as her nature allowed. She was convinced though, that Gene could have done better, just as she was convinced that Fred, who had just married his childhood sweetheart, had made a mistake as well.

After the Philadelphia opening of *Best Foot Forward*, Gene and Betsy returned to New York as man and wife for the Broadway opening of the show. Then on October 2nd, 1941, they began their honeymoon by driving from New York to New Orleans, where they took a banana boat to Vera Cruz. They then drove through New Mexico, Texas, through the Great Smokeys, Nashville, North Colorado and Arizona. They criss-crossed to Wyoming and back, went west to Oregon and south to San Francisco, where they spent five days with William Saroyan, who had written a new one-act play for them called *Hello Out There* which, unfortunately, neither of them were to do. As Betsy hadn't ever been west of the Hudson River, their exploration of America gave her six of the happiest weeks of her life and made the perfect beginning of a marriage to a man she loved very much.

On November 11th they arrived in Los Angeles and made straight for the Hollywood Roosevelt Hotel. Gene pulled up directly in front of the entrance, and stepped out of the car in search of a porter to help them with their bags. While he was away, Edward Arnold walked by and Betsy, convinced that she knew him – for the face was so familiar – waved and said hello. She *did* know him, of course, but only from seeing him on the screen. He said hello back, smiled politely and walked on.

It was, in a way, an appropriate introduction to Hollywood for her. For she did not know it then, but soon she was to find herself playing hostess to the colony's most celebrated stars and personalities.

A few moments later a porter appeared and showed her and Gene to their suite.

The Kellys had arrived.

Part Three

Los Angeles was not entirely unfamiliar to Gene: he and his family had visited relatives there in 1935. It had appealed to him then and, on renewing acquaintance with it, he fell in love with its insane excess all over again. Apart from the sunshine, which added to the pleasure of the numerous sporting activities he had by no means abandoned, a town so single-mindedly involved in the business of making money through entertainment excited him, and from the outset he was eager to meet the challenge it offered. In just over two years he had become the *enfant cheri* of Broadway. How long, he wondered, would it take him to do the same in Hollywood – a city which boasted the greatest array of creative talent in the world?

He was twenty-nine when he arrived in California – not an age to be taken lightly for a dancer, and he knew if he wanted to make it in pictures, there was not a second to be wasted. Only one thing stood in his way.

David Selznick, who recklessly dangled contracts in front of the people he thought worthy of them, did not have a suitable script for Gene. And although there were promises of numerous properties – by the end of the year still nothing had materialised. It was as if Gene had been lured away from Broadway under false pretences.

For the first few months in Hollywood, therefore, Gene enjoyed himself on what he considered unearned income; contacted several of his New York friends who, like himself, had been seduced by the promise of international stardom, friends such as Keenan Wynn, Van Johnson, Jan Sterling; and generally acclimatised himself to the crazy personality of this crazy city. Gene's inactivity and the comforting amount of security bought by seven hundred and fifty dollars a week, gave him and Betsy a chance to look around for somewhere to stay. They were helped by Johnny Darrow who, with Leyland Hayward now in charge of the bulk of his clients in Hollywood, had begun to dabble in real estate, a hobby he was later to convert into a career.

Darrow put them onto a small house in Laurel Canyon called Lookout Mountain Drive. It was charming but minute and without furniture, save for a bed and a large ping-pong table. There were a hundred steps to the top which left their friends panting for breath, but suited Gene splendidly. Betsy, who was unable to cook, thought she'd show willing by learning how to make Gene's favourite fish-stew – and in no time at all the couple settled down to blissful domesticity.

From their earliest days in Hollywood, they created their own entertainment at home, playing charades with their friends, a pastime which, in the next few years, was to become well known throughout Hollywood. Occasionally, Betsy recalled, Gene would go out on a drunken binge with a few of his friends – including David Selznick, who was a regular guest at Lookout Mountain, and who, among many others, would help the Kellys tote up a weekly liquor bill of over a couple of hundred dollars. These binges would end at 6 am with Gene sneaking into the house and grinning good-naturedly from ear to ear. Once he and Selznick staggered back at dawn full of beer and pretzels. Inadvertently they woke Betsy up who, good and attentive wife that she was, came down in her dressing gown to brew some much-needed coffee. Selznick claimed that, apart from his own wife Irene, he was not used to seeing women without their make-up on, and found the experience very refreshing; later that day he sent Betsy a bouquet of flowers with a note which read: 'To an unretouched angel, for her courtesy to drunks at dawn'. 'If I'd have been a few years older,' Betsy said, 'and realised that David Selznick was in the house, I'd *never* have allowed myself to appear without make-up! I mean, he was only one of the greatest producers in the world, and I was a struggling actress. But at the age of eighteen what did it matter how I looked? I was young, wildly in love and far more concerned with Gene's career than with my own.'

The Kelly tenancy at Lookout Mountain lasted no longer than about six weeks for, towards the end of December, a torrential downpour practically washed away the steps, making their continued existence there impossible.

On January 1st, 1942, they accepted an invitation from actress Lois Moran's mother to move in with her in North Elm Drive until they found a suitable place of their own – which, a couple of months later, they did – much to the relief of Mrs Moran who, though she liked the Kellys, didn't like the noise they and their friends made – and was, according to Gene, relieved to see the back of them.

Their next home was in Alta Drive, which they rented from lyricist Yip Harburg. By the time they moved into it, Betsy was pregnant. Gene, meantime, was still not working, and was convinced that it would only be a matter of time before Selznick realised he had made a costly mistake, and would send him back to Broadway where he belonged. But the money continued to arrive regularly. Betsy, who earned thirty-five dollars a week in New York, was given a weekly personal allowance now of a hundred dollars, which she deposited straight into the bank and hardly touched. Her clothes were bought on a charge account, Gene paid for the food, and the petrol for her car was paid for on Gene's account at their local petrol station. Eventually, she found herself feeling guilty at having so much money at her disposal and started giving a lot of it away to various charities, or buying presents for friends. Occasionally, if Gene thought she was being extravagant, he'd give her a lecture on what he called 'the eternal verities' – but at the beginning of 1942, with practically no responsibilities in the world, it was generally a case of easy come, easy go, and he rarely questioned what she did with her money.

Yet while money – the lack of it, the earning of it, the saving of it – had always played an important part in his life, thanks to his mother's scrupulous training in this direction, Gene was a woefully inadequate businessman; instead of investing his weekly pay cheque in property or stock, he simply opened a deposit account 'like a farmer or coal-miner', and shoved it all in the bank, perfectly content to pay tax on the interest his money accrued. 'If,' he confessed, 'I had known more about those things at the time, I'd be an extremely wealthy man today. As it is, I'm comfortable, but nothing to what I could have been.'

To anaesthetise some of the frustration he felt at not working, he continued to encourage his friends to drop by – any time of the day or night – and soon their home on Alta Drive became known as the 'game house', the main attraction each evening being 'the game' – a charade Gene picked up when he was living in New York. It was perfectly simple and straightforward. Two teams stationed themselves in different rooms, and someone who wasn't part of either, was chosen to make out a list of phrases or words that he secretly imparted to the two captains. Each captain then rushed back to his own team and acted out the phrase or word until some-one guessed what it was. Thereupon the one who guessed would return to the man with the list for the second phrase, and repeat the process all over again. The team to guess all the phrases first won.

From so simple a party piece developed an activity which, according to those who participated at the time, was insanely competitive and extraordinarily physical. Gene soon established himself as the champion player (he once guessed the phrase '*dementia praecox* is very unfortunate hanging on the family tree' in forty seconds flat), with Betsy coming a close second. So seriously was 'the game' taken, that once Selznick brought out a team from New York in an attempt to beat Gene and Betsy. He lost. Tyrone Power had his own group as well, and often he and the Kellys would play together until early morning as their respective teams pitted their wits against each other.

As long as Gene wasn't working during the day, Selznick thought it might be a good idea if he were to visit the major studios and 'get to know the environment'.

Though there was a war on and many top stars and technicians had enlisted, activity was brisk in 1942 as each studio pushed out dozens of films, most of which were designed to keep the popu-lation's mind off reality.

20th Century Fox contributed to the morale of the country by dazzling it with a series of lushly made musicals, such as *Sun Valley Serenade, Moon Over Miami, Springtime in the Rockies* and *That Night in Rio* with stars like Sonja Henie, Alice Faye, Carmen Miranda and Betty Grable, the GI's favourite pin-up girl who embodied the most striking American virtues.

At Warner Brothers they were making engrossing soap operas with Bette Davis and Paul Henreid. Their big musical for 1942 was a biography of George M. Cohan called *Yankee Doodle Dandy* with James Cagney; while Ingrid Bergman, that bright promise of a Europe Americans were fighting to save, was the star, with Humphrey Bogart, of the memorable *Casablanca*. Metro-Goldwyn-Mayer, the wealthiest and most prestigious of the major studios and the one with 'more stars than there are in heaven', made inoffensive wholesome family entertainment such as *Random Harvest* with Greer Garson and Ronald Colman, *Andy Hardy's Double Life*, with top box-office star Mickey Rooney, as well as a clutch of musicals with such stars as Jeanette MacDonald, Ann Sothern, Red Skelton, Virginia O'Brien, Kathryn Grayson and Eleanor Powell.

From Paramount, the 'Continental' studio, came a series of comedies with a sophistication and a sheen rarely matched else-where in Hollywood. Preston Sturges' *The Lady Eve* with Henry Fonda and Barbara Stanwyck and his *Palm Beach Story* with Joel McCrea, Claudette Colbert and Rudy Vallee were two excellent examples; so were Billy Wilder's *The Major and the Minor* with Ginger Rogers and Ray Milland, and René Clair's enchanting fantasy *I Married a Witch* with Veronica Lake and Fredric March.

It was during his visit to Paramount that Gene first met Astaire, who was filming *Holiday Inn* with Bing Crosby. Having been a fan of the incomparable Fred throughout the thirties, he regarded the encounter as one of the most exciting things to have happened to him since his arrival in Hollywood. The two men were mutually complimentary about each other's work and over the years became good friends, although they were only to work together once.

At Paramount, Gene also met Carole Lombard, who was filming Ernst Lubitsch's brilliant comedy *To Be or Not To Be* with Jack Benny for United Artists. 'She overwhelmed me completely,' he said. 'There was just something about her I found uncannily wonderful, and I remember telling her how marvellous I thought she looked and asking her how she managed to get up at the crack of dawn, looking so incredible. And she just threw her head back, laughed and said I should try it sometime as it had a lot to recommend it because, she said, at four in the afternoon she was no good at all. She told me how much she'd enjoyed my performance in *Pal Joey*, and just as I was becoming totally smitten by her, she was called onto the set. I saw her once more after that, and was afraid to approach her in case she didn't recognise me – but she did. A few months later she was killed in a plane crash. She was the only Hollywood 'legend' I found totally accessible and felt I could shake hands with. The others, like Garbo and Hepburn were polite and friendly, but somehow in the Hollywood of the early forties, untouchable. I got to know them all much better a few years later, but as a newcomer to the world of motion pictures, they were as formidable as you'd expect. Which is fine. It's not good to have all one's illusions shattered at a stroke.'

In the spring of 1942, Selznick finally offered Gene a script. It was the screenplay of A. J. Cronin's *The Keys of the Kingdom*, and the part he wanted him to play was a missionary priest. Gene, however, knew what he could and what he couldn't and shouldn't do, and while flattered at Selznick's faith in him, persuaded the great producer that he simply did not have the necessary dramatic equipment to undertake such a role. *The Time of Your Life* was the only straight play he had done, and his acting, he felt, was not sufficiently 'honed' to be relied on. The whole idea made him ill at ease and very afraid.

Selznick listened to Gene's objections patiently, still convinced he was capable of playing against type, then offered him the part of the Scottish doctor which, if anything, was an even more difficult role than the priest for a newcomer. His Scottish accent, he told Selznick, was phoney as hell.

Selznick remained unmoved. 'We'll put you onto a vocal coach in Pasadena,' he said, 'and in a couple of weeks no one will know you're not Scottish.'

Gene, who desperately wanted to work, allowed himself to be

talked into it. Selznick's suggestion that he spend some time with a coach sounded reasonable, and each day he drove out to Pasadena where he worked with the man for a couple of hours at a time. Two weeks later, a test was made at the Selznick Studios in Culver City.

While it was being screened in the viewing theatre the next day, Gene began to giggle. He looked at Selznick, and Selznick glowered back at him. Then both men began to laugh uncontrollably and, according to Gene, fell about with convulsions. It was, he said, the best comic performance he had ever given, but it had nothing whatsoever to do with A. J. Cronin. Even Selznick, finally, had to admit that it had all been a ghastly miscalculation. When he recovered his composure, he told Gene not to despair and, in the meantime, made Gregory Peck the priest and James Gleason the doctor and sold the 'package' to 20th Century Fox who made the film in 1944.

Two months passed, and still nothing. Gene and his ever-expanding circle of friends – the latest acquisition being the portly Laird Cregar, fresh from his role in the Alan Ladd–Veronica Lake thriller *This Gun for Hire* – continued to do battle each night with 'the game', and although he was still unable to label himself a Hollywood star, Selznick's money continued to provide him with the where-withal to live like one.

Then in April, five months after he and Betsy had arrived in California, Arthur Freed, who was to become the greatest producer of musicals in Hollywood's history, was preparing a new musical at MGM called *For Me and My Gal*, and offered Gene a leading part in the film opposite Judy Garland and George Murphy.

'The first time I ever saw Freed,' Gene said, 'was backstage at the Booth Theatre after a performance of *The Time of Your Life*. He came into my dressing-room and for a moment just stood there – this imposing man with his kind face and blue eyes – and smiled. I didn't know what he was thinking, but I liked him immediately. So, when he offered me a picture a couple of years later, I was very tempted – in spite of how I felt about Louis B. Mayer. Well I was older now, and not quite so headstrong as I'd been on Broadway.

Besides, I was aching to work and the thought of doing a picture with Judy Garland really excited me.'

Gene discussed the offer with Selznick, who realised finally that if he was to become a star in Hollywood, it would be as a song-and-dance man and not as a dramatic actor. And as Selznick International had no intention of making musicals, he agreed to loan Gene to MGM at a price that more than recouped the money Gene had been costing him over the last five months.

For Me and My Gal, written by Richard Sherman, Fred Finkle-hoffe and Sid Silvers, was to be directed by Busby Berkeley, one of the great Hollywood originals, whose dance direction for a handful of memorable Warner Brothers musicals – *42nd Street, Gold Diggers of 1933, Footlight Parade, Dames* – rightly assured him of a place among the top musical talents of the thirties. At the beginning of the forties, however, the Hollywood musical was changing in style and Berkeley's elaborate, awesomely inventive kaleidoscopic routines were being replaced by more intimate numbers in which visual opulence was subordinated to the talent of the individual star. Berkeley's début for MGM as a fully-fledged director in charge of the overall production rather than only the dance numbers, was with *Babes in Arms* in 1939. This was the first of a series of Rooney–Garland musicals in which a group of kids get together and 'put on a show'. They perfectly illustrated Louis B. Mayer's vision of America, and are paeans to family life and to the potentiality of his (adopted) country's youth – themes Mayer held most dear for he believed they represented the very foundation on which America was built.

These films were highly successful and in Rooney, Garland and Berkeley, MGM had found a winning combination.

For Me and My Gal, however, was slightly different in subject-matter though, like *Babes in Arms,* it was vaudeville orientated, and Bobby Connolly was engaged to stage the musical numbers.

Its simple story concerns a hoofer called Harry Palmer, who teams up with Jo Hayden, a girl from Clinton Junction, Iowa, and her boyfriend Jimmy. Inevitably there are complications. Jimmy is in love with Jo, Jo is in love with Harry, and Harry is in love with Harry. And Success. For, unless they play the Palace Theatre in New York, they won't have achieved a thing.

Then, just as it looks as if they're about to make it, war inconveniently spoils their plans, and Harry, in order to avoid being drafted, smashes down the lid of a trunk on his hand. Jo and Jimmy are disgusted with him, and dissolve the act in order to go off and entertain the troops. Harry, however, soon sees the selfishness of his ways, joins the army, and becomes a hero in battle. The film ends with the three of them united, particularly Jo and Harry, and the finale takes place where you knew it would all along – at the Palace Theatre, New York.

Garland was cast as Jo, George Murphy as Jimmy and Gene as Harry Palmer. Originally Freed had intended to use Murphy as Harry Palmer, but when he realised how similar the characters of Harry and 'Pal' Joey Evans were, he switched roles hoping that Gene would bring the same dynamic quality to the screen that he had brought to the stage, and give the role 'more scope'. Murphy was understandably disappointed at the switch, for Harry Palmer was the more colourful of the two roles, and throughout the shooting he could not forgive Gene – although the decision had been entirely Freed's. There was friction too between Gene and Busby Berkeley, who would also have preferred Murphy to play Harry Palmer, and for several weeks the director was decidedly hostile towards Gene. Gene's staunchest ally during his initiation into movies was Judy Garland whom he had first met during the run of *Pal Joey*.

She had sent someone backstage to ask him to join her and a few people for dinner after the performance and, of course, he was delighted to do so.

The 'few' people turned out to be her mother, three press agents, her own personal agent, and an 'adviser' of sorts, whose exact function he never did discover. Gene was somewhat floored by the entourage, but Judy took it all in her stride, and said she wanted to have a bit of fun. So they all went to the Copacabana where they danced and sang until about three in the morning, when she asked her mother whether she and Gene could go for a walk and see a bit of the city. In those pre-mugging days it was possible to stay out late in New York without jeopardising life and limb, and her mother granted her permission, much to the dismay of her press agents. 'I took her to Central Park,' Gene said, 'and we walked and talked until five o'clock, then I left her at her apartment, and said goodnight. In the course of our walk she said it would be great if we could make a picture together, so when the opportunity arose to do so, she was delighted. So was I. Without her, my first few weeks at MGM would have been even more miserable than they were.'

For, not only were George Murphy and Busby Berkeley resentful of his presence, but big boss Louis B. Mayer, vividly remembering the letter Gene had sent him a couple of years back, was hardly enamoured of this new boy on loan from his son-in-law. Nor was Sam Katz, an executive in charge of musicals. But Arthur Freed, who enjoyed a privileged relationship with Mayer, and whose judgement Mayer respected implicitly, went ahead and employed him in spite of the opposition.

It wasn't until the full complement of MGM executives attended the preview of *For Me and My Gal*, which was held in a small theatre near Riverside, about a mile away from Louis B. Mayer's ranch (thus enabling Mayer to attend screenings without being away from his horses longer than was absolutely necessary), that they realised no one else under contract to the studio could have played the role of Harry Palmer as well as Gene.

Though Busby Berkeley's animosity towards Gene disappeared after about the third week of shooting, Murphy refused to be placated and the set was never entirely free of tension. It was left to Judy to keep the peace, although she herself (though she never showed it) was at the time having marital problems with her first husband, composer David Rose, who was twelve years her senior. It was Judy, too, who gave Gene all the help and guidance he needed, in return for which Gene taught her all he could about dancing – a skill she was eager to acquire.

For Me and My Gal opened at the Astor in New York on October 21st, 1942, to generally favourable reviews, though Bosley Crowther in the *New York Times* had reservations about Gene, whom he claimed had been pressed a bit too far in his first film role. 'Mr Kelly,' he said, 'gets embarrassingly balled up.'

It was the script, however, that got embarrassingly 'balled up'. Its combination of corn and sentiment, and the transition Harry Palmer makes from ruthless, ambitious 'ham' to self-effacing hero, was more contrived and unsubtle than anything in vaudeville itself.

The story-line put Gene at a disadvantage, too, in that once again he was asked to play a character audiences would find basically unsympathetic. The scene in which he disfigures his hand to avoid the draft is too dramatic for the slender plot and disfigures the film just as badly.

Yet in its early scenes *For Me and My Gal* must have given people who had never seen Gene in *Pal Joey* some idea of his performance in that show; for the two characters are strikingly similar. It also gave film audiences the first chance to sample Gene's energetic dancing (including the bit where he bounces across the stage on the palms of his hands), which made up in vigour what it lacked in originality. In fact, the musical numbers throughout had pace and energy, and although predictable (and what else is vaudeville if not predictable?) certainly evoked the mood and flavour of the period.

What was entirely unpredictable, however, was the superb professional mating of Gene and Judy Garland. The rapport they established with each other was quite magical and their rendition of the title number, sung simply but joyously at an upright piano in a restaurant, is the undoubted highlight of the film. The contrast between a vulnerable, hesitant Judy, and a confident give-it-all-you've-got Gene was effective too and, despite the somewhat maudlin story, audiences who in 1942 were in the right mood for chunks of undigested patriotism anyway, turned the film into a considerable box-office success, and made a star of Gene Kelly.

Though Gene refused to be impressed by MGM and the entertainment empire it represented, accepting his personal success in *For Me and My Gal* as a matter of course, and as the logical outcome of everything he had been working towards, he was completely stunned by some of the advertisements which Howard Strickling, head of MGM's publicity department, showed him after the New York opening of the film. The one that particularly thrilled him was a large advertisement in the *New York Times* which, in spite of Mr Crowther's unflattering pronouncements in the same paper, proclaimed to the world that a great new star had burst onto the cinema scene.

'That bowled me over completely,' Gene admitted, 'because it was back on my own piece of turf so to speak. I guess my heart, basically, was still on Broadway, and I was thrilled, for some reason, to be acclaimed like that over there.'

Gene's reaction to seeing himself on the screen, however, elicited from him a completely different comment. Few things in life, he remembers, were more distasteful or made him feel more un-comfortable than that first preview of *For Me and My Gal* at River-side when MGM's top brass congratulated him and told him how much the picture was going to gross. The perfectionist in him was outraged by every fault and blemish he saw on the screen, and the minutest miscalculation to him in his timing assumed titanic proportions.

Yet, when the initial shock had worn off, and he was able to temper his criticism with objectivity, instead of ruthlessly demolishing himself, he began to learn how to adjust his particular style to motion pictures. What really upset him at first was the realisation that steps and routines which, on the stage, would have had every-body in the theatre stomping their approval and yelling 'Bravo!' – fell rather flat on the screen. If he was to make any impression at all in movies, he would have to rethink his style and reassess his approach completely. It was just one more challenge in a career full of challenges, and his initial irritation with the problem turned to fascination.

The first secret he learned about dancing for the cinema, was concerned with time. What lasts on the screen for a minute could last on the stage for three to five minutes, the reason being that the stage is three-dimensional. A film, on the other hand, is two-dimensional, like a painting, and the dancer who is just pasted on the screen, must somehow make up for that lost third dimension. There is a lack of kinaesthesia on the screen, he discovered – that physical force a live audience feels when a live actor is projecting towards them. On stage, if he threw a kick or a punch to the audience, there would be a reaction, depending on how close they were to him. They would react to the force of it by involuntarily leaning back or turning their heads. But on the screen the very same gesture would receive no reaction at all.

There were ways, he learned, to get round this. For example, a dancer rushing towards the camera from a fair distance away *can* create some sort of kinaesthetic effect if, as he moves towards the camera, the camera stands still. But this presented him with problems because, unless one has a stage as long as Manhattan Island, there is, physically, a limit to how far back a camera can go. One can also pan sideways, but this too is problematic. For, when a camera follows a dancer from left to right – in other words, when they're moving parallel with each other – the effect is rather like two trains travelling together at sixty miles an hour, and to anyone peering out of the windows of those trains, the impression given is that the trains are standing still. And so it is with dancing on film. If the camera moves at the same speed as the dancer, there's hardly any movement at all.

This was one of the first things he noticed about putting a dance on film, and he managed to overcome the problem, but only partially. What he did in his panning shots, was to place vertical props in the background or even the foreground – the equivalent of, say, telegraph poles to further the train analogy. So, as the camera panned, and the props shot past, one did at least get some feeling of speed and movement. But it was not a particularly satisfactory solution, for how often can this be repeated in one dance number?

The second thing he learned about choreographing for the screen, was that films often diminish the personality of the dancer. With straight actors, he found it was often just the reverse. A close-up did wonders for establishing what was going on in an actor's head. But with a dancer it was necessary to show his whole anatomy – and not only from head to toe, but often from his raised arms over his head to the tips of his toes.

To get all this into the frame, the camera has to pull back; but the further back it goes, the smaller the image becomes. And the smaller the image becomes, the less personality the dancer projects.

After working on *For Me and My Gal*, he realised that the eye of the camera wasn't in any way like the eye of a human being. The eye of the camera will only enclose a certain area of the 'environment'. So if a dancer is standing in the middle of a room, all that is seen of the room is the portion behind the dancer. On the stage this did not apply. With good, or even fair peripheral vision, one is able to see the dancer in his complete environment in the theatre, and if he is square in the centre of the stage, you see the whole stage which, Gene said, is as it should be in ballet, because the environment and the dance are inextricably linked. The one enhances the other – that is why the settings for ballet are so important, and why so many great artists have designed ballet sets.

With photographed dance most of the environment is eliminated – unless, of course, the camera is kept as far back as possible. But what happens then is that while the whole environment is seen, the dancer is so small he could be a midget. And in a close shot of him, the background goes out of focus due to the technical limitations of the camera. One way and another, Gene found, he just could not win! He realised that unless he invented a whole new way of filming a musical number, these problems would never be satisfactorily overcome, and would put a ceiling on his impact as a dancer in pictures. In trying to find a way to overcome these problems, he remembered what John Murray Anderson had taught him about the correct use of colour, and he discovered how to enhance the mood of a dance emotionally by putting some of Anderson's theories to work. But that came later, in films like *The Pirate*, *On The Town* and *Singin' in the Rain*.

He also began to put into practice what he had learned on Broadway in *The Time of Your Life* and *Pal Joey* about characterising a dance. If a man was playing a sailor looking for a broad on 42nd Street, he must move and dance appropriately. It was his old truck driver theory again. 'Whoever, or whatever you're portraying,' he said, 'you *have* to remain totally in character when you dance.' This was an important discovery for him, because it helped overcome many of the drawbacks inherent in imprisoning a three-dimensional art into only two dimensions. These discoveries, of course, did not happen overnight. It was a very gradual process. But most of the musicals he made after *For Me and My Gal* were, in some way or another, an advancement on the one that came before.

After *For Me and My Gal*, Gene devoted himself to staging numbers for the screen which, quite simply, would not be possible to do in the theatre. This was hardly an innovation. In the thirties

Busby Berkeley created routines which no stage in the world could accommodate – with his vistas of swaying pianos, illuminated violins and dazzlingly inventive kaleidoscopic formations. But they had very little to do with the dance and were more concerned with the opportunities the screen offered to create elaborate spectacles.

Though his first film gave no indication of what Gene was later to achieve as a dancer and choreographer, MGM was sufficiently impressed to overlook their initial resistance to him, and shortly after the film was released, Arthur Freed persuaded Louis B. Mayer to buy up his contract from Selznick.

A deal was made between Mayer and Selznick, and Gene was signed to MGM for seven years with options at a salary of a thousand dollars a week.

On October 16th, 1942, Betsy gave birth to a daughter. Gene wanted to call her Bridget, but Betsy thought Bridget Kelly sounded too relentlessly Irish. They compromised and called her Kerry – just as relentlessly Irish, but at least, Betsy argued, it had a lilt to it.

Life for the Kellys right now could not have been sunnier. *For Me and My Gal* was a hit; Kerry was a beautiful baby, Gene and Betsy were firmly establishing themselves as part of Hollywood's élite, and money was plentiful and regular.

Back in Pittsburgh, Mr and Mrs Kelly and Louise were still in control of the dance schools, which were doing better than ever as a result of Gene's name both on Broadway and in Hollywood. They continued to employ assistants to handle the teaching, and maintained the high standards Gene had set ten years before. Fred Kelly, meantime, went straight from the road company of *The Time of Your Life* into the army, where he stayed for the next four and a half years, and wound up appearing in morale-boosting shows.

In Hollywood, Gene too felt he should be in the service. But as the Government wanted pictures to keep the nation's mind off the war, almost as much as they wanted recruits, MGM had no difficulty in getting their thirty-year-old star deferred.

The closest Gene came to war at that time was on the set of

Pilot No. 5, a trite, episodic drama directed by George Sidney, the son of Louis B. Mayer's right-hand man, L. K. Sidney. The story, told in flashback, concerns an ambitious young lawyer who becomes involved with a fascist-minded politician, who realises too late what sort of man the lawyer is. In order to break the politician, the lawyer sacrifices his promising career and enters the air force to continue his fight against fascism.

Franchot Tone was cast as the pilot, and Gene played a flyer called Vito D. Allesandro (no Italian accent required) who, alone among the group of pilots, knows the whole story. Van Johnson was in the picture; so was Marsha Hunt.

Gene's performance was barely competent, which is still more than can be said for the film.

What had initially appealed to Gene about *Pilot No. 5* was its social content, but between the script and what finally appeared on the screen, it had been considerably diluted. More concerned with internal than international politics, the studio refused to burn its fingers on 'inflammable' material – particularly in 1943. Still, Gene enjoyed working with Franchot Tone, who put him totally at ease during the first days of shooting; and it was pleasant to have his friend Van Johnson on the set as well.

But the best thing about *Pilot No. 5* was the opportunity it gave Gene to see himself in a non-musical role. 'On Broadway,' he said, 'I was a damned good actor. I could hit that fourth balcony without any trouble at all. But I needed to *see* three thousand pairs of eyes to do it. On the screen it was a different story altogether. In *Pilot No. 5* I looked fine in the long shots – but the close-ups weren't any good. In fact, I've never learned how to do a close-up the way, say, Spencer Tracy has. Orson Welles once said that the camera close-up was kind to a chosen few. Tracy was one of the few. I wasn't.'

In *Pilot No. 5* Gene felt a conscious need to 'act' if he was not to be totally eclipsed by Franchot Tone. It was his first 'straight' film, and he wanted to make as much of an impact in it as he had done in *For Me and My Gal*. 'The result,' he said, 'is that in *Pilot No. 5* I had a tendency to overact. Of course, my initial defence was to say, "but why the hell didn't the director tell me?" – like a kid blaming his mother for not telling him that if he walked down the street without looking where he was going, he'd fall into the sewer. And in some of my straight roles, I often fell into that sewer.'

As with dancing, Gene realised, after watching himself in *Pilot No. 5*, that acting for pictures also had a language of its own, one that he had better learn quickly. 'I was trying to give a performance all the time, and in pictures that's about the worst thing you can do. Some of the best acting I ever did was in *For Me and My Gal* when I didn't worry about competing with Barrymore, or Tracy, or Franchot Tone. There is a scene with Judy Garland in that picture in which we just talked – which is as good as anything I've ever done, because I played it easily and as naturally as I could. Nothing I did in most of my other   straight   movies was as good.'

Before Gene went into *Pilot No. 5*, there were two notable additions to his and Betsy's close circle of friends. One was Stanley Donen, the other a chorus girl called Jeannie Coyne whom Gene had taught when she was seven years old in Pittsburgh, and who had taken over from Betsy in *Panama Hattie*, when Betsy did *The Beautiful People*. Both Stanley and Jeannie had been friendly with Gene in New York, and as soon as they arrived in California, resumed their friendship. They became regulars at Alta Drive, with Gene presiding over them as a sort of guru at whose shrine they sat, listened, worshipped and learned. Though Jeannie was never much interested in books or politics, or intellectual matters, she was, said Betsy, 'a gorgeous, lovable girl' who adored Gene and was great fun to have around.

Stanley Donen, from South Carolina, was virtually adopted by the Kellys. He was a 'nice, eager, funny youngster, with an attractive voice, a lively personality and large, brown, glamorous eyes like those of a gazelle'. He soon became 'the boy around the place' and was known as 'the kid'. He had no particular identity or evident talent in the way that some of the New York set who visited Alta Drive had, and was just 'a kid' from the South, who wanted to make it in show-business. So when Gene persuaded Charles Walters, who had been signed by MGM as dance director of the film version of *Best Foot Forward*, to find something in it for Stanley, he was extremely grateful.

Earlier that year, Charles Walters had replaced Felix Seymour as dance director on Gene's third film, *Dubarry Was a Lady*. Gene found he was unable to work with Seymour, an elderly man whose ideas were, so far·as he was concerned, antediluvian, and asked the studio to engage Bob Alton instead. But Alton had just signed to do a show with the Shuberts on Broadway, and was unavailable. Gene then suggested Walters (as Walters, a few years earlier, had suggested Gene for *The Time of Your Life*), who happened to be in Hollywood just then. The studio agreed, and as a result of his work on *Dubarry Was a Lady*, Walters was put under contract to MGM where he remained for the next twenty-two years.

Although *Dubarry*'s basic story was similar to Cole Porter's Broadway original, in which a night-club hat-check boy wins a sweepstake, drinks a Mickey Finn, and dreams that he is Louis XIV and that his Dubarry is the night-club singer with whom he happens to be hopelessly in love, practically everything else that made the Broadway show a hit was changed or discarded in Hollywood's characteristically meddlesome way. A couple of the Porter songs survived, but most of the numbers were written by Burton Lane and Ralph Freed, E. Y. Harburg, Lew Brown and Roger Edens, and were considerably less *risqué* than the originals.

The film, which was photographed in colour and lavishly produced, starred Red Skelton, Lucille Ball, Rags Ragland and Zero Mostel. It was directed by Roy del Ruth, whose chief interest in the property seemed to be in the challenge of drawing as many laughs as possible from Red Skelton and Lucille Ball, at the expense of everyone and everything else. Rags Ragland and Zero Mostel, with no guidance at all and being basically stage actors, gave two wildy uncontrolled performances that not even Cinerama could comfortably have accommodated.

Dubarry showed very little advancement in Gene's dancing, though the routine he does at the beginning of the picture, called 'Do I Love You', staged by Charles Walters, is an effective fusion of music and movement, with Technicolor contributing greatly to the overall excitement. The sequence's 'big finish' as Gene, dressed in white tie and tails, once again bounces on the palms of his hands through a row of chorus girls, is stunning. If *Dubarry* was to any degree meaningful to Gene, it was in the way he took some of his well-worn stage routines, cut them in length, and reworked them for the camera. But the personal Kelly style which was to characterise his best work had yet to emerge.

1943 was a busy year for Gene, but none of the pictures he made during it were particularly memorable.

After *Dubarry* came MGM's contribution to the war effort called *Thousands Cheer* (which had nothing whatsoever to do with Irving Berlin's Broadway revue *As Thousands Cheer*).

What originally started as a small film about a romance between a colonel's daughter and a circus aerialist turned soldier, became a full-scale musical crowned with a jewelled tiara of guest stars, all of whom appeared in a show-to-end-all-shows finale. Gene played the private, Kathryn Grayson was his girlfriend, John Boles the colonel and Mary Astor his estranged wife. The finale, set in a servicemen's camp, had Mickey Rooney as MC, again giving the imitations of Clark Gable and Lionel Barrymore which he had done four years earlier in *Babes in Arms*. If MGM's proud boast was that it had more stars than the heavens, they were all in *Thousands Cheer*.

Eleanor Powell, no longer quite as youthful as she was in her Broadway Melody series, still managed, however, to tap out machine-gun rhythms with her shoes, Red Skelton, MGM's most popular comedian, did an item in which he and little Margaret O'Brien have a competition to see who can eat the most ice-cream; Frank Morgan as a phoney medic, leeringly examined three WAVES, one of whom was Lucille Ball; dead-pan Virginia O'Brien sang 'In A Little Spanish Town', flanked by Gloria de Haven and June Allyson (who'd finally made it into pictures in *Best Foot Forward*); Lena Horne was memorable with 'Honeysuckle Rose', Kay Kyser, Bob Crosby and Benny Carter represented the big bands so popular at the time, while an edgy Judy Garland accompanied by José Iturbi belted out a number which should have worked, but didn't, called 'The Joint Is Really Jumpin' In Carnegie Hall'. The climax was an aerialist act presented by Gene and his circus family in which Gene had little involvement, as an aerialist from Ringling Brothers was recruited to do the trapeze work.

The only chance Gene got to dance in *Thousands Cheer* was when he was confined to quarters for insubordination and made to clean the local PX. He did what was called the Mop Dance, using not only a mop but other props which were on hand, including a soda fountain and all its trappings. It was effective in that, for the first time, Gene attempted to construct something which, if not impossible to do on a stage before a live audience, would have been extremely difficult. Its complicated rhythms and skilful synchronisation of beats (involving the soda-jerking apparatus) demanded the kind of split-second precision that only the camera can provide, and was cinematically inventive. The actual use of the mop was not all that spectacular in itself, but the sequence showed Gene's now obsessive eagerness to break out of the confines of the stage and try something new. Astaire, of course, had worked with props, and nothing in the mop routine was an advance on any one of his brilliant solos. But before Gene could begin to innovate, he himself needed to reach the point Astaire had reached, which could not happen overnight.

So, as relatively unimportant as the mop routine was, it did represent advancement and growth, and Gene was happier with it than with any of the other numbers he had so far done on the screen. Though he received no choreographic credit for the dance (at that early stage in his career he had not yet realised how important and prestigious a credit could be) the idea and presentation of it were entirely his, and he was happy that Joe Pasternak, the producer, allowed him to execute it without interference. He was less happy, however, with Metro's decision to tag on its all-star finale, believing that with so much talent around, his own contribution would be wasted. But it was the best thing that could have happened. Far from being swamped or overshadowed, his mop dance easily stood comparison with the star turns that followed it. Quite simply, it was the best thing in the film and everyone at MGM knew it.

Gene went straight from *Thousands Cheer* into *The Cross of Lorraine*, the third film with a wartime background he had made since *For Me and My Gal*.

Once again he was drawn to the content of the screenplay – it was an anti-Nazi story about a group of Frenchmen who surrender, without much resistance, to the Germans. They are taken to a POW camp, where the brutality of their captors appalls them, and at the same time gives them the courage and strength to escape and resume the life of dignified, freedom-loving Frenchmen. It had an impressive all-male cast headed by Jean-Pierre Aumont, Richard Whorf, Cedric Hardwicke, Peter Lorre and Hume Cronyn. The director was Tay Garnett.

But as with *Pilot No. 5* the previous year, the script of *The Cross of Lorraine* was somewhat diluted. Regardless of how clear-cut the political issue was, MGM refused to stick its neck out further than it thought necessary, and the result was a worthy, earnest, not altogether satisfying film. Nor was the script entirely to blame. Peter Lorre's joke Nazi, for example, was unconvincing and im-parted a levity to many of the scenes that the writer could not have intended.

Gene, who played a French patriot called Labiche (no accent required!), was slightly more convincing than he had been in *Pilot No. 5*. It was not a large part, and what there was of it required him to act out the after-effects of gruesome torture. 'I thought I did quite well in the first half,' he said, 'but missed towards the end. I had several close-ups which just weren't registering what I wanted them to. Still, it was fun doing the picture. I didn't have to wear any make-up – nor did I bother about shaving. And it was a great pleasure to be able to get dirty without having the wardrobe department jump down your throat.'

With five films to his name in less than two years, Gene's career was solidly, if not spectacularly, launched. The two war dramas did average business at the box-office, but the musicals were popular and this popularity clearly indicated (as if indication were necessary) where Gene's real abilities lay.

Betsy had, by now, temporarily shelved her own career (though she was attending dancing classes for her figure), and had become a full-time wife and mother. She did, however, plan to return to the stage when Kerry got older, for it was now her ambition to succeed as a dramatic actress. Occasionally she attended an audition 'just for fun' but without much luck. Her particular quality was not easy to cast, and her looks – unconventional by contemporary standards – were not quite what producers were looking for at the time.

So she continued to enjoy her private life in Hollywood to the full, playing 'the game', making friends with the famous, and becoming more and more involved in left-wing politics. The thoughts and ideals which had been planted in her imagination way back in New York at Louie Bergen's, were now beginning to bear fruit. In a few years' time they were to prove troublesome.

In spite of the inevitable tensions that exist between a husband and wife who are both in the same profession, but whose respective careers are in no way comparable in terms of success, Betsy and Gene continued to be blissfully happy together. 'He treated me like some strange phenomenon that had constantly to be watched, cosseted and protected,' she said. 'My mother always taught me that it was a woman's job to brighten up the corners of the man in her life, but that I should never forget that the person whose corners I was brightening was very lucky to have me. In other words, that I was something special. Well, that's exactly how Gene saw me— as something special; and he was protective and very fatherly about his possession. I was only twenty at the time, and I needed his guidance and concern. To me he was the most marvellous man a woman could have.'

Towards the end of 1943, Gene was again deferred from active service (against his wishes), which left him free to continue his career in pictures, and the next film he made was also to be his most notable so far. It was a lavish Technicolor musical with Rita Hayworth called *Cover Girl*, for which he was loaned out to Columbia Studios. The producer was Arthur Schwartz, a gentle, soft-spoken man who, with Howard Dietz, had composed *The Bandwagon*. The director was Charles Vidor, and the songs were by Jerome Kern and Ira Gershwin.

Originally Harry Cohn, the bellicose boss of Columbia Pictures, intended to make *Cover Girl* with artists already under contract to him. For some reason he started shooting it without a leading man – only to discover that there was no one at Columbia who fitted the bill.

'As far as I was concerned,' said Arthur Schwartz, 'there was only one man in Hollywood who could do it, and that was Gene Kelly. But each time I mentioned this to Cohn, he would explode. "That tough Irishman with his tough Irish mug?! You couldn't put him in the same *frame* as Rita!!" he growled. "Nonsense. Forget it. Nothing doing. Besides, he's too short. I saw him in *Pal Joey* and he's too goddam short."'

But Schwartz was convinced Gene was his man, and without Cohn's permission went to see Benny Thau, an executive at MGM in charge of actors and their contracts, and told him he was in trouble, and lied that Harry Cohn had sent him to see what he could do. Thau told Schwartz he could have Gene – but only for four weeks. Schwartz then returned to Cohn's office, took a deep breath before entering – and told him that their problems were over. At last, he said, they had a leading man.

'Who?' growled Cohn.

'Gene Kelly,' said Schwartz, and waited for the heavens to open.

'But,' said Schwartz, 'Cohn got up, put his arms around me and said, "Thank God!" Strange man, Harry Cohn.'

Harry Cohn was actually intrigued at the prospect of working with Gene – but his main concern, still, was that he would be too short for Rita Hayworth. So he asked Schwartz to arrange a meeting with Gene, and when Gene walked into his office, saw that he (Cohn) and Gene were the same height exactly. 'All right,' said Cohn to Schwartz. 'So I made a mistake. But it wasn't my fault. It was those seats they put me in. Right on the side. Those goddam lousy seats!'

Fortunately the four weeks extended indefinitely because the picture Gene had been scheduled to do at MGM was cancelled, and within a matter of days he began work on *Cover Girl*.

One of the first things Schwartz did was to show Gene the footage that had already been shot, some of which he liked, some of which he hated. One of the things he hated was a routine at the beginning of the film called 'The Show Must Go On', set in a night-club and designed to establish the club and its girls. But Cohn did not want the footage scrapped or reshot and there was nothing that could be done about it. So, as a compromise, there is a shot of Gene in the wings watching the number with an expression of distaste on his face!

Schwartz listened to Gene's comments, and when they extended to the music and the lyrics, Kern and Gershwin were called in. Gene felt that several of the songs were overlong, and while they might work on a stage, had three choruses too many for the screen. After the cuts were reluctantly made, Kern agreed that Gene had been right, and at the end of shooting sent him a plaque which was simply inscribed: 'To G.K. who is OK with J.K.' Gene's instincts for what would or what wouldn't 'play' were developing fast.

Cover Girl, which was written by Virginia van Upp (the producer of Hayworth's most famous film, *Gilda*) tells the rather conventional story of a Brooklyn night-club dancer – played by Rita Hayworth – who deserts her lover and becomes a famous Cover Girl, much sought-after by society. But she soon learns that money and fame are not enough, and returns to the simple life and the man she loves. The story is told against a series of flashbacks set at the turn of the century, in which Rita's grandmother (also played by Rita) is shown to have followed exactly the same course.

Lee Bowman and Otto Kruger were cast as the rich men for whom Rita deserts Gene; Phil Silvers played Gene's faithful friend and side-kick, and Eve Arden was chosen to put some zing into the role of a high-powered executive searching for the ideal Cover Girl.

Apart from an uninspired plot, there is a great deal in the film that is trite and unoriginal – not least of which, is the main production number glorifying the American Cover Girl through giant 'blow-ups' of the country's most famous magazines. The sequence, staged by Felix Seymour, with whom Gene had been unable to work on *Dubarry Was a Lady*, is Hollywood kitsch *par excellence*. Nor are all Kern's and Ira Gershwin's songs their best. Also, the period flashbacks are tiresome and unnecessary.

Yet *Cover Girl*, for all its blemishes, is one of the most innovative musicals of the forties, and through his association with it, Gene Kelly 'came of age'. For in *Cover Girl* he was given a chance to experiment in a way that had not been possible before. The film also marked his promotion from hoofer to dancer, and for the first time Kelly, the athlete cum ballet-dancer, emerged in one glorious, inventive leap. It was the film in which the ideas and theories that had been formulating in his imagination ever since he saw himself in *For Me and My Gal* blended into a cohesive whole.

'Right after I'd been jilted by Rita in the picture,' he said, 'there was a spot where I wandered out into the street – alone and unhappy. At this point I wanted to express what I felt in a dance. And I wanted the dance to further the plot emotionally, and not just be a musical interlude. But unless you're in a ballet, you can't just begin to dance. You have to state your "thesis" in a song, first, and then go into the dance. Take the number "Singin' in the Rain". I tell the audience in a song what I'm going to do, and then I do it. So, in *Cover Girl*, what I decided to do at this point was state my thesis not in a song, but in a few words which came over the sound-track as if they were my "stream of consciousness", and then go into the dance.'

The sequence, one of his most famous, known as the 'alter ego' dance, is remarkably advanced for what was being done in the musical film at that time. The number begins in a mood of tranquillity. Gene, walking alone through Brooklyn late one night, suddenly sees himself reflected in a shop window. The reflection turns into flesh and blood and steps down from the window and into the street. At first Gene and his *doppelgänger* dance in unison. Then one challenges the other and, in a competitive spirit – akin to Gene's real-life personality – they try to outdo each other, leaping over each other's heads, until in the end the ego image is destroyed – and the dance ends quietly, as so many of Gene's dances tend to do.

It was the first number he had done that could not be duplicated on the stage and was uniquely cinematic. It was also, technically, the most difficult to accomplish, and to help him with it Gene brought over Stanley Donen to assist him in what was to be the first of many successful collaborations.

Cover Girl further illustrated Gene's belief that a dance number can be emotionally enhanced by the proper use of colour, and he and Charles Vidor, the director, worked painstakingly on the particular processes used in the film to ensure that they had the correct tints and tones in each of the main songs. The street scenes at night are particularly effective.

He was also given the chance to demonstrate his theory that, in order to feel the full kinetic impact of a number, the dancers must move towards the camera, as in the exuberant 'Make Way For Tomorrow' number. To achieve this effect, Gene persuaded Harry Cohn to give him more 'breathing space' by knocking down a couple of walls and joining two studios into one. At first Cohn was reluctant to do so because he couldn't see what Gene had in mind. But he admired and recognised talent when he saw it and, after showing his obligatory resistance, allowed himself to be browbeaten into agreement.

'Cohn had to be convinced about everything before he gave the go-ahead,' Gene said. 'He automatically said no – and left it up to you to see if you were strong enough to persuade him otherwise. Most times you could put something down on paper, and he could more or less see what you were driving at. But when we came to selling him the idea of the "alter ego" number, it was a battle because he couldn't visualise it. After all, how do you tell a man with not very much creative imagination that you're going to dance with yourself for five or six minutes, and that the dance is meant to represent a man fighting with his conscience? The only way to do it was to be as persuasive as you could – then threaten to walk out if he said no.

'Half the time I realised that Harry Cohn didn't know what the hell I was talking about. But I must have been pretty convincing because he'd listen with a blank expression on his face, then say, "All right. Go ahead. Just get the fucking hell out of here." I think he knew I wouldn't nag him for something if I didn't believe it was possible to achieve.

'At the same time, he knew he was gambling, but he was prepared to take a chance, and I admired him for that. At MGM Arthur Freed and, to a lesser extent, Joe Pasternak, gambled as well. Most of the time they didn't know what I was on about either – because how do you describe a dance in words – any more than you can accurately describe music in words? There was a time at MGM when they insisted that all their choreographers write synopses of their dances. Which was a joke. But that's the directive we got, so we'd all sit down and try to describe what was in our imagination, and out would come the biggest load of bullshit you ever saw. This synopsis writing lasted six months before they realised they'd just have to trust us.'

Though Harry Cohn respected talent, there was something in his nature which refused to allow the people he most admired to get on with their jobs without constantly needling them, and on one occasion during the filming of *Cover Girl* he called Gene into his office and accused him of creating routines that favoured him at the expense of his star, Rita Hayworth. Gene was flabbergasted at the accusation, for he had worked particularly hard to create steps that would flatter Rita and make her look better than she had ever looked before, and he threatened to punch Cohn in the jaw if he didn't retract the remark. Cohn then smiled benignly at Gene who was ready to slam his fists into the man's face and said, 'Of course you're making Rita look good. I just wanted to see what you'd say.'

Like Astaire's, Gene's singing voice – once described as 'gargling with pebbles' – was serviceable, and helped him into his routines without too much pain. In *Cover Girl*, however, he was given a chance to sing one of Kern's loveliest ballads, 'Long Ago And Far Away', a difficult song which needed more than the simple ability to remain in the right key. Phil Silvers tells a story that, on the day the number was shot everyone was nervous, for Kern himself was to be on the set, and no one knew how he would react to Gene's singing, or the fact that this most romantic of numbers was set in a dingy Brooklyn night-club against a backdrop of chairs piled high on tables. 'The great man arrived,' Silvers said, 'sat himself down, and Gene began to sing. When he was through, Kern was silent. Not a single word did he utter. We all thought the worst – that he'd hated what had been done to his beautiful song. Then very quietly he said to Gene: "If you want to make an old man happy, please sing it again."'

Gene himself has no recollection of the incident – but whether or not the story is apocryphal, his passionate rendition of the song almost convinces one that his singing is as good as his dancing. For in *Cover Girl*, Gene not only found his feet but his voice as well. Those light, high, slightly grainy notes are heard to marvellous effect as they caress Kern's tender melodies and joke with the rousing, more sprightly ones.

Cover Girl is important, too, in that it contains elements which Gene was to refine, rework and enlarge in some of his later musicals at MGM. Who, for example, can deny that the street setting of the 'alter ego' dance was to influence the title number in *Singin' in the Rain*? Or that the 'Make Way For Tomorrow' routine had the sort of exuberance which was repeated in *On the Town*?

After *Cover Girl* was released and became one of the biggest money-makers of the year, Gene was hailed as an original talent who was bringing to musicals a freshness and vitality they had not had since *42nd Street*, and the Astaire–Rogers musicals in the early thirties. Harry Cohn was delighted at the box-office returns (which broke records in spite of Bosley Crowther's dismissal of the film in the *New York Times*), and Gene became the blue-eyed boy of Hollywood.

'But if the picture had flopped,' he said, 'Cohn would have kicked me in the derrière. That was the way Harry operated, and the reason I could never have been under long-term contract to him. He would have exhausted me long before I could have exhausted him.'

At the same time, while Gene never had the sort of fights with Louis B. Mayer that he had with Cohn, he preferred Cohn who, he said, was at least no hypocrite and would admit he was a bastard. 'Mayer, on the other hand,' said Gene, 'would put on a veneer of benevolence and self-righteousness which fooled the innocent into believing he was a nice avuncular old man when, in fact, he was just as ruthless as the worst of them. During the Communist witch-hunts in 1947, Mayer remarked to someone that I couldn't possibly be a commie because I was a Catholic who loved his mother. The difference between Mayer and Cohn was that, if Cohn believed me to be a Communist, which I was not, he would have said "Kelly's a Catholic, *and* he's a Communist. And if he's going to make money for me, I'll put him in my next three pictures." There was a toughness and an honesty about Cohn which I liked. I may have recognised something of myself in him – especially in my tough early Pittsburgh days. But whatever it was, I think I understood him better than most people. I liked Billy Rose for the same reasons. Now Mayer, who was outwardly more respectable than both Cohn and Rose put together, I didn't like at all. I could laugh and have fun with Rose and Cohn. But Mayer I avoided.'

In spite of Cohn's constant interference in matters artistic, Gene was stimulated by the work he did on *Cover Girl* and grateful to Cohn for allowing him to try out some of his ideas in public. He adored working with Rita Hayworth and found her to be a most sympathetic dance partner, as adept as himself at picking up new dance steps and routines. Gene also enjoyed Phil Silvers' zany humour, and Silvers became the next regular visitor at Alta Drive where, between sessions of 'the game', he would entertain and improvise at the piano for hours at a time.

After the success of *Cover Girl* Cohn was eager to make a second musical teaming Rita and Gene. And as Columbia had bought the film rights to *Pal Joey*, there was no problem of finding a suitable subject.

Louis B. Mayer, however, had other ideas. After the acclaim Gene received in *Cover Girl* he was far too valuable a property for MGM to loan out as easily as it had done before, and Mayer asked Cohn for an unrealistic sum of money. 'Goddamit,' Cohn would keep telling Gene, 'the bastard wants too much for you, I just can't do it.' Cohn even offered MGM Rita Hayworth, his biggest money-making star. But MGM was not short of famous ladies. They had under contract Lana Turner, Ava Gardner, Greer Garson, Katharine Hepburn and Hedy Lamarr – so what did they need Hayworth for? Besides, Cohn and Mayer were hardly the David and Jonathan of Hollywood and Mayer was not about to put a fortune Cohn's way by releasing Gene to make a film he knew would be another money-spinner for Columbia.

Every three months – for several years – Cohn tried to secure Gene's services from MGM, but always without success. Eventually, Columbia made *Pal Joey* in 1957 with Frank Sinatra as Joey Evans. Rita Hayworth, who would have been far too young for the role of Vera Simpson in 1944, was now the right age – and was cast opposite Sinatra. The film bore little resemblance to the Broadway original and was not a success.

MGM realised that in Gene they had a useful 'contract' player who could play in both musicals and straight subjects. But they had not quite bargained for his star potential. It took Harry Cohn at Columbia to make a name out of Gene. Naturally, MGM were now anxious to cash in on their windfall, in the hope that he would do for them what he had done for Columbia.

Unfortunately, they did not have a suitable vehicle for him just then, but in order to keep him working, tested him for the role of a Chinese in Jack Conway's *Dragon Seed*, adapted from Pearl Buck's novel about a Japanese invasion of a Chinese village. The film was to star Katharine Hepburn, Agnes Moorhead, Akim Tamiroff and Walter Huston.

Gene was delighted at the prospect of working with Miss Hepburn, but the screen test he made was just as funny as the one he had made for David Selznick a few years back. Though Jack Dawn, head of MGM's make-up department, had a field day flattening his nose and slanting his eyes, he looked, as he says, as convincing as a Chinese Irishman and, once again, everyone watching the test roared with laughter. Understandably he was terribly disappointed at the outcome, for he would have given anything to work with Katharine Hepburn, whom he adored. But he saw how ludicrous he would be if cast, and agreed it would be a mistake. For all MGM's proud boasting about how many stars it had, there was no one on its books who could play the Chinese role – and Conway was forced to offer the role to Turhan Bey, who was under contract to Universal.

In Hollywood, however, no studio helped out a rival without making sure it was worth its while, and Universal demanded Gene's services in return for the indispensable Mr Bey. They owned a property called *Christmas Holiday* which they had bought for Deanna Durbin, still one of their biggest money-making stars, and there was a part in it which Gene could play to perfection. A deal was made, and Gene was despatched to Universal. He read the script of *Christmas Holiday* and wasn't at all happy with it. But as he was under contract, he had to do as he was told – or go on suspension, which he wanted to avoid, as he felt that to be out of work in wartime (when he should have been in the forces anyway), was quite the most unpatriotic thing he could do. So, grudgingly, he made the picture.

Once again Gene found himself cast as an unlikeable character, a murderer and wastrel, in fact, whom Miss Durbin marries shortly after meeting him at a symphony concert. After killing a bookmaker, he is sent to jail – but escapes, and makes straight for his wife, whom he plans to murder as well; disaster is averted (only in the plot, that is) and Gene is killed instead. *Christmas Holiday*, directed by Robert Siodmak, was not one of Gene's happiest films, although the slightly homosexual quality he brought to his role gave it marginally more interest than it would have had, had he played it absolutely straight. Miss Durbin, however, was unable to make the transition from child star to adult without becoming overwrought and self-conscious in certain scenes, and is never convincing as the put-upon young wife. If anything, *Christmas Holiday* is notable in that it contains the only scene in Gene's career in which the scene changes the moment he (and Miss Durbin) walk on to a dance floor!

The public, however, enjoyed the film – or Gene and Deanna Durbin in it – and it was one of Universal's biggest successes of 1944.

After the completion of *Christmas Holiday*, Gene returned to MGM and filmed a sequence with Fred Astaire for *Ziegfeld Follies*, a somewhat overblown Technicolor tribute to the great showman whom MGM had glorified twice before, in *The Great Ziegfeld* in 1936, and again in *Ziegfeld Girl* in 1941.

It was the only time Gene and Astaire were to dance together and the occasion should have been more noteworthy than it was. The item they chose was a Gershwin number called 'The Babbit and The Bromide', which Astaire had used once before in a stage revue, and the basic story it told was of two stupefyingly boring men who meet each other on a park bench and get into 'conversation'. Vincente Minnelli staged the sequence, and apart from the quite amusing notion of changing the attitude of the equestrian statue behind the bench as 'the Babbit and the Bromide' dance through the various ages of man together, the number was left entirely to the two protagonists.

The relationship that developed between Gene and Astaire was cautious, guarded and polite, with neither daring to criticise the other's work. 'It was,' said Minnelli, 'quite, quite fascinating to watch.'

137

The dance was a piece of straightforward hoofing, and the rivalry the world thought existed between the two great dancers was hinted at good-naturedly throughout the routine. The choreography, however, seemed to suit Gene more than Astaire, being nearer in mood to *For Me and My Gal* than to *Swingtime*, for example. It was a pleasant divertissement, but notable only in that it offered the unique opportunity to see both of them together – though individually they had each done, and were to continue to do, much better work.

To the majority of America's film-going public, who were largely unaware that other great dancers existed in the world, Astaire was the finest there was. As he had had little competition in motion pictures at the time of his greatest successes in the thirties, it was predictable that as soon as another star dancer came along, whoever he was would be considered a rival, regardless of how different the new man's style might be. The most frequently printed sentence Gene read about himself at the time of his emergence – particularly after *Cover Girl* – was: 'here we finally have a fellow who can give Astaire a run for his money.'

'The fact that Fred and myself were in no way similar – nor were we the best male dancers around,' Gene said, 'never occurred to the public or the journalists who wrote about us. There were people like Igor Youskevitch and Jean Babillé who, as all-round dancers, I thought superior to us in many ways. But they were unknown to the mass audiences we reached – so Fred and I got the cream of the publicity and naturally we were compared. And while I personally was proud of the comparison, because there was no one to touch Fred when it came to "popular" dance, we felt that people, especially film critics at the time, should have made an attempt to differentiate between our two styles. Fred and I both got a bit edgy after our names were mentioned in the same breath. I was the Marlon Brando of dancers, and he the Cary Grant. My approach was completely different from his, and we wanted the world to realise this, and not to lump us together like peas in a pod. If there was any resentment on our behalf, it certainly wasn't with each other, but with people who talked about two highly individual dancers as if they were one person. For a start, the sort of wardrobe I wore – blue jeans, sweat shirt, sneakers – Fred wouldn't be caught dead in.

Fred always looked immaculate at rehearsals, I was always in an old shirt. Fred's steps were small, neat, graceful and intimate – mine were ballet-oriented and very athletic. The two of us couldn't have been more different, yet the public insisted on thinking of us as rivals. In fact, after Fred announced his retirement in 1946, there were people who felt he did so because he no longer could compete with the "new boy". Well, nothing could have been further from the truth. Fred was still at the height of his powers, and the reason for his retirement was that he was so saddened by the death of his wife, he just felt that he no longer wanted to work. Two years later I persuaded him to put on his dancing shoes again, and replace me in *Easter Parade* after I'd broken my ankle. If we'd been rivals, I certainly wouldn't have encouraged him to make a come-back.'

Today Gene and Astaire are no longer 'lumped together like peas in a pod', and both dancers have been interestingly and provocatively assessed and compared. Arlene Croce, the distinguished dance critic says, quite simply, that the difference between Gene and Astaire 'is a difference not of talent or technique, but of levels of sophistication'. Pauline Kael, on the other hand, sees it another way: 'The difference starts with their bodies. If you compare Kelly to Astaire, accepting Astaire's debonaire style as perfection then, of course, Kelly looks bad. But in popular dance forms, in which movement is not rigidly confined as it is in ballet, perfection is a romantic myth or a figure of speech. Nothing more. Kelly isn't a winged dancer – he's a hoofer and a man – a hurting man. Now Astaire is impervious to emotion, no matter what calamity he has to face with Ginger, it's an "oh gosh, oh gee" emotion he gives out, and he handles it in a stylish fashion. He is almost a dance version of Buster Keaton. Whereas Kelly is a suffering human being; and one can almost say, without using the term as a perjorative, that he is "wet" in comparison to Astaire's "dryness". Kelly bleeds and Astaire doesn't, because Astaire's dried out to start with. Astaire is a great stick figure – a grasshopper with no flesh. He is not a man who suffers, but a dancer who does things through stylised dance. Kelly, on the other hand, is a hoofer who acts and as an actor he's also highly vulnerable. He brings a freshness to his line-readings which no song-and-dance man has done before, and his voice is a beautiful emotional instrument.'

139

But even more important, Gene – his personal qualities apart – is an innovator.

Astaire's breathtaking routines were rubies, emeralds and diamonds in scripts constructed out of paste. They were merely adornments, and we are grateful to them as such. Gene's dance routines, on the other hand, sprang more naturally from the plot and were totally integrated into the structure of the film. Gene changed the shape of the Hollywood musical.

At MGM, he and Arthur Freed took the form out of its claustrophobic confines and into the streets; and just as all good Broadway musicals have integrated scores which are not interchangeable with other shows but belong uniquely to themselves, the best of Gene's films have a homogeneity and a dramatic integrity which thrusts them into the realm of art in a way totally alien to Astaire's musicals of the previous decade. *Singin' in the Rain* is a more unified work of art than *The Gay Divorce* or *Follow the Fleet*.

In the middle of 1944 Gene made *Anchors Aweigh* for producer Joe Pasternak, with Frank Sinatra and Kathryn Grayson – an archetypal Gene Kelly musical, many of whose ideas would later be repeated in other Kelly vehicles – most notably *On the Town*.

Like *On the Town*, *Anchors Aweigh* is about sailors on leave. Their port of call, however, is not New York, but Hollywood, and there are two of them, not three. Priority number one is picking up a couple of girls, a habit which comes easy to the wise-cracking Gene, though less so to his gauche buddy Sinatra, who hasn't had much experience with women. Gene, however, assures him he'll take care of things, and the two of them set out on their Hollywood girl-hunt. But they don't get very far before they stumble across young Dean Stockwell, who tells them he has run away from home to join the navy. Being responsible sailors, they do what any responsible sailors would do – and return the boy to his home, where they meet his aunt, Kathryn Grayson. Miss Grayson, they learn, is a film extra, who also happens to be a singer, and whose ambition is to audition for the great José Iturbi. Before you can say 'gob', Gene is smitten and, in order to impress Miss Grayson, lies to her that he and Iturbi are good friends and that with a word in the maestro's ear the audition is as good as arranged. Miss Grayson believes him, and for the remainder of the film (which runs a hundred and forty minutes) Messrs Kelly and Sinatra rush around Hollywood trying to find José Iturbi, in the course of which Sinatra bumps into a girl from Flatbush, his home-town, and pairs off with her, thus leaving the way clear for his buddy to pursue Miss Grayson and Mr Iturbi, whom he never manages to find, but who finds Miss Grayson instead, thus ensuring a happy ending.

So much for the plot, a typical Pasternakian trifle in which audiences are offered equal quantities of popular standards and light classics – not unlike his formula for *100 Men and a Girl*, which he made for Universal in 1936 with Deanna Durbin in the Grayson role and Stokowski in the Iturbi role.

Though Pasternak's middle-European schmaltz was thickly spread over the story-line, Gene's energetic presence and lively imagination gives the story a freshness and a vigour it lacks in synopsis, and in George Sidney's pedestrian direction. And once one suspends disbelief and accepts Sinatra, then the bobbysoxer's idol, as a 'nebbish' incapable of finding a date for himself, it is even possible to follow the unlikely adventures of the two sailors without letting the more mawkish elements in the story stand in one's way.

The three major dance numbers Gene devised for himself are brilliantly characteristic of his personality and clearly show the way his mind was working and the progress he was making towards formulating a personal style. In one of the routines, a fantasy sequence in which he woos Kathryn Grayson on the sound stage of a film studio, the set becomes a romantic Spanish courtyard, wherein Gene, dressed in a dazzling gold shirt, red and black cape and black trousers, gives full expression to his athletic prowess in a fandango-style routine that has him scaling battlements, leaping over parapets and making a forty-five foot vine-swinging jump from a rooftop to the balcony of his señorita in the noblest Fairbanks tradition.

Apart from being a bravura demonstration of his athleticism, the number provides him with a blueprint for much of *The Pirate*'s choreography, four years later.

In the Mexican Hat dance, performed in a studio reconstruction of Olvera Street, the Mexican settlement in Los Angeles, with its colourful market-place, Gene partners a charming little girl called Sharon MacManus in a routine which, although self-consciously cute, has some delightful moments – particularly when Gene and Miss MacManus link arms and dance round the fountain in the middle of the square together.

Though working with children was hardly new to Gene, this was the first time he had done so in a film. But by no means the last – for he had a Pied Piper quality to which children readily responded. The big trick to working with children, he discovered during his teaching years in Johnstown, was simply getting them to like him, and in *Anchors Aweigh* he was especially concerned that Sharon MacManus adored him off the set as well as on it, otherwise the particular quality he wanted would not be there.

'To work successfully with kids,' he said, 'you *have* to have the wherewithal to make them laugh. Then you need the energy to keep them laughing, for children want you to do everything three or four times before they're satisfied – and that can be tiring. Conversely, when they do something funny, they'll repeat it over and over again – and that can be tiring as well! I've always wanted to please kids because I enjoy it when they laugh, and I'll become something of a whore, if necessary, in my desire to keep them happy – whether I have to wiggle my bottom or stand on my head. And, of course, you have to retain that child-like thing of being able to fantasise or imitate people. And not only people, but things. In "I Got Rhythm", from *An American in Paris*, which I do with a group of French kids, I not only imitate Hopalong Cassidy and Charlie Chaplin, but an aeroplane and a train as well. I found I could generally get children to work for me if I appealed to their imaginations and had the energy to keep going. So in "I Got Rhythm", I simply did in front of the cameras what I would have done behind them, and it worked.'

While Sharon MacManus and Dean Stockwell adored Gene because he made them laugh, little Miss MacManus was also required to dance, and this presented certain problems to Stanley Donen, who was once again Gene's assistant on the film, and to whom fell the thankless task of teaching her the routines. Once he spent three hours in the morning and a further four in the afternoon preparing a single step with her which involved a skipping-rope.

At the end of the session he did not wish ever again to see another little girl, or a skipping-rope, unless the rope was for the purpose of hanging the little girl. Every half hour Gene would pop into the rehearsal room and airily enquire whether Sharon had got the 'rope bit' yet, and Stanley would reply with an icy 'no' – and glower, at which point Gene would call him aside and say, 'Stanley, but the secret is to make her believe you *love* her.' To which he'd reply: 'But I loathe her!' Eventually, little Sharon began to loathe Stanley just as much, so that by the time the scene came to be shot, she would have done anything for Gene, if only to spite Stanley. Consequently the dance went beautifully.

The third dance in *Anchors Aweigh*, which was quintessential Kelly, was a cartoon and live action sequence in which Gene plays a Patagonian sailor in white trousers, a blue-and-white striped vest and a beret with a red pom-pom, who teaches a grumpy mouse (Jerry from the *Tom and Jerry* cartoons) how to dance. Together man and mouse slide, glide and cakewalk, joyously demonstrating the simple philosophy that we can bear anything life has to offer if we dance our gloom away.

As MGM had never attempted anything quite like it before, the cartoon idea had initially to be sold to Louis B. Mayer who, like Cohn with the 'alter ego' number, couldn't at first visualise what Gene was after. Joe Pasternak saw its possibilities, and as he was the one producer whose musicals always made money for the studio, tried to convince Louis B. Mayer and Eddie Mannix, the general manager of the studio, that the idea could work. Mannix, however, was not entirely sold and suggested that Gene and Stanley Donen pay a call on Walt Disney for some first-hand advice. Disney, who was himself at the time experimenting with live action and cartoons in *The Three Caballeros*, was most enthusiastic and admitted that what Gene had in mind was far in advance of anything he was doing. What, in effect, Gene wanted to do, was to choreograph a number with a cartoon mouse in mind, then have the cartoon synchronised with the live action so that when the two were matched the impression given was that he and the mouse were dancing together.

'To his eternal credit,' Gene said, 'Walt immediately 'phoned Eddie Mannix on our behalf and told him what a great idea he thought it was, and that technically it was certainly possible to achieve. That was all Mannix and Mayer wanted to hear, and they gave Pasternak permission to shoot it.'

Once he knew he had the go-ahead, Gene asked Disney whether he would agree to carry out the animation work for them. Disney said he couldn't because his staff were busy with their own work as well as being involved in the making of propaganda pictures for the war effort. He just was not able, he said, to take on another thing.

So they took the work to their own cartoon department at MGM, in which, for some reason, Eddie Mannix had little faith and the long, laborious process began. Gene was photographed against a neutral blue background then, following the action frame by frame by the rotoscoping or tracing process, Jerry mouse was animated – and, after a complicated matting process, a composite picture was made optically with a cartoon background.

As soon as he was assigned to *Anchors Aweigh*, Gene realised he would have to bring to it every ounce of creativity he had in him, if he wanted to save it from being a tired, routine piece of schmaltz. Every night he and Isobel Lennart, who wrote the screenplay, held script conferences and spent hours attempting to turn situations of pure dross into forty carat gold. Pasternak's working methods and his belief that once you had an idea, a few good songs and a couple of stars everything would automatically jell, was not shared by Gene, who was a perfectionist who left nothing to chance. And as most of the ideas came from the dancer himself, rather than the director, Gene felt a responsibility to see those ideas realised to the best of his ability – at the same time making sure that all other elements in the picture maintained a certain standard of competence as well.

One of the things Gene learned on *Anchors Aweigh* was that unless the people he shared his scenes with were as good as he was, his own contribution to them would be reduced. He knew from the outset that he would have to work especially hard with Frank Sinatra, who had made several bad films at RKO and whose reputation for not wanting to rehearse was already well known. In recalling his first venture with Gene, Sinatra admitted that if he had any ideas of walking through the picture, he was quickly shown the error of his thinking. 'Gene somehow tricked and cajoled me into working harder than I had ever done in my life before, and I found myself locked into a room rehearsing some of the routines for as long as eight weeks. Eight weeks! You can shoot a whole picture in that time!'

Gene's capacity for hard work was fast becoming the curse of the studio, and others less energetic than he resented his industry. Sinatra became one of the first victims of Gene's mania for perfection: on one occasion, early on in the shooting schedule, he felt he was about to collapse from physical exhaustion and decided to take the day off, pleading fatigue. Such a thing was unheard of at the studio, and the entire MGM executive hierarchy marched onto the set to insist that Sinatra continue working. Even Louis B. Mayer, who rarely appeared on a sound stage, visited him in his dressing-room with the purpose of 'telling him off'. But Sinatra refused to be told off by Mayer or anyone, and went home. Gene was entirely on his side. He knew he'd been working Sinatra too hard, and that singers did not have the same stamina as dancers. At the same time, he felt his slave-driving was the only way to draw a decent performance from him.

When Sinatra finally saw the finished product, he was grateful to Gene, who in spite of working Frank much harder than he had been used to, had also helped him through the picture emotionally.

'When I arrived at MGM to do *Anchors Aweigh*,' said Sinatra, 'I was a nobody in movies. And because I didn't think I was as talented as some of the people I was working with, I used to go through periods of depression and get terribly embarrassed at myself. After all, what was I then? A crooner who'd been singing for a big band for seven years and whose only claim to fame was that girls swooned whenever I opened my mouth.

'But after working with Gene, who always saw me through my depressions and encouraged me to do a little better than I thought I was capable of doing, I felt I actually had some talent. I was born with a couple of left feet, and it was Gene and only Gene who got me to dance. Apart from being a great artist, he's a born teacher. I felt really comfortable working for him and enjoyed his company, in spite of his insane insistence on hard work.'

To Gene, 'hard work' is a prerequisite of the job. He saw nothing unusual in working between ten and twelve hours a day, for how else could one achieve perfection? 'I only wish,' he said, 'that I could have started out in pictures at twenty-one and not thirty, and given myself ten more years of discovery and fun. For that's what hard work is to me: discovery and fun.'

Unlike many dancers who, after a few weeks of arduous rehearsing 'want to go home and commit Hara-kiri', Gene was always ready to come back for more. 'I suppose there's a certain masochism in it,' he said, 'but in a way I like the training period, the weeks and weeks of endless rehearsing, much more than the actual shooting – like a sportsman who enjoys the warm-up more than the game. There was something about achieving a perfection during rehearsals, which I found even more exciting than committing that perfection to celluloid. And I imagined everyone I worked with felt the same.'

Anchors Aweigh was released in August 1945, and was an instant success with the Press and public. James Agee praised Gene, who, he noted, 'dances and acts excellently', while in the *New York Times* Bosley Crowther said, that 'Kelly proves to be the par, if not the superior at rigadooning of Fred Astaire', thus falling into the trap of comparisons both dancers so much abhorred.

The film was nominated for a Best Picture Award, and Gene was nominated as Best Actor. (The awards, in fact, went to *Lost Weekend* and Ray Milland for his performance in that film.)

Before *Anchors Aweigh* had been completed, however (part of the intricate cartoon sequence had still to be done), Gene finally got his wish and in November 1944 was given leave of absence by MGM to join the navy – and this time not just on the screen, but for real.

After enlisting, Gene was sent to Bootcamp in San Diego, where he spent thirteen tough weeks learning how to kill. He hated every brutalising moment of the experience and was shocked by the way the men were 'dehumanised' and treated like cattle. Worse, he was amazed at the complacency with which the men accepted their rough-house treatment (in much the same way as the boys at college put up with their degrading fraternity initiations). Most of them were from the south-western part of the States, ten years younger than he was, and although they were capable of spotting an enemy plane in profile with a keener eye than he ever could, were basically kids with whom Gene had absolutely nothing in common.

It was a most depressing thirteen weeks. Not only did he hate the regimentation of the armed forces – being told when to get up, when to eat, when to turn out the lights – the whole thing was like living in a police state, and was anathema to his philosophy of life. But this was war, and there wasn't much he could do about it.

On his last day in camp, he was called in by the CO in charge, and told that he was being sent East to appear in a movie. A movie! Gene was furious. He'd been training, he said, to fight fascism in the Pacific. If he wanted to entertain or make another picture, he could just as well have remained in Hollywood and earned better money than the navy was paying him!

But he soon learned that the film to which he had been assigned, was extremely important. It was to be made for navy personnel who were suffering from battle fatigue, and was by no means just 'another movie'. So, in order to prepare himself for it, he checked into a convalescent hospital near Philadelphia, pretending to be one of the patients. For the next two weeks, he observed the behaviour of the men around him. At night, he would slip out into Philadelphia itself, a privilege extended to the patients who were almost better. Inevitably though, Gene was recognised, and it wasn't long before newspapers printed items about him suffering from chronic shell-shock and battle fatigue.

A few weeks later he made the film and, at the age of thirty-two, became an officer. As he had a reserve officer's Training Diploma from college, he was inducted as a lieutenant junior grade, and eagerly recruited into the photographic division of the naval airforce.

Most of Hollywood's better writers and directors were working for the army or the airforce. So the navy wasted no time in putting Gene to work. His first assignment was top secret.

'At the time,' he said, 'the Japanese were kicking the hell out of us. They had something called Bakka bombs which caused so much devastation on our aircraft-carriers that ordinary fire-fighting equipment couldn't put the fire out quickly enough. The result was that men on board those ships were dying most terribly. Admiral King told me he wanted to stage a fake bombing raid in which new fire-fighting equipment would be demonstrated, and that I was to film the results. So about twenty men, eleven of whom were camera operators, were despatched to a suitable location on the East Coast, together with a tough Irishman who claimed he knew of a foam that could lick the Japanese Bakka bombs pretty effectively.'

It was a massive and expensive operation. Twenty planes, all drenched in gasoline and filled with explosives were used as 'props', and the thirteen cameras were strategically placed to record every last detail of the operation. The explosives were ignited, the fire-fighters jumped in with their experimental foam and, in a matter of minutes, the conflagration was over. The foam was a triumphant success. Gene took the film which recorded the good news to Admiral King in Washington, on the strength of which thousands of tons of the new foam were shipped over to the Pacific. A camera, Gene realised, was as important to the service as a gun, and he no longer felt upset about his particular role in the navy. What did upset him though, was the embarrassment he felt when people recognised him (particularly on war bond rallies), and rushed over to him for his autograph. 'I hated that,' he said, 'and wanted to get as far away from them as possible, because invariably I was accused of having landed myself a "cushy" job in the navy. "Oh, you're Gene Kelly," they'd say, "I saw you in *Cover Girl*." Then they'd ask me where I was stationed – and the moment I told them I was with the Photographic Service, they'd say: "Well, that figures. All you Hollywood guys have an easy set-up." They were making the same mistake I made to begin with. I also thought that what I was expected to do was cushy . But I was wrong. Boy, was I wrong. I had a pretty important job to do, and my only regret was that I wasn't sufficiently well trained in Bootcamp to cope with the technical side of things. Instead of just teaching us to kill, I'd like to have learned more about the machines and the equipment it was part of my duty to photograph, particularly as my next assignment was to join a cruiser called *The Fall River* in the Philadelphia naval yard, and make a detailed photographic survey of its various parts, especially the radar equipment, which I then had to send to Naval High Command so they could study it.'

His knowledge, however, did not extend beyond recognising radar equipment when he saw it, so as soon as he began his work, he had to ask his way around the ship, much to the amusement of the eighteen-year-old youngsters, who, with every justification, must have wondered how the hell he got his job in the first place.

The Fall River happened to be a brand new vessel, and as little as he knew about other cruisers, he knew even less about this one. He was hopelessly ill-prepared for the job, and just as he was about to start despairing, he discovered that the commander of the ship was one of the boys who had worked for him in a Cap and Gown show in Pittsburgh. Gene levelled with him, and by the time the cruiser reached its base in Cuba, he had all the footage he needed. He was then put on a plane and a few hours later was back at photographic headquarters in Anacostia, near Washington.

It wasn't until America dropped the Atom bomb on Hiroshima that Gene finally reached the Pacific.

'I was all set to go to Japan with a crew of eleven and only a camera for a weapon, and I was scared to death. When the bomb dropped, I thought: well, this is it. We're now going to start the invasion of Japan. But I was stopped at Hawaii and brought back to San Francisco, and the number of days during the first and second bomb was a sort of drunken nightmare to me, as I sat waiting to see what was going to happen next.

'After the second bomb was dropped and the Japanese surrendered, they brought me back to the naval air base at Anacostia. Peace, I was told, was going to be declared, but there was still a lot of unfinished work to do, and I mustn't think of going home just yet.'

He was then transferred into the submarine service, which filled him with mortal dread. Being a dancer to whom space was as necessary as oxygen, the thought of being confined under water horrified him. He had only once before been in a submarine – which had remained on the surface – and even then had felt as though he were trapped in an elevator. But he went through with it, and found to his relief that once the ship submerged, a strange feeling of serenity cancelled out his fears.

His assignment, even at that late stage in the war, was to make a propaganda film about the submarine service and its daring raid on the Japanese coast earlier in the war. Apart from the scenes which would depict life in a submarine, most of the stuff Gene shot was faked or taken from stock library footage. The purpose of the film was to show how exciting the submarine service could be and to allay the fears of men, who, like himself, imagined that living under water for any length of time would be claustrophobic.

'We did the whole thing at very little cost,' he said, 'because we had the men and the imagination. The whole exercise was as invaluable to me as I choose to imagine it was to the navy.'

Another propaganda film to which he was assigned concerned the destruction by Kamikaze pilots of the huge US aircraft-carrier, the *Benjamin Franklin*. 'The purpose of the picture was to show how terrible the Japs were being to our boys at a time in the war when we were getting a real pounding from them. So I got a fellow called Jules Epstein to write a scenario for me, and together we went to the Brooklyn Navy Yard, where the *Benjamin Franklin* was docked, interviewed those members of the crew who had survived the blazing inferno by escaping through air holes and kitchen hatches, and began to reconstruct the appalling incident for the cameras.'

The actual shooting of the film lasted a week. Gene checked into the St Regis Hotel in New York, and spent whatever free time he had seeing some shows and visiting old friends.

After his two directorial stints, he was sent back to Anacostia, where his job was to edit thousands of feet of film, most of which simply showed planes landing and taking off, though occasionally the footage would include an exciting battle, or even captured Japanese film. As he had never worked with a moviola editing machine before, he was, at the same time, learning one more vital aspect of film-making.

Just before the bombing of Hiroshima, Gene was put in charge of the navy edition of the *Army–Navy* screen magazine, a weekly film compilation which was shown to the fleet. It was his job to assemble the week's most interesting footage and supply the commentary. Again, the experience proved invaluable. He was stationed in New York for his work, which enabled him to spend some time with Betsy and Kerry. For, shortly after Gene enlisted, Betsy had given up the house in Alta Drive, and come East. She landed a job understudying Julie Hayden in Tennessee Williams' *The Glass Menagerie* and, now that Kerry was no longer a baby, set out to try and re-establish herself as an actress.

Though she and Kerry had spent some time visiting Gene in

Washington, her base was her parents' home in New Jersey. When Gene was sent to New York to edit the *Army–Navy* magazine, however, they took an expensive apartment on 59th Street and Central Park South. Kerry remained with her grandparents in New Jersey and saw her father once a week. To this day Gene regrets what he feels to be his selfish and unfatherly neglect of Kerry during that period. 'But I guess Betsy and I fancied ourselves as Zelda and Scott Fitzgerald and just wanted to have a good time. A child would have been in the way.'

Shortly before Gene was discharged from the navy in May 1946, Betsy returned to Hollywood with Kerry and, with the help of Johnny Darrow, Gene's erstwhile agent who was now permanently involved in real estate, started looking for a house.

She found one in North Rodeo, Beverly Hills.

She called Gene as soon as she had seen it, and told him about it. It was, she said, the last farm-house extant in Beverly Hills, and at $37,500 an absolute bargain. She described each room to him in great detail over the 'phone, and such was her enthusiasm for it, that without waiting to see it himself, he gave her the go-ahead to buy it.

A few weeks later he followed Betsy to the coast – convinced that Hollywood was waiting for him with open arms.

He was in for a shock. The eighteen months he had been away had all but erased his name from Hollywood's fickle memory, and those arms were dangling indifferently.

It was as though *Cover Girl* and *Anchors Aweigh* had never happened.

He would have to start all over again.

Part Four

When Gene returned to California in 1946, he brought back with him an attractive young secretary called Lois McClelland, who had been a WAVE assigned to the Naval Photographic Science Laboratory at Anacostia, DC, and whose efficiency had impressed him enough to offer her a permanent job. Lois, who is still in Gene's employ, was to prove invaluable almost immediately, for the new house in North Rodeo was desperately in need of renovation and repair, and she was as efficient with a paintbrush as she was with a typewriter. Gene had paid cash for the house (being ignorant of the benefits of the mortgage system), with the result that he did not have enough money in the bank to hire a team of professional decorators – so all the help he could inveigle out of friends and associates was appreciated. He even made several pieces of furniture himself, the irrefutable evidence of his impecunious position. But he was still under contract to MGM (who had continued to pay him a stipend during the time he was in the navy), and on his return to Hollywood, began to draw his full salary. Within a few months, he was once again comfortable.

Comfortable, but not happy, for MGM had nothing to offer him, and again he found himself in the same situation as he had done with Selznick five years earlier. The 'wonder-boy' who had set Hollywood aglow with his last two films was unemployed. To

Gene, who expected to resume his career exactly where he had left off nearly two years before, his position was ego-deflating and humiliating. It was particularly hard for him to take, as Hollywood in 1946 was in the throes of the most productive period in its chequered history.

While the world agonised during five years of war, the movie capital had prospered obscenely and, by 1946, had made so much money (the box-office receipts for that year alone were $1,750,000,000!), that pictures were as plentiful as rice at a wedding. Few people, however, had the foresight to realise that the honeymoon would soon be over. Naturally enough Gene, who had only scratched the surface of what he wanted to achieve as a dancer and choreographer, was anxious to return to work and become a part of this boom.

His temporary unemployment may have had something to do with his image, which was inextricably linked with war pictures (five out of the eight films he had made had him involved with the services – even in *Cover Girl* he leaves Rita Hayworth to enlist) and audiences by then had had enough. It may also have been connected with the return of the studio's most popular male stars, such as Clark Gable, Robert Montgomery, James Stewart, Van Heflin and Robert Taylor who, like Gene, were equally anxious to resume their careers and who, because of their immense popularity, were given priority.

In fact, the hiatus in Gene's career lasted no more than a couple of months. But to Gene, itchy with ambition, it seemed like an eternity. Finally, he was offered a comedy called *Living in a Big Way*, to be directed by Gregory La Cava, in which he was once again to play a soldier, who this time meets and marries a girl the night before he is drafted, only to discover, once the war is over, that she is a millionairess, always has been, bitterly regrets the marriage, and wants a divorce.

Gene could not believe it. Not only were audiences no longer sympathetic to this sort of subject, but he felt it gave him no scope to extend himself. Quite the contrary, it would nullify everything he had achieved in pictures before the war. But Benny Thau urged him to take the role if only for the sake of his co-star, Marie MacDonald, whom the studio were moulding into another

Lana Turner type. 'You were once given a chance with Judy Garland,' Thau reminded him, 'so why not do the same for someone else?'

Reluctantly Gene began work on the film.

The experience, he says, was one he would rather forget. He hated the script, loathed working with Miss MacDonald 'a triple threat who couldn't sing, dance nor act', and considered the film a monumental waste of time.

He was right inasmuch as *Living in a Big Way* was a box-office catastrophe and is rarely seen today. But wrong in his assessment of its qualities. Though by no means an unqualified artistic triumph, it was a stylishly made comedy. Its theme – the proletariat (represented by Gene) versus the good life (represented by Miss MacDonald) was a favourite of La Cava (the director of *My Man Godfrey*) who, although working in familiar territory, was able to eschew stereotype characterisations and avoid sentimentality. It certainly deserved more serious consideration than it received at the time. Its setting was 1946 – but the mood of the film, especially in the way it looked, had a thirties feel to it and, had it been made a decade earlier with, say, Joel McCrea and Carole Lombard, would most certainly have been a success.

Still, La Cava, who was one of the few directors with complete autonomy at MGM, managed to draw a cool, controlled, most accomplished performance from Gene, who, despite his misgivings, revealed a flair for comedy not many people realised he possessed.

Living in a Big Way is not a musical, although it does contain three musical numbers, which Gene staged with the assistance of Stanley Donen. In the first, Gene and Marie MacDonald dance in an Astaire–Rogers fashion to 'It Had To Be You', falling in love as they do so. By the time the music stops, they have convinced us that it is indeed possible for two people who have just met to do something as silly as marry on the spur of the moment. The second number, called 'Fido and Me', which Gene dances with a little dog, takes place after he has returned from the army. Both Gene and the dog have been spurned by Miss MacDonald; and the routine, which revolves around a statue in a garden and is all about rejection, is rich in ideas and steps which Gene was later to develop and refine.

Finally there is a production number of sorts which takes place in, under and over the skeletal frame of an incomplete apartment house, and is an athletic routine in which Gene makes effective use of metal rings, step-ladders and planks of wood. The number is done with children, and the easy, spontaneous way he involves them in the action is again quintessential Kelly.

Living in a Big Way took nine months to complete because of a union strike which occurred midway through shooting. Gene was on the board of directors of the Screenwriters' Guild (he was becoming increasingly active in politics) and he was given permission to travel to Chicago for talks with the heads of the Carpenters' Union who were blocking the strike. The studio was far more concerned with overcoming their labour problems than with finishing *Living in a Big Way*, and as Gene was involved in meetings with the management as well as with union officials, he was kept busy for several months before the issues were finally resolved.

During the course of his negotiations, he was accused by the Right of championing the cause of the strikers, which was not true. His only concern in this instance was to see a fair settlement on both sides. But his and Betsy's reputations as free-thinking liberals were fast gaining ground in a Hollywood that was soon to be thrown into political turmoil. Nor did his anti-Establishment sentiments go unheeded, and a few years later he would not have been surprised had he found himself on Senator McCarthy's notoriously destructive black list and labelled a Communist.

Shortly after completing *Living in a Big Way*, Gene decided to go abroad. Neither he nor Betsy had been to Europe before, and they both welcomed the opportunity to leave Hollywood temporarily and visit Rome, London, Paris, Florence and Venice – cities they had always longed to see. There was also a possibility that Betsy might do a film in Europe with Montgomery Clift – but the deal fell through, and she had to content herself with just having a holiday instead. When they returned to California six weeks later, Gene was assigned to the new Judy Garland musical *Easter Parade*, which had a score by Irving Berlin. But after rehearsing for nearly a month, he broke his ankle playing volley-ball with a group of kids, and had to withdraw from the production. It was one of the few occasions when Louis B. Mayer actually called on him in person. 'I told Mayer I'd been rehearsing a rather complicated dance step,' he said, 'and that I'd damaged my ankle, because I didn't think he'd respond too well to the truth. Well, Mayer was beside himself. He didn't have a replacement, he said, and what was he going to do? I said "Why don't you give Fred Astaire a ring and ask him to do the picture?" So he called Fred. Then Fred called me and said he didn't know whether he should. He'd been in retirement for a couple of years; and was worried that the routines which had already been arranged wouldn't suit him. I told him they could easily be rearranged and not to worry. He was still a bit reluctant, but finally said okay.'

In the meantime, while Hollywood continued to produce lush escapist musicals like *Easter Parade*, the industry itself was entering the unhappiest period in its history.

Apart from the Labour Strike, the Department of Justice introduced a law which protected independent motion picture exhibitors from being forced to screen a particular studio's 'B' pictures as part of an overall package which also included the better ones as well. The studios had been in no way concerned with the personal tastes of their exhibitors, and by insisting that they take the good with the bad, had guaranteed themselves a profitable return on all their product, regardless of quality.

On December 31st, 1946, however, the Department of Justice won a battle which it had been fighting for twenty years. Major film studios which also controlled their own cinema chains, were now allowed merely to produce, but no longer to distribute or exhibit their product. Each of these operations had to be divorced from the other if the company was not to fall foul of the monopolies' commission. The result of this was a fairer deal for the cinema owner but a drastic decrease in the studios' annual profits, as well as in the number of films being made. In short, it marked the beginning of the end of Hollywood. For, although the 'block-booking' system as it was called, was certainly unfair in one respect, it necessitated a steady flow of product, which in volume and variety contributed incalculably to Hollywood's reputation as the film capital of the world.

In August 1947, the industry faced a further crisis when Hugh Dalton, Britain's Chancellor of the Exchequer, announced that seventy-five per cent of all the profits accrued by American film companies would be subject to heavy taxation.

The Midas days of Hollywood, when movie-making was a synonym for money-making, were over. Even Louis B. Mayer, the highest salaried man in America, was forced to take a twenty-five per cent cut in his salary, the same percentage, in fact, by which he reduced his staff at MGM in September 1947. With the war over, the American public no longer felt the need to go to the pictures three or four times a week as they used to. Life, they began to discover, was full of other diversions. Also, the rise in the country's cost of living was another reason Hollywood's fortunes declined. People seemed to be spending less on entertainment and more on necessities.

Against this background of financial uncertainty, the industry, confused by its changing fortunes, suffered its greatest humiliation. At a time when many Americans seriously believed that their country was fast becoming the victim of a heinous Communist plot, it was inevitable that the film capital, with its vast concentration of left-wing intellectuals and the power they possessed to express their socialist views through the potent medium of motion pictures, would become the most conspicuous target in Senator Joseph McCarthy's 'final solution' to Communism.

In Hollywood, an insurance broker called J. Parnell Thomas headed the committee of the House UnAmerican activities, and by the autumn of 1947, the hysterical witch-hunt, designed to ferret out all known and suspected Communists in the entertainment industry (especially writers) was at its height.

Both Gene and Betsy were deeply concerned at what was happening and were determined to fight Thomas and his committee. In October 1947 with his leg still in plaster because of the broken ankle, which kept him out of *Easter Parade*, Gene and a group of actors and directors led by John Huston and William Wyler, and which included Humphrey Bogart, Richard Conte, Lauren Bacall, Paul Henreid, June Havoc, Danny Kaye, Evelyn Keyes and Sterling Hayden, flew to Washington where the first official hearings were being held in the Customs Chamber of the Old Office Building.

The hearings were climaxed by the arrest of the 'unfriendly ten', a group of writers who failed to co-operate with Thomas and his committee.

Gene himself was approached by the American Legion and asked straight out whether he was a Communist. He said he was not, and furthermore held no sympathies with Communists. In fact, ever since his fraternity days at college, he loathed anything that smacked of regimentation. And although he had never foresworn his belief in social justice, Communism, he said, was not for him. He was a liberal who believed in democracy and equality. He also believed implicitly in the creative freedom of the artist and, therefore, could not remain inactive while the careers of his friends and colleagues were being ruined in this senseless purge, even though it meant jeopardising his own career at MGM, the most outspokenly right-wing studio in Hollywood.

Before his trip to Washington, L. K. Sidney, Mayer's right-hand man, came to Gene's home and begged him not to go. 'You'll only make trouble for yourself,' he said, 'and who needs trouble?'

But Gene insisted he was only doing what he had to do. Besides, he said, he wasn't a Communist, so what had he to fear?

Betsy, on the other hand, had been actively involved in the Joint Anti-Fascist Refugee Committee, the committee to elect Henry Wallace, and the Hollywood Committee for the Arts, Sciences and Professions; and for a period did, in fact, believe in Soviet Communism. 'But I learned better,' she said, 'although by then most of the studios considered me untouchable and my career definitely suffered. There's no doubt about that.'

Mayer, however, had a two-hour talk with her one day, convinced himself she was as American at heart as he was, and allowed her to appear in a film opposite Angela Lansbury called *Kind Lady*, which she had come perilously close to losing because of her outspoken political beliefs. She did not work again for four years, then she was offered a part opposite Ernest Borgnine in the film version of Paddy Chayefsky's *Marty*. And even then there was a proviso. She was to write a letter to the American Legion in Washington explaining away her political ideologies, naming names, and admitting that she had been 'misled'. This she emphatically refused to do. She was, she said, prepared to voice her belief in democracy and the US, but no more.

At the time Betsy was offered *Marty*, Gene was in the middle of shooting *It's Always Fair Weather*. When he heard that she might lose the role if she refused to write the required letter, he stormed into Dore Schary's office (Schary had replaced Louis B. Mayer as head of the studio in 1951), and demanded that he do something about the situation. 'You know Betsy very well,' he said to Schary. 'You've known her for fifteen years. You know she's no threat to anyone.' Then he delivered an ultimatum. Either Schary used his influence to clear Betsy's name, so that she got the part, or he would stop work on *It's Always Fair Weather*.

Put like that Schary had little choice, and in Gene's presence he called the American Legion in Washington and personally vouch-safed her good character. She got the part.

Gene's career, however, continued without political prejudice and after his return from Europe in 1947, he was put to work in a rather strange property Arthur Freed had recently acquired and was developing for the screen. It was a romantic satire by S. N. Behrman called *The Pirate* which Alfred Lunt and Lynn Fontanne had appeared in on Broadway. As a play *The Pirate*, a most daring experiment in artifice, had not been a success, but Freed was convinced it would work on the screen as a musical. He saw it as a vehicle for Judy Garland and her husband Vincente Minnelli, and commissioned Cole Porter to write the music and lyrics. Albert Hackett and Frances Goodrich, a successful husband and wife team, were signed to do the screenplay with the brief that they were to change the emphasis of the story from the man to the woman.

Gene, who was offered the role of Serafin after the Hacketts had reshaped their screenplay for the third time, was well aware that the story was being rewritten from the woman's point of view. But he wanted to work with Judy Garland again, particularly after the *Easter Parade* incident, and agreed to take second billing. Besides, there was something that appealed to him about this rather exotic, pastiche of a strolling player (Serafin) who pretends to be the notorious Caribbean pirate Macoco in order to win the love of the wealthy Manuela (played by Garland). Robert Alton was brought in to assist Gene with the choreography and from the start, the

ST. RAPHAEL'S SCHOOL
PITTSBURGH, PA.
Rev. J. P. GALLAGHER, Pastor

...ort of *Eugene Kelly*   Grade *7*

	September	October	November	December	January	February	March	April	May	June
...istian Doctrine		85	72	94	12	90	91	95	98		
...e Stories		85	72	94	12	90	91	95	95		
...S. History		83	70	92	94	90	92	94	96		
...ding		86	72	95	96	91	92	96	100		
...ding		83	91	90	92	90	93	95	100		
...iting		85	90	91	86	92	90	96	98		
...mmar		87	72	90	91	90	92	92	94		
...position		87	72	90	91	90	92	92	94		
...ebra		59	71	93	82	87	91	96	98		
...ctical Arithmetic	Absent	90	72	95	96	91	93	98	94		
...ntal Arithmetic		90	93	95	96	91	93	98	94		
...graphy		83	72	92	93	90	91	94	98		
...giene		87	74	95	92	87	90	95	96		
...ics		80	75	91	90	80	87	95	97		
...sic		90	70	98	95	97	95	98	100		
...me Work		86	95	95	92	83	87	91	100		
...awing		83	90	86	86	80	82	87	89		
...plication		82	95	95	15	85	90	98	100		
...atness		80	100	100	96	87	92	95	100		
...'s Absent	10	½				1					
...es Tardy											
...portment		80	75	95	95	85	90	96	95		

...NING OF NOTES
...00 Perfect
...0 Very Good
...00 Good
...0 to 75 Passable
...50 to 65 Unsatisfactory

Sister M. Euphrosia
TEACHER

(Top left) Gene's seventh-grade report card.
(Below) Gene, back row, second from left. *Playcast*, 1929.

PLAY CAST — 1929
COURTESY THE PITTSBURGH PRESS

(Opposite page) Gene at age fifteen: His first derby.

(Top) Mary Martin in *Leave It to Me*. To her right, Gene Kelly in his first Broadway show.

(Below left) Gene Kelly and Nell O'Day in *One For the Money*.

Bruno
Hollywood
nyc

(Opposite page) Gene Kelly: A Broadway postcard, 1938.
(Above) Gene rehearses for *Pal Joey* with Betsy Blair looking on.
(Below) A scene from *Pal Joey*.

(Opposite page) Betsy Blair, Gene, and daughter, Kerry, Hollywood, 1942.
(Above left) Gene Kelly, Judy Garland, and George Murphy in *For Me and My Gal*.
(Above right) Franchot Tone, Marsha Hunt, and Gene Kelly in *Pilot No. 5*.
(Below) Gene Kelly takes the MGM chorus line through their paces in a rehearsal for a routine in *Dubarry Was a Lady*.

(Above) Red Skelton, Lucille Ball, and Gene Kelly in *Dubarry Was a Lady*.
(Below left) Gene Kelly dances with his alter ego in *Cover Girl*.
(Below right) Gene dances with mop in *Thousands Cheer*.

(Above left) Gene Kelly and Rita Hayworth in *Cover Girl*.
(Below) Frank Sinatra and Gene Kelly making *Anchors Aweigh* ... (Above right) ... and how it looked to audiences.

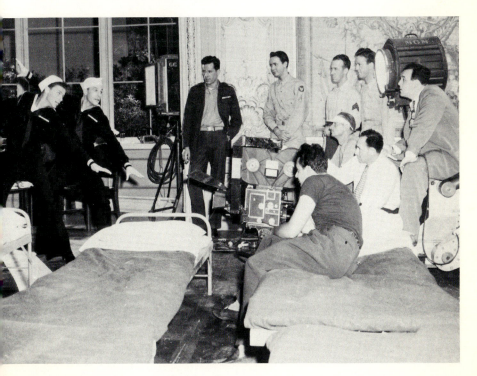

(Opposite page) Gene Kelly dances with Jerry Mouse in *Anchors Aweigh*.
(Above) Star line-up for *Christmas Holiday*: Richard Whorf, Deanna Durbin,
and Gene Kelly.
(Below) Gene Kelly and Jean-Pierre Aumont between takes of *The Cross of
Lorraine*.

(This page) Gene Kelly and Fred Astaire as the Babbit and the Bromide in *Ziegfeld Follies*.
(Opposite page) Gene Kelly in an energetic routine from *Living in a Big Way*.
(Overleaf) Gene Kelly and Judy Garland in *The Pirate*.

project, with its theatrical emphasis and extravagantly melodramatic plot, pulsated with possibilities.

The shooting of *The Pirate* took much longer than it should have, due to certain difficulties with Judy Garland, who was beginning to show the first ominous signs of her long and protracted illness. There were days when she arrived late, and days when she did not arrive at all. Her marriage to Minnelli was on the verge of crumbling; she resented his close friendship with Gene, being 'decidedly miffed' at the length of time the two men spent together discussing every detail of the picture, oblivious to her constant need for affection and attention.

From the start, Gene's idea of the part was to poke some affectionate fun at his childhood heroes, Douglas Fairbanks in the swashbuckling scenes, and John Barrymore in the romantic ones. Minnelli, too, was charmed with the idea of satirising the entire myth of the adventure yarn.

Alas, the finished product, pitched at a stifling temperature of ninety-five degrees in the shade – so that the very water in the quay at San Sebastian (the Caribbean Island on which the action is set) seems sizzling to the touch – was more than audiences could take. The grossly overdrawn characters; the unharnessed performances of Gene and Judy, who play all their scenes in capital letters and punctuate every gesture with an exclamation mark; and the heady conglomeration of colours which predominate Jack Martin–Smith's balletic sets and Irene Sharaff's carnival costumes – these were all elements that dizzied the public.

Happily though, the musical numbers are splendid. In 'Nina', for example, a routine of sustained inventive brilliance danced to a catchy bolero rhythm, Gene, dressed in black trousers, colourful waistcoat and dashing white hat, curls himself around drainpipes and clambers over rooftops as he courts every girl in San Sebastian in that overtly masculine manner which is his stylistic trademark. Once again he modified basic ballet steps to suit his own athletic approach and the result, as he moves from girl to girl with the seductive grace of a panther, is mesmeric. The dance is an appealing combination of all the elements he had been trying to unify into an effective whole, and the most clear-cut statement of his personal style yet seen on the screen. The apprenticeship he had served on such films as *Cover Girl* and *Anchors Aweigh*, both of which are exciting because they show Gene, the dancer, in search of a refreshingly original persona, was over. In *The Pirate* he became a master of the genre.

It is not only Gene's *bragadoccio* contribution to 'Nina' (the style is more appealing in the dance numbers than the 'straight' sections) which makes it so memorable, but also the editing of the sequence (by Blanche Sewell), the compositions in Harry Stradling's photography, the colours chosen by Minnelli and, of course, the wizardry of Cole Porter's song – whose lyrics work wonders in helping Gene establish his character before he goes on to find its choreographic counterpart.

The Pirate ballet, however, in which Serafin dances out his fantasy as Macoco, and which has Gene cavorting boisterously up, down and across a screen of billowing mauve clouds and black belching smoke is visually quite exciting, but in the end, more orgiastic than artistic. Nor is it of much consequence choreographically and, if anything, adds to the overall staginess of the film. It is also excruciatingly noisy.

Midway through filming, Gene felt the picture needed a light-hearted and unashamedly commercial number at a point in the story where the action seemed to flag. Minnelli, Arthur Freed and Roger Edens, the musical director, agreed. But as Edens was in the middle of a feud with Porter over the arrangement of 'Nina', Gene decided to approach the great man himself. He drove out to the composer's home in Brentwood, and explained the situation. Porter sat in a corner of the room, listened attentively as Gene outlined the sort of thing he wanted, then said he would see what he could do.

The following day, Porter called Gene and asked him whether he was free to drive out to Brentwood as he had completed the song.

As soon as Gene arrived, Porter handed him a drink, sat him down, slowly walked over to the piano, and played him five choruses of 'Be A Clown'.

'When he was through,' Gene said, 'he turned to me and asked me whether it was the sort of thing I had in mind. Had in mind! It surpassed anything I could have imagined. It was brilliant. Each verse was more stunning than the last. I rushed back to the studio and showed the number to Vincente and Arthur, who liked it so much, they used it not only in the spot for which it was intended, but at the end of the picture as well.'

'Be A Clown', a rousing and catchy paean to vaudeville, which Gene staged for himself and the Nicholas Brothers, two brilliant black speciality dancers – became the hit of the film.

It is full of effective 'business' and the perfect antidote to the more sophisticated and stylised 'Nina'. Unfortunately, when *The Pirate* was first released in 1948, cinema managers in Memphis as well as other key cities in the South cut the number from the film on racial grounds.

If *The Pirate* proved anything, it was that there was no mood Gene could not accomplish or express through the language of the dance or the flexibility of the cinema. All things were possible and if, technically, he was assured they were not, he would devise a way of getting around the problem. On one occasion in *The Pirate* he wanted to get a low-angle shot, but was told it was impossible because the sheer size of the Technicolor camera prevented the lens from getting low enough on the ground. So in conjunction with the MGM camera department he invented a mechanism he called 'The Ubangi' – a long lip that projected from the camera, heavily reinforced with iron grids underneath, and with a mirror on it, only a couple of inches off the floor, so that the camera could shoot down into the mirror which, in turn, could be adjusted to reflect the exact angle he wanted.

At the age of thirty-six, Gene Kelly, dancer, choreographer and innovator, had come of age.

Like the play, however, *The Pirate* was not a success when it was first released.

'After the previews,' Gene said, 'Vincente and I honestly believed we were being so dazzlingly brilliant and clever that everybody would fall at our feet and swoon clean away in delight and ecstasy – as they kissed each of our toes in appreciation for this wondrous new musical we'd given them. Well, we were wrong. About five and a half people seemed to get the gist of what we set out to do. And in retrospect, you couldn't really blame them. We just didn't pull it off. Not completely. Whatever I did looked like fake

Barrymore and fake Fairbanks. But that's the result of the damned elusive camera I'd been trying so hard to tame. It all looked so good in rehearsal.'

Today, in spite of James Agee's accurate pronouncement that 'The Pirate has the death's head, culture cute, mirthful grin of the average Shakespearean comic', it is, a quarter of a century after it was made, being 'rediscovered' by cineastes, and is now a cult film its adherents are hailing as a masterpiece.

Gene's superb ability to leap and bound across the screen made him a natural choice for the studio's expensive new production of The Three Musketeers, and after the role of D'Artagnan had been assigned to him, he spent two arduous months learning how to fence, and generally preparing himself for the numerous tricks and stunts he would have to perform. Jean Heremens, the Belgian fencing champion, began by teaching him the rudiments of classical swordsmanship, and gradually Gene adapted what was being taught him to suit his own particular style. His ballet training proved invaluable, for he noticed that a great deal of classical ballet is directly related to swordsmanship. 'In both,' he observed, 'the feet are always placed outward, making it possible to move quickly from side to side and to use your body to the full. Unless your toes were turned outwards, the costumes of the period made it difficult to move easily in a duel. So, when I first started fencing, I had no problem moving around. What I found more difficult was training my reflexes to deflect with speed, then come back at my opponent. That was a skill I had to acquire through sheer hard work and practice.'

In the many hours Gene spent rehearsing the duelling sequences for The Three Musketeers, the sword he used had a small rubber lump attached to its tip for safety purposes. During the shooting of the film, the lumps were removed and the sword-edge blunted and dulled. In spite of the precautions, a few minor mishaps occurred, and once Gene was nicked on the face and lost half his false moustache. The cameras continued to turn for about twenty seconds until the cameraman noticed only half a moustache and stopped the scene.

Throughout filming, Gene was perpetually being bruised; much of the action was pretty rough and, except for a couple of really dangerous stunts, he did most of the leaping about and all of the sword-fighting himself. In the rough-house atmosphere of the picture, Lana Turner as Milady did not have an easy time of it either. In the scene in her bedchamber in which Gene discovers her infidelity, he flung her on the bed with such vigour that she fell off it on to the floor, broke her elbow and was incapacitated for two weeks, during which time Gene took the opportunity to improve his swordsmanship, for even the most complicated duel scenes were to be done without a stand-in. 'Not because I'm particularly brave,' he said, 'but being a dancer, the public knew the way my body moved, and if someone else was suddenly to double for me, the illusion would be spoilt.'

As in *The Pirate*, Gene's inspiration for D'Artagnan was Douglas Fairbanks, although the duel he has with Richelieu on the beach is reminiscent of the Errol Flynn–Basil Rathbone confrontation in *Captain Blood*. 'What I envied about Fairbanks,' he said, 'was the way he registered his satisfaction after completing a particularly dazzling trick without in any way being smug about it. There was something in his expression that acknowledged his own excellence, and it was most engaging. I tried to acquire the same sort of nonchalance for D'Artagnan, but I was never able to be as ingenuous as Fairbanks. With me it came out rather tauntingly – a sort of "come on and fight", as if I were Mohammed Ali sparring with a rival boxer. It was never quite the same. Fairbanks had a combination of naïvety and arrogance which was unrivalled in the cinema. And although there wasn't a trick in his entire repertoire I couldn't duplicate, the "brio" with which he performed them was uniquely his and, of course, made him such a star.'

In *The Three Musketeers* Gene was required to be elaborately clothed for most of the film. His costumes – designed by Walter Plunkett – were bulkier than anything he had been used to before, including *The Pirate*, in which he was colourfully, though less heavily clad. And as most of the shooting took place in summer, the physical discomfort he and the rest of the cast suffered was immense. Yet he remembers *The Three Musketeers* as being one of the most enjoyable of his career because, he said, 'it was like being a kid all over again – playing cowboys and Indians. For what is *The Three Musketeers* if not a Western with plumes?'

But for Gene the really exciting aspect about the film was that all the action sequences were extensions of dancing, particularly the one in which the Musketeers first meet and join forces against Richelieu. Tchaikovsky's 'Capriccio Italien' provided the stirring background music, and the ensuing encounter which takes place behind the Luxembourg gardens between the Cardinal's guard and the Musketeers, was choreographed around the music. Rhythm was everything.

Unfortunately, director George Sidney was unable to give the narrative the same momentum as the action sequences, and whenever the swordplay and the brawling stop, the film becomes heavy going.

Physically, however, the picture could not have been more elaborately or more impressively mounted. That it only jumps into life three or four times when, with more imaginative direction, it could have been constantly animated, is regrettable. The major duels stand out in such high relief against the flatness of the rest, that the disappointment we feel in Sidney's inability to shape the rest of the film with the same tongue-in-cheek bravado, is total.

Gene's D'Artagnan does, however, manage to achieve a consistency. His character, though conceived with no more finesse than his Serafin/Macoco in *The Pirate*, springs directly from the light-hearted agility he displays in the duel scenes; and the panache of his swordplay as well as the ardour of his encounters with Lana Turner, are indistinguishable in tone. It is a well thought out, beautifully integrated caricature, wherein his acting becomes an extension of his swashbuckling – as it did in *The Pirate*. But unlike *The Pirate*, Gene's sense of burlesque in *The Three Musketeers* is more agreeably convincing, his comedy less obvious and his overall presence more acceptable to audiences.

After *The Pirate* and *The Three Musketeers*, Gene desperately wanted MGM to mount a production of *Cyrano de Bergerac* for him, one of his favourite plays, and in which he believed he could excel. When the idea was turned down on the grounds that it would not make money, Gene suggested they do it as a musical. But Eddie Mannix was despatched by Louis B. Mayer to tell Gene that his career would be ruined if he were to appear in a silly, false nose. The failure of *The Pirate* also mitigated against the possibility of his playing Cyrano, for the studio was convinced that Gene's audience did not want to see him in 'sophisticated' roles. So Gene went to Europe instead – to Klosters, in Switzerland – and, now that he could afford it, taught himself the rich man's sport of skiing.

When he returned to California, he found himself a part of MGM's starry tribute to Rodgers and Hart in a musical called *Words and Music* directed by Norman Taurog, featuring Mickey Rooney as Lorenz Hart, insipid Tom Drake as Richard Rodgers, and a roster of guest stars including June Allyson, Judy Garland, Lena Horne, Cyd Charisse, Mel Tormé and Vera-Ellen.

Gene was assigned to choreograph (with Robert Alton) and (with Vera-Ellen) appear in the 'Slaughter on 10th Avenue' ballet – a frenetic item about a gangster and his moll which was adapted from the 1936 Rodgers and Hart Broadway musical, *On Your Toes*, and which was originally danced by Ray Bolger and Tamara Geva.

In the Broadway version, the story of 'Slaughter on 10th Avenue' concerned a young dancer who found himself having to dance with the body of a dead girl in order to stop a gangster's bullet from entering his heart. The complicated plot of *On Your Toes* leading to the ballet, was integrally woven into the dance itself, and when Gene and Robert Alton came to restage the sequence, they simplified it, changing the story-line completely and making it a self-contained ballet in which a gangster and his moll are shot dead in a sleazy saloon while doing an American-style apache dance. The comic element which Ray Bolger brought to the original ballet was gone, and with Rodgers' permission certain bars of music were cut or changed to accommodate the new libretto.

The sequence, staged in garish yellow and red sets, has some exciting moments, most notably the exuberant outburst prior to the slaughter, and is interesting in that for the first time we see Gene playing a character to whom ballet dancing in real life would be unthinkable. (Even in *Anchors Aweigh* there is no ballet as such.) It is a perfect illustration of the 'truck driver' theory he formulated when he first appeared in *The Time of Your Life*, which simply set out to show how, by employing the right choreographic language, it was possible to interpret the most unballetic characters in terms of the dance without stretching an audience's belief in the character.

He rehearsed it for six weeks, and took a further three weeks to shoot it. It runs for ten minutes and is the most memorable ten minutes in the film.

After *Words and Music*, MGM once again decided to team Gene with Frank Sinatra.

Producer Joe Pasternak had a story which concerned two sailors who, after demobilisation, buy a bombed-out aircraft-carrier from the government for a couple of thousand dollars, and turn it into a successful floating night-club. Pasternak thought Gene and Frank would be ideal casting.

But Gene took one look at the story and was horrified. 'It was the sort of thing they dreamed up ten years ago for Mickey Rooney and Judy Garland and in self-defence, I decided I'd write something more suitable myself.' The result was *Take Me Out to the Ball Game*. Years ago, Gene had heard of the existence of two fellows who played professional baseball in the summer, and who, in the winter, went into vaudeville. Using them as models for himself and Sinatra, he began to work on a story-line which he hoped would be more amusing than the one Pasternak was touting around.

'But I got stuck three-quarters of the way through,' he said. 'It was my usual problem of not being able to write a third act. I was in New York seeing shows, and I called Stanley Donen on the coast and asked him to fly out and help me with it. A couple of days later he arrived and looked over what I'd done. He thought it a great idea, and the following day we managed to figure out a suitable ending to the story. Neither of us were "compleat play-wrights" and the work we'd done consisted of no more than a couple of pages of text. But it was enough to give the studio an idea of the sort of picture they could expect. The fact that we'd totally ignored the foreign market and blissfully refused to realise that few people outside America knew or cared what a ball game was (in Britain the title was changed to *Everybody's Cheering*) was irrelevant. We thought it a funny idea and that's all that mattered.'

So they put their names on it, and sold it for twenty-five thousand dollars – not to Joe Pasternak (whose musicals tended to be on the old-fashioned side) – but to Arthur Freed. 'I'll never forget the look on Stanley's face,' Gene said, 'when he heard about the sale. Though we split the fee, 12,500 dollars for a couple of days' work was money from the gods, and we couldn't believe our luck.' Harry Tugend and George Wells wrote the screenplay, Betty Comden and Adolph Green (whose first film at MGM had been *Good News* with June Allyson) wrote the lyrics, and the music was supplied by the studio's Roger Edens, with a contribution by Harold Arlen and Yip Harburg. The director was Busby Berkeley.

Take Me Out to the Ball Game, set at the turn of the century, is about the amorous exploits of two baseball players cum vaudevillians. As in *Anchors Aweigh*, Sinatra is the shy, more retiring of the two men – and falls in love with the lady who happens to be the manager of his baseball team. She, however, only has eyes for Gene, which leaves Sinatra open to the advances of a homely but determined Betty Garrett. Complications develop in the form of a gang of crooks who want Gene and his team to lose a vitally important game – but these shenanigans are speedily disposed of, and the film ends jubilantly with a patriotic, flag-waving finale called 'Strictly USA'.

Though *Take Me Out to the Ball Game* sets out to glorify the all-American male, and is basically a Kelly–Sinatra vehicle, the studio wanted Esther Williams, their popular money-making swimming star to co-star as the lady manager, and it was Tugend and Wells' thankless task to devise situations in which she could take to the water. Happily they only came up with one.

Apart from Gene and Sinatra, Esther Williams and Betty Garrett, Jules Munshin was also cast (as a baseball-playing buddy of the two men), and the chemistry of the three men pleased MGM sufficiently to bring them together again in *On the Town* the following year.

Take Me Out to the Ball Game, which was completed in 1949, was Busby Berkeley's first big musical since *The Gang's All Here*, which he had made with Alice Faye and Carmen Miranda four years earlier at 20th Century Fox. His previous picture, *Cinderella Jones*, made at Warner Brothers, was a nonentity, and its failure aggravated a crisis in the director's private life involving alcoholism and marital problems. Though Arthur Freed realised that Berkeley was not up to par, he felt sure the veteran dance-director was still capable of keeping an experienced eye on the production.

Berkeley's ideas, however, were not always in tune with Gene's, and Betty Garrett remembered how, on one occasion, he was after the sort of overhead shot he had popularised in the Dick Powell–Ruby Keeler musicals and called out to the cameraman, who was attempting to achieve it: 'Back . . . back . . . we have to go back . . .' to which Gene remarked, under his breath, 'Yeah. Back to 1930.'

When it came to shooting the elaborate finale, Gene realised he would have to take over from Berkeley, who was too tired to continue. Berkeley admitted he was 'pooped out' and didn't mind at all. If anything, he was grateful to be relieved of what had become for him a chore. The finale turned out to be a co-direction job between Gene and Stanley Donen, whose solid contribution to *Take Me Out to the Ball Game* helped him earn a real co-director's credit with Gene on their next project, *On the Town*.

Gene deeply regretted that Berkeley had to be relieved of some of the work on the film because, as he said, he owed him a debt and would have liked him to have felt that everything on *Ball Game* was his. Although by the late forties his working methods were old-fashioned, Berkeley taught Gene how to control the timing in a production number by counting out certain beats to which the cameraman had to adhere. It was one of the most valuable things he ever learned about putting on a dance for the cameras.

Take Me Out to the Ball Game is by no means an epoch-making musical, but it has the same vitality that characterised the three great Kelly musicals which followed it. It reunited Gene with Sinatra, introduced Munshin into the group, consolidated Gene and Sinatra's relationship (first established in *Anchors Aweigh*), as well as that between Sinatra and Betty Garrett, and generally served as a sort of 'trailer' for *On the Town*.

On the evidence of *Ball Game*'s story, both Gene and Stanley Donen were grossly overpaid for their efforts. The musical numbers, however, are delightful, and although Gene dances down to Sinatra in the simple but effective soft-shoe treatment of the title song, and mugs somewhat over-enthusiastically with him and Munshin in a celebratory ditty called 'O'Brien to Ryan to Goldberg', he later gets a chance to demonstrate his stunning sleight of foot in a made-to-measure solo called 'The Hat My Father Wore On St Patrick's Day', in which he executes a series of 'barrel rolls' akin to the back bend pirouette of ballet, which are breathtaking. Gene had never hoofed as well in any of his previous pictures, and if for no other reason, *Take Me Out to the Ball Game* is still worth looking at today.

Gene worked an average of fourteen hours a day, but still managed to find time to pursue his social life with equal dedication. The notorious 'game' was still popular in the Kelly household and was as competitive and tense as ever. Once Betsy recalls, Miriam Schary, the wife of Dore Schary who, in 1948, became Vice-President in charge of production at MGM, acted out a certain phrase which her husband was unable to guess. Tension was at its peak, and in a fit of fury, she gave him a wounding kick on the shin which reverberated throughout the house.

Betty Garrett also remembers that the atmosphere during these sessions was so electrically charged that what should have been a pleasant social event, usually turned into a gladiatorial combat. After spending one or two evenings with the Kellys, she and her husband Larry Parks, decided they'd had enough. 'Besides,' she said, 'no one was ever formally invited to the Kellys. If their light was on outside, it was understood you could just drop in. But Larry hated dropping in on people uninvited, even though he knew he would always be welcome, so we just faded out of the group after a while.'

Gene never locked his front door at North Rodeo, and André Previn, then a young man of seventeen working in the MGM music department, and a frequent visitor to the Kelly household, recalled how he and Stanley Donen once thought they'd play a joke on Gene. 'We arrived one afternoon, and the house was empty,' he said. 'So we decided to take all the paintings off the walls and left with them in my car, hoping Gene would think he'd been burgled. But, of course, he put two and two together in about three seconds flat, rang me up, and told me to bring the paintings back!'

Apart from 'the game', they also played 'Botticelli', which Gene usually won because, Betsy said, he knew more names and dates and useless information than anyone else.

Saturday and Sunday were the Kellys' volley-ball days, a sport Gene took as seriously as his work – and according to Bob Fosse, the choreographer who witnessed several of these sessions, Gene played to win. 'It was his backyard, and his volley-ball,' said Fosse, 'and he wanted to be king. I'd never seen anyone so fierce about a so-called friendly game in my life – before or since. He had a competitive streak in him which was quite frightening. At the same time, he had this tremendous Irish charm, and if he saw you were unhappy, he'd flash that smile at you and all was well.'

'The volley-ball games,' Gene said, 'were famous, I guess, because of the high standards we tried to maintain. We used to invite teams from Santa Monica Beach and the YMCA to come out to the house. Then we'd get together a team of our own, usually Hollywood actors, and we'd fight it out. Some of the games were terrific. They provided me with a most enjoyable way of keeping fit. And it wasn't only volley-ball we played. Touch football was in vogue at the time, and we had some rough goes at that. I played a lot of tennis as well so, one way and another, any surplus energy I may have had during those years was burned up.'

Kerry, his daughter, was encouraged to take part in sport as well, and while the adults played volley-ball, she and her friends played kick-ball. The Kellys didn't have a swimming pool until the mid-fifties, and the only way to cool off after the activity was to take a cold shower. 'Having a swimming pool,' Gene said, 'was just too much of a Hollywood status symbol in the forties. And I didn't want Kerry to grow up thinking of herself as a rich man's kid.'

Saturday and Sunday nights were 'open house' at North Rodeo. From about seven o'clock, people would start dropping in. The dining-room table was filled with an assortment of cold-cuts, and throughout the rest of the night as many as fifty people would help themselves to as much food as they could eat. Gene stood behind his bar dispensing alcohol to all-comers, and as the evening wore on, and the room filled with celebrities, the piano became the focal point of attention, as performers and musicians like Johnny Green, or Frank Sinatra, or Phil Silvers, or Lennie Hayton, or Leonard Bernstein casually strolled over to it and began to play.

Other regular entertainers at the Kelly house were Judy Garland, Lena Horne, Betty Comden and Adolph Green (whose respective spouses were subjected to endless repetitions of their repertoire), Kay Thompson, Roger Edens, Noël Coward, Nancy Walker and Peter Lawford. Johnny Green, then General Music Director of MGM believes, today, that he was looked on as an object of derision by several members of the Kelly group. 'I always wore tails, you see, because I came from that sort of family background in New York. I was rarely seen without a flower in a buttonhole, and I adored wearing a morning suit. Nor did I find it objectionable to wear a necktie. Now Gene, of course, is just the opposite. He's about the most informal guy you could wish to meet; and while he often ribbed me about my clothes, he never ridiculed me. And this I appreciated, because several of my other contemporaries did ridicule me. There's no bullshit about Gene. True, he's a talent snob, he's brash, competitive, and one hell of an Irish leprechaun; and if you didn't possess, shall we say, "special abilities", he found it difficult to have much time for you. But that's the way he was and God bless him for it. A lot of people disliked him for this, but that didn't bother Gene. Of course it's nice to be loved by everyone but being loved was not the prime motivation in Gene's life. Artists who expect constant adulation usually land up in trouble. Gene demanded nothing from anyone that he didn't demand from himself – perfection, whether in the studio during the week, or on Saturday nights at home.'

'The thing about the Kelly get-togethers,' André Previn recalled, 'was that you never knew exactly who was going to be there. And there were no rules when to come or go, or how to dress. I think I can honestly say that I have never met so many extraordinary people in one room, on so many occasions in my life. I met Noël Coward there, and Chevalier, and Chaplin. And there was never a fanfare to herald their arrival. The keyword was informality, but the prerequisite was talent. Gene and Betsy had an unforgivably conceited intolerance of untalented people. If, for example, any one of the bachelors in the group showed up with a girl who was pretty – well that was okay. But if the girl opened her mouth and turned out to be a dumb broad, or tried to play "the game" and wasn't particularly good at it, they would be extremely intolerant of her and showed their displeasure.

'When I first started going to North Rodeo at the age of seventeen, Gene took a liking to me and my work, and it was next to impossible to resist those sort of surroundings when you're still young and impressionable. Yet he was the first to come down hard on me if I made what he thought was a conceited remark. At the time, of course, I couldn't see, where Hollywood and its values were concerned, that we were all on the *Titanic* and the band was playing "Nearer My God To Thee". I was seduced happily and willingly, and I learned a great deal from people ranging from the gifted to the merely brilliant.

'But ultimately,' he said, 'my visits waned because the competing for centre stage, not in terms of performance, but in "look how clever I am" precluded having fun, and I realised, after a while, it was an expendable part of my life. I'm as ambitious as the next man, but the sort of competitive streak I encountered in Gene really made me uncomfortable. He had this desperate need always to prove he was the best. I've never known anyone to work so hard at being a perfectionist as Gene.'

Richard Brooks, the writer–director, and a good friend of Gene's, recalled that Gene's perfectionism resulted in a perpetual battle between him and various studio heads at MGM. 'All Louis B. Mayer knew about musicals,' said Brooks, 'was what he saw in the Jeanette MacDonald–Nelson Eddy operettas. Give him a few waltzes and a schmaltzy story where the characters didn't jump around too much, liked each other and wore beautiful gowns, and he was happy. Now Gene, of course, didn't quite fit into that category. He was an unattached live wire who sprang across the stage like electricity. And to Mayer and some of his boys, this was a whole new ball game and one he didn't understand at all. Consequently, Gene was always having problems. And when Gene had problems, he fought like a prize-fighter to get them resolved. And this, in turn, made him unpopular with certain important people at the studio. He refused to be compartmentalised and told what to do. As a result people tended to find him difficult, yet at the same time they were in awe of him. His detractors never learned to talk his language or to appreciate the perfectionist in him. After all, it takes a perfectionist to understand one. And believe me, there aren't many of them about.'

'The thing that first struck me about Gene,' producer Joe Pasternak recalled, 'was that he was a pretty smart cookie. No bullshit. And believe me, this made a change because most actors are ignorant people who let success go to their heads. In the movie business it's easier to live with failure than success. Look what happened to Mario Lanza. He couldn't cope with his success and began to over-eat. It killed him. And there are plenty others like him. Kelly, on the other hand, took success in his stride. He wore it well.

'The next thing that struck me was that he was a perfectionist. Right from the beginning of his Hollywood career he wasn't prepared to settle for anything less than his best. Now, in an actor this can be a pleasure, but it can also be a pain, because most perfectionists are pretty stubborn, unbending people. But Gene, I remember, always listened to my point of view. He was never unreasonable. And, unlike most of the actors I've worked with, he was concerned about such sordid things as the budget of a film. He never let a producer waste money unnecessarily. Even in his expensive production numbers he helped keep the costs down as much as possible by not making unnecessary demands. I guess it was his thrifty Irish upbringing which gave him his respect for the dollar.

'I first worked with him in *Thousands Cheer*, and the highest praise I can give him is that in spite of having practically every heavyweight MGM star in that picture, he is the one who made the biggest impact. I told him from the start: "You want to steal the movie? All you have to do is one dance that is new and original. Everyone else is doing their usual 'shtik' – you be different." So he came up with the mop dance, which is the best number in the picture.

'The thing about Kelly,' he said, 'is that he is one of the handful of Hollywood originals. The two dirtiest words in the English language to him are "second best".'

As a result of the constant flow of talent that passed through North Rodeo each Saturday and Sunday night, Gene and Betsy rarely went out, preferring the comfort and stimulation of their own gatherings to Hollywood's plastic night life. Night-clubs and formal parties, said Gene, were never his style. 'Ever since I can remember,

I've always been awkward at them. They bring the worst out in me. I once went to a lavish Hollywood "do" one night, which I couldn't really avoid because it was being given by Louis B. Mayer and his wife. And in the course of the evening, Vivien Leigh came up to me and said there was only one thing left for her to do in Hollywood, and that was to dance with Gene Kelly. And before I knew what hit me, she was leading me onto the dance floor. I don't know why, but I began to stammer and blush, and said something dumb like "are you *sure* you want to?" She said yes, she was quite sure, and as soon as we began to dance, I realised she couldn't follow me too well. We were both too nervous about it, I guess, and simply out of sync. with each other. Maybe we had both had a couple of drinks too many, but it just never worked out, and after a while, I did something I've never ever forgiven myself for. I asked her if we could sit the rest of it out. Well, of course, I hurt her feelings terribly. It was a cruel, thoughtless thing to have done to anyone – let alone someone as lovely and gracious as Vivien Leigh – and I wanted to kill myself the second after I'd done it. But that's how gauche I became at formal parties. They really brought out the worst in me. I'm sure a lot of people considered me anti-social, which I wasn't. It's just that my social life took place in my home.'

One of the most unusual gatherings in the Kelly household took place one evening, shortly after their cook, Bertha, decided she could do with a new set of pots and pans. She had spotted a pamphlet advertising utensils for cooking without water – the advantage being, or so the literature claimed, that with steam, food retained its vitamins better. Bertha persuaded Gene and Betsy to call the man who sponsored the pots and to ask him round to demonstrate exactly how it was possible to cook without water. The man said he would be delighted to oblige, but insisted on there being at least a half a dozen people present, as he was going to cook a large meal which had to be eaten. Naturally, he was also hoping to off-load as many pots and pans as he could.

So Betsy invited Hedy Lamarr, Nick Conte and his wife Ruth, Ava Gardner, Rita Hayworth and George Cukor.

A half an hour before the guests arrived the salesman, a nice-looking man in his early thirties appeared with his wife, and at eight o'clock the front doorbell rang.

'We knew it had to be George Cukor,' Gene said, 'because he was the only one of our friends who was formal and who didn't just walk in. I opened the door and saw that he'd brought with him Greta Garbo, who was a diet-fanatic and was very taken with the whole idea of cooking with steam.

'When everyone arrived, we moved into the kitchen. Garbo sat on the sink. Hedy Lamarr crossed her legs on the sideboard, Ava Gardner propped herself against the refrigerator, and Rita Hayworth squatted in a corner on the floor. Our young demonstrator didn't have a clue who any of us were, and began by showing us, with the aid of a chart, how to cook carrots without water. An hour or so later he completed the meal – which was absolutely tasteless – and said whoever ate the most would get a prize. Nick Conte accepted the challenge and won. His prize was a pancake cooked without butter. Garbo thought that hilarious and laughed and laughed, just as she had done in *Ninotchka* when Melvyn Douglas fell off the chair, and was utterly charmed by the salesman and his charts and his food and his pots and pans.

'After the demonstration was over, Greta disappeared into the lounge, and returned half an hour later having bought a complete set of utensils for eighty-seven dollars. This most sophisticated Swedish woman – and probably the most famous film-star in the world – was completely won over by the man and took everything he said dead seriously. We just couldn't believe it was the same woman who had played Camille or Marie Walewska. She was so completely naïve. The rest of us, with the exception of Hedy Lamarr, who bought half the man's pans, decided we could live without waterless food and disappeared down the road for a good, honest, unhealthy pizza.

'In retrospect, it is one of the evenings I remember most vividly in all my years in Hollywood: Garbo, Lamarr, Gardner and Hayworth – four of the world's most beautiful women – draped round my kitchen like ordinary *hausfraus*. I wish someone had taken a photograph of them.'

The Kellys, in the midst of all their activities, also found time to maintain their intellectual interests. They read avidly, kept abreast of what was happening in the cinema by screening new films every Sunday night in their living-room, perused the *London Observer* from cover to cover each week, regularly travelled to New York to see the new plays, and even studied a couple of languages.

At the same time, Gene was determined to become a model father, and spent as much time as possible with his awesomely intelligent daughter Kerry, who was seven years old in 1949.

'He was basically a teacher,' said Kerry, who today is a child psychologist, married and living in London. 'His whole conversation was unconsciously or half-consciously constructive. He never talked down to me, and if I didn't know what a word meant, he refused to tell me and made me look it up in the dictionary. Then we'd discuss it together. And after dinner, he might suddenly decide there was something I ought to know about, and out would come the encyclopaedia, and together we'd study and talk about whatever it was he thought I ought to know. We were,' she said, 'a great family for discussing things from volley-ball to the more abstract qualities of life. We were a pretty high-sounding household. I was always treated not as a "little adult" like Liza Minnelli or Portland Mason were, but rather as a child whose opinions were worth listening to. He always thought of me as someone with whom he could reason. For example, I was never forbidden to go to a picture or read a book. But if Gene thought the picture or the book was unsuitable, he'd say so, and leave it up to me to decide if I still wanted to go ahead. He gave me the equipment to make my own decisions. A great deal of care, attention, loving thought and tenderness went into all the things to do with home. He wanted so desperately to be an excellent father – and he was.'

Kerry did, however, find Gene's conscious concern that she should not become a typical Beverly Hills kid somewhat isolating.

He had an obsession about her growing up with the normal everyday values he himself had as a child, and this led to certain paradoxes of which he was not even aware. If there was anything she wanted, such as a toy or a doll, he would make her save up for it. At the same time, he would think nothing of travelling first-class to Europe with her and staying at the best hotels, where she could summon room service as often as she liked simply by lifting a telephone. He expected her to look after herself and do all sorts of chores, although they had a house full of servants. He would take her to New York for a weekend to see a friend's play, and together they would live it up for forty-eight hours; yet at the same time he gave her less pocket-money than any of her friends received. His main concern was that she should develop a decent set of values in an environment notorious for its lack of them. In fact, to Kerry, Gene was a mass of contradictions. He adored living in California, but he felt at heart much more of an Easterner whose intellectual sympathies were in New York. He even hated her Californian accent and desperately hoped that on one of their trips to Europe she would learn to speak properly. The biggest irony of all though, was that he was very anti-Establishment, yet he could comfortably live in Beverly Hills, surrounded by some of the 'wickedest' capitalists in the world! 'Considering the contradictions,' Kerry remarked, 'it was a formidable achievement that the things he taught me actually managed to sink in.'

In spite of the clear-cut, 'short-back-and-sides' values Gene tried to instil into his daughter, the prevailing ethos in the family was slightly avant-garde, providing yet one more contradiction. She wasn't brought up in a classically feminine way, and there was nothing she couldn't do simply because she happened to be born a girl. She and Gene went mountain-climbing together, took off on camping weekends, and generally enjoyed each other's company. He taught her to roller-skate, ride a bike, play tennis and touch-football; until she became a young woman, at which point he concerned himself with the men in her life, he made no concessions, over and above a few overt displays of tenderness, to the fact that she was a girl.

Kerry loved the idea of her father being famous, but again the 'prevailing ethos' in the Kelly household was that one must not be too proud, or boast. 'I was allowed to say "my daddy's in pictures" because everybody's daddy was in pictures in Hollywood,' she said. 'What I wasn't allowed to say was "my daddy's the greatest dancer in the world!"'

Gene involved her in his work as well as in his leisure time, and from about the age of six or seven, she would watch him rehearse at home, giving him his cues and helping him learn his lyrics. She was proud to be included in all facets of his life, and felt resentful of the children with whom he worked in his pictures, particularly little Sharon MacManus in *Anchors Aweigh*. 'I was the same age as she was, and when I saw them on the screen together, I felt positively betrayed!'

What she never realised about her father until much later in life was how complicated and introverted a man he really is.

'Though he was always surrounded by people who believed him to be as outgoing in his private life as he was on the screen, he was very complex and really rather lonely. He was always restless – trying to prove something to himself all the time. And he was at his happiest when he was involved in a project, and doing it better than anyone else could. His reason for being in Hollywood was to acquire a sort of perfection never before achieved. He wanted to make one perfect film, and then he would be happy. His role in life was to be an "original". Anything else was second best. And second best was nothing.'

In 1949, Gene and Stanley Donen co-directed *On the Town*, a glorious culmination of everything he had striven to achieve during his nine years in Hollywood, and the most innovative musical of the decade.

When, in 1944, Louis B. Mayer was prevailed upon by Arthur Freed to see the original Broadway musical on which it is based, Mayer was offended by a scene in which a black girl danced with a white man and condemned the show as 'smutty' and 'Communistic'. But Freed, whose judgement he respected, persuaded him to buy it all the same, which he did, and which the studio then sat on, making *Anchors Aweigh* instead.

Gene, who had also seen *On the Town* on Broadway, was enchanted by it. It had been developed from a Jerome Robbins ballet called *Fancy Free*, and though now a full-blown Broadway musical, still retained its balletic flavour.

The idea of sailors featuring prominently in ballet was by no means new. *Les Matelots* from France and *The Red Poppy* from Russia had both been variations on the theme. As the well-known song has it, 'there's something about a sailor' (which Gene had already discovered in *Anchors Aweigh*), and whatever it was, audiences liked it, especially if the sailors were on leave, because they knew then, they could expect some fun.

The story of *On the Town* which Betty Comden and Adolph Green adapted from their Broadway show, changing *en route* the character of Gabey to suit Gene's personality and leading man status, is hardly shattering. Three 'gobs' disembark from their battleship in the Brooklyn Navy Yard at six o'clock one morning, and spend the next twenty-four hours in search of women and fun. Gene falls in love with a poster of Vera-Ellen, who is the subway's Miss Turnstiles for June, and spends half the film looking for her, until he finally tracks her down to Symphonic Hall where she is receiving some ballet coaching from an inebriated Ouspenskaya-type ballet mistress (Florence Bates), whose proud boast is that she has taught everyone from Nijinsky to Mickey Rooney.

Frank Sinatra, again cast as the timid, butter-wouldn't-melt-in-the-mouth innocent, is chased with relentless zeal by a lady cab-driver called Brunnhilde Esterhazy – played to the hilt by Betty Garrett, while Jules Munshin (never quite convincing as a lover-boy somehow), makes quite a hit with Ann Miller, an anthropologist he happens to meet at the Museum of Anthropological History. Which more or less takes care of the story, except that Gene and Stanley Donen invested it with so much that was new and exciting – from the expressive Miss Turnstiles' ballet, to the scintillating se-quence atop the Empire State Building – that they changed the entire concept of musical films. *On the Town* will always find a place in cinema history for being the first purely dance-orientated film musical. The Astaire–Rogers musicals of the thirties, full of match-less delights as they are, are basically light comedies with music appended. It wasn't until *The Pirate* that Gene's physical presence lent a balletic aura to most of the scenes in which he appeared. And even then the predominating impression of his performance is more athletic than balletic.

On the Town, however, is saturated with dance: even when the leading players are standing still (which isn't very often), you feel they're about to take off any second. So concerned was Gene that the film retains its balletic flavour that in the 'Day In New York' ballet he substituted two trained dancers for Sinatra and Munshin.

Agnes de Mille had done this six years earlier in the Dream ballet in *Oklahoma!*, but it had never before been attempted on the screen. The boldness of the concept confused audiences in 1949, and today Gene regards the substitution of the two dancers as the least successful element in the film. He is also disappointed that the charming soft-shoe shuffle called 'Main Street' which he and Vera-Ellen danced, didn't come across on the screen with sufficient impact. For the rest, he was fully aware that *On the Town*, a sort of ballet with songs, was going to change the complexion of the movie musical.

'I really believed it would be a milestone,' he said, 'because I set out to try to make it so. Everything we did in the picture was innovative – from the way we flashed the time of day across the screen as if it were a news flash (an idea which came from John dos Passos' *USA*), to the way we cut the picture, which was pretty revolutionary for its time, and which was greatly admired and copied by the French. The fact that make-believe sailors got off a real ship in a real dockyard, and danced through a real New York was a turning-point in itself.'

From a choreographic point of view, the big test was whether Gene, personally, would be able to make the transition from wise-cracking sailor to ballet-dancer without jarring the audience. He realised if he managed to pull it off, he would have achieved a major breakthrough for himself. For although he portrayed a gangster in 'Slaughter on 10th Avenue', he did not sing, nor did he have any dialogue in the sequence which might juxtapose uneasily with his dancing. His problem in *On the Town* was to retain his sailor-boy characterisation in the ballet and convince audiences that what they were watching rang true and was in no way incongruous.

A similar problem applied to the film's opening sequence, which started at dawn in the Brooklyn Navy Yard, and continued into Manhattan as the trip took in the main tourist sights of the city. Never before had a musical combined realistic settings with song and dance in quite so bold a way (if, indeed, at all) and again, the problem Gene and Stanley Donen had initially to acknowledge was that audiences would find the combination of the real and the unreal confusing.

From the beginning there was executive opposition to the unit's flying to New York to film location shots of the city. Mayer and Sam Katz, who was in charge of musical production, could not visualise the effect Gene and Donen were after and thought the whole idea indulgent and a waste of money. Why not just do it on the back lot – like everyone else? It was left to producer Arthur Freed to mediate and once again persuade Mayer and Katz that at least it was worth a try.

Reluctantly Mayer said they could go to New York – but stipulated they *had* to return in five days. Not an hour more.

'I desperately wanted one extra day to wrap up shooting,' Gene said, 'but our cameraman on location was very much an old studio man who didn't realise what I was after either, and told Mayer we were getting nothing we couldn't have got on the back lot. So they made us come home as arranged. When I think that we managed to shoot stuff at Brooklyn Bridge, Wall Street, Chinatown, the Statue of Liberty, Greenwich Village, Central Park, Columbus Circle, Rockefeller Centre and Grant's Tomb, I still can't believe it, particularly as two of our five days were spoiled by bad weather. We had to "steal" and "cheat" every shot, and somehow keep our cameras hidden from the passers-by who would only delay us further and crowd around if they knew a picture was being made. If it hadn't been for Stanley, who was still considered by the studio to be my whipping-boy, I don't know how I would have managed. He alone knew what I was after in those opening scenes of *On the Town*, and what I wanted to achieve in the picture as a whole. Even Arthur Freed, I think had his doubts this time. And when the picture was finally finished and cut together, most of the big boys at MGM, including Mayer, still didn't know what to make of it. They'd never seen anything like it before and that, as far as they were concerned, was bad. If, however, the public liked it and it made money, it would be a good picture. If the critics liked it and it didn't make money, it would be a dud. Such were their criteria.'

The public and the critics – as it happened – liked it, and accepted without any difficulty the numerous innovations, with the exception of the two dancers taking over from Sinatra and Munshin. Gene's choreography and dancing were highly praised, and his fears that an audience would not accept a sailor who expressed his innermost thoughts through the medium of ballet, were groundless. And instead of alienating his male audiences, which he feared he might do, he made them identify with him and won them over by the virility of his dancing. There was nothing sissy or effeminate about him, and they relaxed completely in his presence. Gene was 'safe'. 'Like a guy in their bowling team – only classier,' as Bob Fosse put it. Women found his smile and the cockiness of his personality most attractive and responded to his sex appeal.

After *On the Town*, his popularity soared and the next three years of his career were also to be his most golden. He seemed incapable of failure, and even *Summer Stock*, a minor and rather unhappy musical sandwiched between *On the Town* and *An American in Paris* contains at least one dance as inventive as anything he has ever done.

To derive the maximum entertainment from *On the Town* today, it is necessary to place it squarely in its cinematic perspective, and to realise that if some of its freshness has evaporated (which it has) and that if at times one has a feeling of *déjà vu*, it is because films such as *Hit the Deck*, *Skirts Ahoy*, *It's Always Fair Weather*, *All Ashore*, *So This is Paris* and *Three Sailors and a Girl*, all of which are in many ways similar to *On the Town* have, over the years, blunted our appetite for this kind of simple-minded yarn. And in an era when the movie musical has come to explore the sort of territory traversed by *Cabaret*, the somewhat undergraduate antics of the three sailors in *On the Town* can only appear to be dated.

Also it is to be regretted that most of Leonard Bernstein's memorable score written for the original Broadway production was ditched in favour of a more commercial one by Roger Edens – a particularly unfortunate loss being the ballad 'Lonely Town', one of Bernstein's most moving songs. All the same *On the Town*, which cost $1,500,000 to make, paved the way for *West Side Story* and pushed the Hollywood musical out of its claustrophobic confines in search of new ideas. Lovers of the genre should indeed be grateful for it.

Apart from Stanley Donen, two other people proved invaluable to Gene. One was Carol Haney, a brilliant dancer who joined MGM after working as a dancer with Jack Cole, the choreographer; and Jeannie Coyne, Gene's erstwhile pupil from Pittsburgh, who had come to Hollywood at about the same time as Stanley Donen.

Without them, Gene's work would have come to a standstill. He could not have appeared in the picture and done the choreography as well. He needed people behind the camera to make sure he hit a certain mark on a certain beat and this took expertise.

While Gene was in the navy, Donen, who did not pass his physical, and was forced to fight the battle of Culver City instead, picked up as much as he could about the technique of filming a dance number along the lines previously laid down by Gene in *Cover Girl*, and when Gene returned to California after the war and began work on *Living in a Big Way*, Stanley proved invaluable. Then together they trained Jeannie Coyne and Carol Haney, so that, although the ideas behind most of the numbers were Gene's, what finally appeared on the screen was very much a team effort. Carol Haney was a particularly gifted dancer whose ambition, originally, had been to perform rather than choreograph. But she didn't photograph well, and Gene persuaded her to join him and Stanley on a full-time basis, which she did. She returned to performing, however, when Bob Fosse offered her a part in the original Broadway production of *The Pajama Game*. She received rave reviews but, a few nights after the show opened, she sprained her ankle and was replaced by an unknown young actress called Shirley MacLaine.

Jeannie Coyne, who had arrived in New York from Pennsylvania in 1939, and worked with men like Robert Alton and Jack Cole, both of whom thought highly of her abilities, decided to try her luck in Hollywood in 1942. She was hard-working, intelligent and, though no beauty, had an appealing face which directors found 'cute and perky', and which meant that she was invariably made the captain of whatever chorus line she might be in. It was obvious to Gene, however, with whom she had resumed a long-standing friendship, and whom she adored, that her 'wisdom and her taste' were wasted in the chorus, and like Carol Haney, she could be more valuable to MGM in general and to him in particular if she joined his team as an assistant, which she did.

In 1948, Jeannie married Stanley Donen. They were divorced the following year, but continued to work together.

Gene, Stanley Donen, Carol Haney and Jeannie Coyne were all part of the ever-expanding repertory company which MGM's musical department began to develop in the mid-forties – this most talented group being known (and revered) as the Freed Unit, captained, of course, by the formidable Arthur Freed. The unit included Roger Edens, one of Hollywood's most accomplished music men; Lennie Hayton, husband of Lena Horne; André Previn; Johnny Green; Saul Chaplin; Vincente Minnelli; and Conrad Salinger, the finest orchestrator (together with Ray Heindorf at Warner Brothers) ever to work in films, and the man responsible for giving the classic MGM musicals their particular sound.

The other two major musical producers at MGM were Joe Pasternak and Jack Cummings, a nephew of Louis B. Mayer. Both had their successes: Pasternak produced *Anchors Aweigh* and most of the films featuring Mario Lanza, Jane Powell and Kathryn Grayson; Jack Cummings was associated with most of Esther Williams' work, and produced one great musical: *Seven Brides for Seven Brothers*, directed by Stanley Donen.

But neither Pasternak nor Cummings had Freed's genius for spotting talented people or properties. Besides, Freed himself was an exceptionally gifted lyricist who understood the creative temperament better than any of his colleagues, and had faith in original untried ideas even when he did not altogether grasp them himself. But Freed not only believed in originality, he believed in the ability of his legendary unit to turn their dreams into cinematic reality; in the property rather than in how much money it would make. Faith of his sort culminated in such films as *On the Town*, *An American in Paris* and *Singin' in the Rain*.

'The most marvellous thing about the MGM musical department,' Gene said, 'quite apart from its conglomeration of talent, was that we were one great confraternity. We liked each other professionally as well as socially. We understood each other's temperaments and talents, so that when we came to work together on a project, there was usually a most wonderful blending of ideas. And, of course, we all helped each other out of a jam. If Judy Garland was having problems with Minnelli, Chuck Walters would step in, as he did on *Easter Parade*. If Connie Salinger was unable to complete an arrangement on time to meet a deadline,

Saul Chaplin or André Previn, or Lennie Hayton would finish off the job. And so it went. On certain projects, like *An American in Paris* or *Singin' in the Rain*, they'd all pool their resources without bitching over who was going to get which credit, and the result was a unique repertory company, in which we all boosted one another's egos and worked together as a really inspired team. It was no accident that MGM musicals were the best in the world.' Gene, Stanley Donen, Jeannie Coyne, Comden and Green, Judy Garland, Kay Thompson, Roger Edens, Conrad Salinger and Johnny Green, were, Green reminisced, 'the laughingest bunch of people in Hollywood. When we were all dining together in the MGM commissary it was a disgrace. We were so loud and raucous and behaved as if we owned the place that a lot of people couldn't stand us, or the private jokes we had at their expense. I have to admit it, but the Freed boys and girls were not liked. Talent frightens people. It makes them insecure and there were many of our fellow workers who hated us. We were, in short, regarded as the snob, inconsiderate, self-centered pricks of the studio. And all we were doing was making MGM money!'

Nearly twenty-five years later, André Previn remembers it somewhat differently. 'The thing about the Almighty Freed unit,' he said, 'was that it became a bit inbred – with the same people, the same talents and the same style. We all did our thing over and over again, and while it certainly made life very pleasant, the films we were making became like very expensive home movies. We were all showing off to one another but, happily, never to the same nauseating extent as some of those Sinatra-and-his-clan pictures, all of which looked like they had been made in some backyard, then flogged to Warner Brothers. But there was, it has to be admitted, something of that syndrome in the Freed pictures. They had a look and a sound and a style that ultimately became interchangeable.'

At an age when most male dancers begin to lose their stamina, Gene was still in the peak of condition and, if anything, had greater physical resources than he had ten years earlier.

'As a man of thirty-seven,' he said, 'I combined the energy I still had with an intelligence and an awareness of my capabilities that I certainly could not have had when younger, because at thirty-seven I began to develop something of an aesthetic sense. Not only did I know exactly what I was striving for in my pictures, but I felt that I now knew how to achieve it. And it was this constant sense of adventure I felt every time I embarked on something that kept me going. And I can only be grateful that when I finally matured as an artist, I had the physical stamina – which came upon me like post-adolescence comes on some people – to explore my ideas to their fullest. Most male dancers are at their best between the ages of eighteen and thirty. After that they tend to go "over the hill" and have to adjust their dancing to their diminishing capabilities. But I was still taking leaps and bounds over tables in my forties. Without the mental stimulation my work gave me, I don't think this would have been possible.'

At the same time, he continued to lead a full life, 'eating, drinking and carousing' without ever thinking about his 'condition'. It was his work that kept him fit, and he never consciously exercised. Maintaining 'the body beautiful' was not part of his plan.

Shortly after he completed *On the Town*, Gene was offered the lead in Richard Thorpe's new drama *The Black Hand*. He was to play Johnny Columbo, an Italian immigrant whose father was murdered by the Mafia at the turn of the century in New York, and whose death he is honour-bound to avenge.

The picture was originally scheduled for Robert Taylor who decided he couldn't play it. Taylor felt his matinée-idol good-looks were wrong for the part and the studio agreed. So Gene was signed instead.

The first thing he did was to discuss with Jack Dawn, head of the make-up department, how he might be made to look convincingly Italian. The most effective way, it was decided, was to give him curly hair. The wardrobe department finished the job by shoving a Fedora on his head and slipping a bow-tie around his neck. Finally, the dialogue coach stuffed his mouth with a few Italian sentences, and he was all set to go.

The Black Hand, which also starred J. Carrol Naish and Teresa

Celli, began life as a 'B' picture but it proved popular, made money and was finally considered a 'programmer' – a term used in the trade to describe a routine feature which usually formed the top half of a double bill. It is a competently made thriller in which no single element is worthy of special attention, and although Gene's performance is perfectly in tune with Thorpe's workmanlike direction and Luther Davis's routine script, it is not one of the films by which he (or anyone) will be remembered.

Next came *Summer Stock*.

Joe Pasternak, the producer of *Summer Stock*, had bought a story from Cy Gomberg about a New England farm girl called Jane whose peaceful, bucolic existence is suddenly devastated when her stage-struck sister Abigail invites a troupe of show people to use their barn as a theatre during the summer. Jane is furious at this invasion of her privacy, and insists that the actors help out on the farm to pay for the use of the barn and the food they eat. As the story unfurls, Jane falls in love with Joe Ross, the author of the show, and on opening night steps into Abigail's shoes (Abigail having received an offer from Broadway) and becomes the star attraction. At the final fade, Jane deserts her irritating asthmatic fiancé Orville for the smooth-talking Joe Ross, and she and Joe live happily ever after.

There was nothing happy about the film, however.

Pasternak, who was at least ten years behind the times – and whose professional credo has always been, 'if at first you succeed, try again' – saw the property as a vehicle for Judy Garland and Mickey Rooney. But as Rooney was no longer the box-office attraction he had once been, Pasternak decided to up-date the story by inviting Gene to play the part of Joe.

It was the last thing in the world Gene wanted to do. He had already turned down one of Pasternak's ideas as being too old-fashioned, and after trail-blazing in *On the Town*, he was hardly enthusiastic about doing yet another musical in which a group of people put on a show. But he agreed to do it as a favour to Judy Garland who, a year ago, had lost the prize role of Annie Oakley in *Annie Get Your Gun* to Betty Hutton and been put on suspension.

By 1950, Judy Garland had reached the nadir of her career, and *Summer Stock* was the studio's bid to keep her working and, in some small way, to atone for the many sins they had perpetrated against her over the years. The very least they could do was to provide her with a crutch during this difficult period of her life.

Charles Walters, the director, also felt obliged to accept the assignment as a favour to Judy or, as he put it, 'to baby-sit for her'. 'Gene took her left arm,' he said, 'and I took her right one, and between us, we literally tried to keep her on her feet. But it wasn't easy. Emotionally she was at her lowest ebb. Physically she was pretty unsure of herself as well. There were even times when we had to nail the scenery down and provide her with supports so she wouldn't fall over. Once, I remember, she had to walk up a few steps, and she couldn't do it. So I had to cheat the shot, and shoot the scene from a different angle. The whole experience was a ghastly, hideous nightmare which, happily, is a blur in my memory. I do remember, however, that she'd call me around two or three o'clock in the morning to tell me she didn't think she was going to be able to come in for work the next day, and would I please try to shoot around her. She had always been a neurotic and insecure performer, but never as bad as this.'

After a while, the studio found it necessary to bring in a psychiatrist from Boston who nursed her on the set and helped her get through the day. As in *The Pirate* (but now more frequently) there were days when she failed to materialise at all.

'Chuck Walters was directing the picture, so naturally he was worried silly,' Gene said, 'even though he had the sophistication and the grace to realise that what he was working on was a piece of crap. I, on the other hand, was in the more luxurious position of just being the leading man. So when Judy didn't show I got together a couple of basket-ball teams and played a few games in the main rehearsal hall. It was a way of turning adversity into fun, and it helped pass the time. The thing about Judy,' he said, 'was that she only worked when she thought she was going to be good. If she felt she wasn't up to giving her best, she didn't appear on the set. It was as simple as that. Marilyn Monroe was exactly the same.'

But no studio can readily afford to indulge so erratic a temperament, even where legends are concerned, and after the first few weeks of shooting, Pasternak decided to abandon the picture.

'I'd had just as much as I could take,' he said. 'The picture was costing the studio thousands of dollars in delays, and there was no point in carrying on. Naturally we all tried our best to help Judy, but it was no use. I told Mayer to cut his losses and forget about *Summer Stock*. I thought he'd welcome the idea. But surprisingly he said no. "Judy Garland," he said, "has made this studio a fortune in the good days, and the least we can do," he went on, "is to give her one more chance. If you stop production now, it'll finish her." So we all sighed heavily and went back to work.'

As a result of Garland's stop–go activities, the shooting dragged on so long, that several of the dancers had to leave the film as they were committed to other jobs.

'Every time one of the kids left,' Gene said, 'we'd have a farewell party. Judy was always invited, and she always came. And not only did she come, but the same woman who the day before was incapable of uttering a sound, would sing her heart out. We had about nine or ten parties during *Summer Stock*; each time Judy was the star turn. She'd perform for hours and the kids just loved and adored her. Everybody did. As long as the camera wasn't turning, she was fine.'

On those rare occasions when she did feel well enough to perform in *front* of the cameras, she was, Gene recalled, nothing short of amazing. 'We did a number in the barn together called "The Portland Fancy", and though she was pretty overweight at the time – obese might be the more appropriate word – she danced magnificently, far better than in *For Me and My Gal*, and it wasn't an easy routine. I gave her some very difficult turns to do. But she was fine. Just fine. She was in a good mood that day, and it was hard to believe she had anything else on her mind but her work. The only thing she couldn't lick in that number was her size.'

Though Judy's relationship with Gene was as warm as it could be, the man she turned to in desperation when she was at her most depressed was Walter Plunkett, who designed the costumes for

Summer Stock, and whose job was to see that Judy looked as appealing as possible. Plunkett, who wasn't happy with his own contribution to the film (for he considered himself to be more at home with period costumes, such as those he'd done on *The Three Musketeers*, than with modern farmyard gear), recalled that during the shooting Judy developed hallucinations in which she saw everyone connected with the picture standing in a semi-circle and pointing accusingly at her.

'She was paranoid about her inability to work,' he said, 'and felt she was letting Gene and Chuck Walters down terribly. And the more she tried to pull herself together, the more hysterical she became. It was heart-breaking to see. She developed a hatred for herself and the way she looked which was quite alarming.

'We tried to make her look as thin as possible, but we weren't miracle workers and we didn't succeed.'

During one of her extended absences, a hill-billy number called 'Heavenly Music' (inspired by Irving Berlin's 'Couple of Swells' from *Easter Parade*) was scheduled for shooting when Pasternak decided they could no longer wait for Judy; Gene and Phil Silvers did the number without her. However, a scene showing Judy in her hill-billy costume backstage had previously been shot as it was necessary to the plot, and although she never performed the number, the impression given in the film is that she did. There was also no explanation for her remarkably *svelte* appearance at the end of the picture when she sang 'Get Happy'.

'What happened with "Get Happy",' said Charles Walters, 'was that after we were finally through with shooting, we decided we needed one more number. Judy meantime had gone off to Carmel with a hypnotist fellow who was trying to get her to lose weight, and I called her to ask whether she'd like to do one more number for us. She said she would, but that I would have to stage it personally, and that the song she wanted to do was "Get Happy". She also stipulated she wouldn't spend more than a week on it.

'Well, by the time we were ready to shoot, nearly three months later, Judy had lost a couple of stone and was looking fabulous. Better than she had looked in years. Her state of mind was much improved, and we shot the number, one of the best she has ever done I think, in less than a week. But, of course, she was a very different Judy in appearance from the one at the beginning of the picture. She was dressed only in a black jacket which showed off her legs magnificently, and she had on a little black hat which was pulled seductively over her right eye. She performed stunningly for us.'

As effective as 'Get Happy' is, the most striking number to emerge from *Summer Stock* is a solo Gene does in the barn, and in which he uses a piece of newspaper and a squeaking floorboard as props. It is built around the sounds made by the paper and the board, and is the most original number in a show constructed almost entirely out of clichés. And it all came about while Gene was waiting for Judy to recover from one of her lapses. He still had one more number for himself, and while wondering just what to do, he went to visit Nick Castle, who was choreographing some of the picture. As soon as he arrived Castle produced a piece of newspaper and began to tap on it. Then he asked Gene what he thought of the sound it made. Gene told him he thought it very effective and that it would be a great sound to build a number around. So the following day – when Judy still hadn't shown – Gene went into a rehearsal room and began to work on a routine that would have him tapping on newspaper. But it just didn't work. It was nothing but a gimmick. It needed more to it. Another sound, maybe. And he began to think to himself that if he used the theme song of the picture – 'You Wonderful You' – together with the newspaper sound, plus one other sound, he would have the basis for a number. The problem was finding that other sound. There were lots of things he could do with paper. He could tear it; he could tap on it; he could crumple it – but it still needed something else. So he took a walk and tried out all sorts of sounds, from crunching pebbles to kicking empty tin cans or anything else that came under his foot. But it was all pretty useless.

Then he decided to go back to his old hobby-horse of developing something that sprang naturally out of the environment he had been working in. 'I asked myself: where is the dance set? In a wooden barn. What's it like dancing in a barn? Difficult. Why? Because of the uneven floorboards. And that,' he said, 'was when it hit me. A squeaky floorboard! That would be my other sound.

After that it was easy. I completed the story-line of the dance in about an hour. I'd be reading a newspaper and whistling. Then, accidentally I'd step on the squeaky board – then on the newspaper. Suddenly the sounds would come together, and *voila!*' But what he had not bargained for was the temperamental quality of newsprint. On the screen it all looks pretty simple, with the paper doing what he wanted it to do. But in order to get it to tear at the right spots, he had to experiment for days. He tried to serrate the paper at various points, but that was useless because it just came apart the minute he stepped onto it. Newsprint, he discovered, has many peculiar qualities. If it's old, it will tear in the middle easily. If it's new it won't tear at all – unless with much effort. Then he experimented with different types of shoes. And when he found a pair that seemed to be sympathetic towards what he was doing, he discovered after a couple of days, that the quality of the shoes would change and they would be useless. Then, quite by chance, he and one of the prop men stumbled on the fact that the most suitable newsprint for the dance had to be at least three months old. So they collected as many three-month-old back numbers of the L.A. *Times* as they could, and after a lengthy process of elimination, Gene settled on a pair of shoes that would not do too much damage, and finally they shot the sequence.

The idea of beginning a number utilising only sound is hardly new. Rouben Mamoulian opened his memorable *Love Me Tonight*, with Jeanette MacDonald and Maurice Chevalier, by creating a mélange of sound effects, all of which represented the city of Paris first thing in the morning, and which grew through a rhythmic crescendo into 'Isn't It Romantic'. But it had never been done purely in terms of the dance before, and remains as effective a number as any Gene has devised for himself. It is purely cinematic too for, simple as it appears, it could in no way be duplicated in a stage performance.

The other glorious moment in *Summer Stock* takes place when Judy Garland drifts onto the brightly coloured stage which has been erected in the barn, where Gene talks tenderly to her about the unreal world of greasepaint and his dedication to it.

No other musical during MGM's golden period was as much a hodge-podge as *Summer Stock*. Three people, Gene, Nick Castle and Charles Walters divided the dance numbers between them and each is markedly different in style. Nick Castle, described by Saul Chaplin as a 'meat and vegetable choreographer' handled the less sophisticated routines such as the energetic 'Dig For Your Dinner', which Gene danced on top of a long wooden table while the rest of his troupe (which included Jeannie Coyne, Carol Haney and Arthur Loew, Jr., grandson of Marcus Loew, one of the founders of MGM), supplied a counterpoint accompaniment of hand-clapping and feet stomping; Gene himself choreographed his number with the newspaper and squeaky board, as well as the routines shared with Judy Garland; while Charles Walters was responsible for the aforementioned 'Get Happy', whose elegance is at variance with the rest of this 'barnyard entertainment'.

But possibly the most disturbing element in the film is the intensity of Judy Garland's opening scene, which is far too dramatic for the lightweight subject-matter. Because of her emotional problems she brings the same kind of controlled hysteria to the scenes in which she opposes the arrival of Gene and his troupe, as she was later to bring to *A Star is Born* and *Judgement at Nuremberg*. Yet the talent invested in *Summer Stock* does, in the end, produce dividends, and the film has enough high spots to make one overlook its old-fashioned formula. And in spite of Judy Garland's difficulties on the picture, one cannot help being struck by the warmth and tenderness of her relationship with Gene, once their romance begins to blossom. Temperamentally Gene and Judy are ideally suited and, as Pauline Kael has observed, they balance each other's talents. 'She joined her odd and undervalued cakewalker's prance to his large-spirited hoofing, and he joined his odd, light, high voice to her sweet deep one. Their duets together, especially "You Wonderful You" have a plaintive richness unlike anything in the Astaire-Rogers pictures. They could really sing together. There was a vulnerability both Gene and Judy brought out in each other and which neither had with anyone else.'

As for the rest of the cast of *Summer Stock* – Phil Silvers, Gloria de Haven (as Judy's sister Abigail) and Eddie Bracken as Orville – they were all too old for the roles they played, yet they perform with a charm and freshness that almost manages to convince us that it is perfectly natural for grown-ups to behave like adolescents. *Summer*

Stock may have been ten years behind the times, but it remains a pleasant musical in spite of its unhappy background.

One night, Arthur Freed and Ira Gershwin were at a concert listening to George Gershwin's *An American in Paris* suite. Later that night, Freed told Gershwin that he had always wanted to make a film set in Paris, and asked whether he would sell him the title *An American in Paris*. Gershwin said he would, on condition that, if the picture were made, the music would be by his brother George. Freed told his friend this was no hardship, and a few days later a deal was made with Ira and the Gershwin estate.

Freed's next step was to select a director for the embryonic project, and the man he chose was Vincente Minnelli, whose visual flair and knowledge of musicals was unsurpassed. He then discussed the possibility of hiring Alan Jay Lerner to write the screenplay. Minnelli thought it an excellent choice and personally approached Lerner for a reaction. 'We didn't for a minute think Lerner would do it,' Minnelli said, 'because he was, after all, a lyric writer himself and in our picture all the lyrics would, of course, be by Ira Gershwin. But he liked the idea, and to our delight said yes.'

So, at this point, Freed had a director and a writer, but not a leading man. He knew it would be Gene Kelly or Fred Astaire, but had not committed himself to either. The choice was made for him when he decided to include a ballet in the picture. He had no trouble in selling the idea of a musical about an American in Paris to Louis B. Mayer, who was still head of the studio, nor to Dore Schary, who was head of production and just as important now as Mayer.

'I remember,' said Schary, 'there was a knock on my door one day and in came Freed, Minnelli and Gene Kelly. They were all tremendously enthusiastic about this new project of theirs, and were anxious to tell me about it. They didn't have a story, but they had the title, and they had the entire Gershwin catalogue to choose from. Then Gene told me he was particularly excited about this ballet he was going to do in the middle of the picture, which would probably involve a search for a girl. Not a Cyd Charisse type of girl, but someone more gamine and, if possible, French. Anyway, they all chatted away about this brainchild of theirs, and they did so with such conviction that, without having the vaguest idea of what it was all going to be about, I gave them the go-ahead. When a triumvirate of people as talented as the three men facing me across my desk are so enthusiastic about something, it's hard to say no.'

Thus, with the approval of both Mayer and Schary and with the Gershwin estate being paid three hundred thousand dollars for the title alone (Ira Gershwin received an extra fifty thousand dollars and was made musical consultant on the project), work began on *An American in Paris*. Alan Jay Lerner went into hibernation to think up a story, and Gene, Vincente Minnelli and Saul Chaplin (who with Johnny Green replaced Roger Edens as Music Director, when Edens was despatched to work on *Showboat*) spent the next few weeks rummaging through the Gershwin catalogue at Ira Gershwin's home, playing each song through and deciding what to use in the picture and what to discard.

Finally, after much soul-searching, they narrowed down the list to a handful of the composer's more famous songs and began to communicate with Alan Jay Lerner who, working quite independently, had thought up the simple story of an American painter who lives a happy existence on the Left Bank, until two women come along and tie knots in his life. One is rich, beautiful, and a patron of the arts, the other an ingenuous young girl working in a *parfumerie*.

In order to win his affections, the older woman arranges an exhibition for the painter, introduces him to the right people, and even buys him a luxurious studio in a fashionable part of Paris. But it is in vain. The painter is in love with the girl at the *parfumerie*, and pursues her – only to learn that she is about to be married to someone else.

Dore Schary, one of the first to read Lerner's screenplay, found it serviceable, but nothing more. It seemed to him to lack sophistication, and to be really rather trite. But he was persuaded by Gene and Vincente to leave it more or less as it was because, they said, it provided them with exactly the sort of framework they were looking for.

The next problem was casting. Two years before *An American in*

Paris had even been thought of, Gene had seen a young dancer in Paris whose name was Leslie Caron. She was appearing with the Roland Petit Company in a ballet by David Lichine called *The Sphynx*. She had, he recalled, 'such an incredible quality, and moved so beautifully' that he felt he must meet her. But when he went backstage she had already gone home because she was only fifteen years old, and her mother did not want her to stay up later than was necessary. He never forgot her, however, and when Minnelli came to cast the role of the young girl, he suggested that this girl he had seen in Paris would be ideal. He described her to Minnelli, who said she *sounded* fine, but that he would have to see a test. Gene then persuaded Arthur Freed to send him to Paris, where he tested not only Leslie Caron but the actress Odile Versois. 'Odile,' said Gene, 'was adorable, but she hadn't danced for quite a while and wasn't really in good enough shape, although, had we chosen her, I'm sure she would have been fine by the time we started shooting. But what worried Minnelli more was that she didn't quite have the naïveté for the role. She was too sophisticated and that was the one quality we didn't want.

'Leslie, on the other hand, was perfection. I directed a test with her in which she didn't do any dancing, but just acted, because the test was for the benefit of Arthur and Vincente who had never seen her before, and who were more concerned with her acting than anything else. They took my word that she could dance.'

Gene returned to Hollywood with the two tests, and everyone agreed that Caron had just the right quality for the role.

The part of the 'other man' was offered to Maurice Chevalier who turned it down. Freed was quite unprepared for a negative reaction from the great French star, and offered him all manner of perquisites, as well as enormous sums of money (to which he was always susceptible), if he would change his mind. But Chevalier was unable to reconcile himself to losing the girl at the end of the picture (eight years were to pass before he agreed to act his age in *Gigi*, also directed by Minnelli and produced by Freed), and refused on the grounds that he 'could not warm to the plot'. So Gene made a second trip to Paris, and signed Georges Guetary, although he knew Guetary was too young for the role Lerner had written. 'We greyed his temples a bit,' said Gene, 'but it didn't really help, and this weakened the central issue between Leslie and myself.'

There was never any doubt, however, that the part of Gene's best friend in the picture – a musician claiming to be the oldest child prodigy in Paris – would be played by Oscar Levant, who, in life had always been a close friend of George Gershwin, and was certainly one of the greatest exponents of Gershwin's music. Besides, Levant's cynical sense of humour and rather hang-dog appearance would contrast effectively with Gene's bravura quality and Guetary's matinée-idol looks. Nina Foch, whose stock-in-trade, like Eve Arden's, was flaunting the sophisticated, brittle aspects of her sex, was cast as the painter's benefactress.

Finally, after months of preparation, shooting began on August 1st, 1950. Almost at once there were problems with Leslie Caron, who simply did not possess the physical stamina to rehearse the long hours Gene demanded. 'During the war,' Gene said, 'she suffered slightly from malnutrition with the result that she was never a particularly strong girl. And when things got really bad and she was way behind in her work, I'd go up to her and say, "Look Leslie, if we don't finish this number today, I'll lose my job" and she'd make an extra effort. But I could see how difficult it was for her and after an hour or so, she'd just collapse. And there was nothing we could do about it. We just had to be tolerant and under-standing – even when she did silly things such as the time she decided to cut her hair because she wanted to look like Zizi Jeanmaire. Well, she's no more like Zizi Jeanmaire than I am like Laurence Olivier. But she went ahead, which wouldn't have been too bad, because she *did* look cute, except that she'd already been established in the picture with longer hair, and suddenly, to have her arriving at the studio one morning looking like a boy was pretty devastating. It was charming enough, but it just didn't match what we'd already shot. All we could do was wait a few days until it grew a bit, and Helen Parrish, the hairdresser, could do something with it.'

Apart from Leslie's inability to rehearse long hours, and the occasional show of temperament from Oscar Levant, who felt there was nothing he could be told about Gershwin, and resented it when others proffered an opinion, shooting progressed smoothly. The big set piece, of course, was the ballet. But half-way through filming Lerner's screenplay, it had still not been decided just what form the ballet would take, nor whether it would be shot on location in Paris or at MGM. Initially, it was decided that the ballet *would* be filmed in Paris, using real backgrounds in just the same way that Gene and Stanley Donen had done with *On the Town*. The music chosen as the basis of the ballet was a Gershwin standard called 'Somebody Loves Me', an arrangement of which Conrad Salinger and Saul Chaplin had worked out, and Gene and Leslie started rehearsing some of the steps together. The ballet would tell the simple story of two men who love the same girl, and it would be placed about half-way through the film.

Arthur Freed then decided against taking a camera crew to Paris because of the expense involved and the problems of location shooting. Or, as Gene put it, 'We would have needed the "chutzpah" of Mike Todd to stop the traffic around the Place de la Concorde or the Avenue de l'Opera.'

After the decision had been taken to remain in Hollywood, Gene decided that 'Somebody Loves Me' was too slight a piece on which to build a full-scale ballet. What he had in mind was bigger and more lavish – a spectacle that would excite audiences and leave them breathless. He wanted to do something which had never been done before, something fresh and original, by which the film would be associated years after its simple story had faded from memory.

Once he decided not to use 'Somebody Loves Me', he began to search around for something else. He and Minnelli then abandoned the idea of telling a story completely, and made up their minds to do a ballet which would be a series of impressions depicting the painter's emotions. One thing led to another. If it was to be a ballet about a painter and about his impressions, and if it was to be set in Paris, why not use Impressionist painters as the inspiration for the whole thing? It wasn't a great deal to go on, but at least it was the germ of an idea. What they needed most now, was the time to develop the idea, and this they got when Nina Foch went down with chicken-pox. Minnelli shot as much as he could without her, then retired to his office with Gene and Irene Sharaff, who was engaged to design the costumes for the ballet, and during the next couple of weeks, while Miss Foch was recuperating, they worked out a definite scheme and synopsis.

'Mainly,' said Minnelli, 'we decided it would interpret our painter's delirium and state of mind on losing his girl to another man, and gradually we evolved an idea which would depict various parts of Paris in the style of famous Impressionist painters, regardless of whether the particular painter had ever painted the scene or not. For example, we had the Paris Opera in the style of Van Gogh, although Van Gogh never painted the Opera House. We didn't want to copy – just to evoke.'

Three questions, however, remained unanswered. At what point in the picture should the ballet take place? to what music? and would MGM buy the idea?

Arthur Freed solved the first two. Against much opposition, he insisted that the ballet should come right at the very end. 'You're not going to be able to top it with anything else, so you should finish on it,' he argued. Gene thought it risky to end a musical with a lengthy ballet, but Freed insisted he knew what he was talking about. Secondly, he suggested they use the *American in Paris* suite, for not only was it the piece of music which inspired him to do the film in the first place, but it was thematically interesting and contained enough colour and variation in mood and tempo to provide the basis for what, as he understood it, Gene and Minnelli had in mind. As for the third question – it was simply a matter of salesmanship.

So, once again, Gene and Minnelli marched into Schary's office, this time to persuade him to spend hundreds of thousands of dollars on a ballet which would probably run between fifteen and twenty minutes. To help give him some idea of their conception, they arrived armed with a portfolio of sketches by Irene Sharaff and Preston Ames, the designer, told Schary to sit back and relax, then outlined the libretto of the ballet thus:

The painter, they explained, finds himself separated from the girl he loves. He is at the Beaux Arts Ball and wanders out onto a terrace. With inconsolable grief in his eyes, he looks across a panorama of the city's twinkling lights. He begins a sketch with a black crayon, but tears it up. Suddenly there is a breeze, and amid the confetti and streamers strewn about the terrace from the costume ball, the two halves of the torn sketch come together and form a backdrop against which the painter appears. At his feet he sees a red rose. He picks it up, the black and white background bleeds into colour and the ballet begins jauntily at the Place de la Concorde with sets and costumes modelled after Dufy.

Then, as the painter sees and pursues the girl he loves, the setting changes to a flower market near La Madeleine and the style of the décor pays homage to Renoir. The mood is sad and tranquil. The pastel colours of Utrillo inspire a street scene followed by a spirited George M. Cohanesque dance (in a Rousseau setting), performed by four Americans in Paris (all wearing different coloured jackets), who are celebrating the fourth of July. In the next section, the emotion changes from exuberance to passion as the painter returns to his mood of longing and regret. The dance depicting this passion takes place in and around a fountain specially designed for the film and placed in the Place de la Concorde. The scene then changes to the Paris Opera *à la* Van Gogh, and then to Lautrec's Montmartre, when the painter becomes the character Chocolat. Once again the scene changes to the fountain at the Place de la Concorde, where the music erupts in a frenzy and becomes a statement for the excitement of the city of Paris. Then, suddenly, everyone disappears as the mood changes from ecstasy to disillusion. The painter is left all alone with his rose.

Schary listened patiently as Gene and Minnelli took him through the various stages of the piece, and after they were through said: 'Well, I don't understand what the hell you're driving at, but it sounds exciting and the sketches look great, so why not go ahead?'

Schary wasn't the only one who couldn't visualise what it would look like once completed. Gene recalled that Irving Berlin, whom he bumped into at the studio one day, said to him: 'I hear you're doing seventeen minutes of music with no words (he didn't use the word ballet). Well, I wish you luck, because it can't be done.'

In fact, it could be done and had been done. In 1949, two British film-makers, Michael Powell and Emeric Pressburger, had made *The Red Shoes* which featured Moira Shearer, Robert Helpmann and Leonide Massine in a seventeen-minute ballet. The film was well received and did excellent business – a fact which Gene was not slow to point out to any MGM executive who, like Irving Berlin, insisted it couldn't be done. There was no arguing against the facts.

The Red Shoes was a money-maker and if it could be done once, why not again?

The *American in Paris* ballet turned out to be the most expensive production number ever filmed up to that point. The scene in the Place de la Concorde alone required a backdrop over three hundred feet long and forty feet high. (Gene recalls how Fanny Brice used to come to the studio each morning to watch the set designers painting these backdrops, and how she would sit for hours just looking at their recreations in utter wonderment.) Over five hundred costumes were designed for the ballet before a final selection was made, and the whole thing took six weeks to rehearse and a month to shoot. The total cost of it was $450,000.

After a preview at a Pasadena theatre at which Arthur Freed and Dore Schary argued about the sound – Freed wanted more, Schary less – the picture was trimmed slightly and a ballad sung by Gene called 'I've Got A Crush On You' removed, as it stated the obvious and served no particular point.

An American in Paris was finally released in October 1951, fourteen months after shooting first began – at the Radio City Music Hall in New York to good reviews and even better business. And the ballet which, until then had had MGM's executives trembling in case the public turned it down, was, as Gene and Minnelli hoped it would be, the hit of the show, and which Bosley Crowther in the *New York Times* pronounced as being 'whoop de doo . . . one of the finest ever put on the screen'. Leslie Caron's début was also noted enthusiastically, and Gene felt especially proud at his discovery. In fact, for Gene *An American in Paris* was an unqualified triumph.

Though nothing in the film was as difficult, technically as, say, the 'alter ego' number in *Cover Girl*, or even the squeaky board item in *Summer Stock*, in the range and scope of its choreographic ideas it was an advance on everything he had done so far. In it he explores his uniquely hybrid style of dancing ('a synthesis of old forms and new styles') more exhaustively than in any of his earlier films.

Nothing in *An American in Paris* was particularly easy for him to do, and nothing could be taken for granted – whether in the ballet itself, or singing the seemingly simple ballad 'Our Love Is Here To Stay' with Leslie Caron on the quay near Notre-Dame.

Even the opening scene, which establishes him as a struggling artist living a frugal existence in a Paris attic, was something of a challenge and required days of preparation. The idea behind the scene was to show Gene living in so confined a space that the only way he could cope with his physical restrictions was by inventing a series of mechanical contrivances (such as his bed sliding upwards at the tug of a rope, or a makeshift table appearing from behind a door), in order to make life more comfortable and smoother running. The idea crops up in numerous silent comedy shorts, but the challenge for Gene was to do the scene in one take, for otherwise it would look phoney; and in order to achieve this, he had to choreograph the sequence. He did, however, receive one invaluable piece of advice from Minnelli, who told him to play the scene as if he were under water.

Leslie Caron's introductory dance solos in the film (to various arrangements of 'Embraceable You') also needed careful planning. The sequence showed her as a student, a party girl and a demure young thing; Gene felt he needed something extra to make it different from Vera-Ellen's introduction in *On the Town*. At Minnelli's suggestion, therefore, he used different colour schemes for each of the vignettes and different styles of choreography. The effect was most striking, particularly when all the images were projected on the screen at the same time.

The problem with 'I Got Rhythm' was to find a way of presenting a song which had already appeared in two films – *Girl Crazy* and *Rhapsody in Blue* – in a way that was entirely fresh. Gene's solution was to do it with a group of children, using the number to demonstrate the time-step, the shim-sham and the charleston. Though Gene was used to working with children, his handling of them in this particular number is somehow less contrived, less obviously cute than it had been in *Living in a Big Way* or in *Anchors Aweigh*, where his dancing with Sharon MacManus on Olvera Street, delightful as it was, had had an air of commercial calculation about it. Precisely the same sort of calculation is present in the 'By Strauss' number, which he, Oscar Levant and Georges Guetary dance with an old lady in a street café, and which is one of the most blatant pieces of schmaltz-peddling in Gene's career – certainly the low spot in *An American in Paris*.

Another item which fails to elicit joy is Oscar Levant's dream sequence in which he imagines himself as a conductor, soloist, as well as every member of the orchestra in Gershwin's 'Concerto in F'. On paper it is a pleasing, Walter Mitty-ish idea. But it simply does not come off.

Gene and Guetary have more luck belting out the infectious 'S'Wonderful', while Gene and Leslie Caron dancing with each other in 'Our Love Is Here To Stay' on the quay near Notre-Dame, are superb.

But it is undoubtedly the ballet which is the highlight of *An American in Paris*. Quite apart from the brilliance of its design – and the numerous other technical aspects which have contributed to its success, such as Adrienne Fazan's mellifluous editing and John Alton's camerawork, Gene's dancing and choreography are magnificent. Whether being set upon by four crimson women like tongues of fire, or hoofing with a quartet of blazered and straw-hatted men in the Rousseau segment, in both departments he shows himself to be a master of his craft. It is not that his work in *An American in Paris* is better than in *On the Town*; just that it has more range, breadth and, most conspicuously, depth, a quality rarely associated with Gene's choreography. The surface emotions of the 'Day in New York' ballet are overtaken in *An American in Paris* by genuine outbursts of love, sensuality, or longing, as the case may be, while the *pas de deux* which takes place around the fountain to the accompaniment of the haunting New Orleans blues theme, is most ardent and deeply felt.

The overall impression left by the *An American in Paris* ballet is of an artist's palette forever changing its colours. Yet, while bright and brilliant to the eye, it is never gaudy and, like the Impressionist canvases from which it draws its inspiration, full of light and movement. Nothing of its kind from Hollywood has quite possessed its class, sense of style and chic. It was, and remains, a unique achievement.

For the rest, *An American in Paris* is an entertaining, if somewhat self-consciously prestigious musical – not as innovative as *On the Town*, and falling short of the perfection which *Singin' in the Rain* was to achieve the following year. Its importance, where Gene is concerned, is that it gave him an opportunity to extend himself further than he had ever done before, both as choreographer and dancer, and in these fields showed that he was to be taken as seriously as Jerome Robbins and Agnes de Mille.

There was nothing now that Gene could not express through the language of the dance. His choreographic armoury was complete.

After making a brief appearance as a Greek soda-jerk called Icarus Xenophon in MGM's all-star tribute to America, *It's a Big Country* – a bouquet of eight stories about the colourful cross-section of people who make up the United States – Gene's next film was *Singin' in the Rain*. This was to establish him as Hollywood's greatest one-man band, or as the French put it, *homme orchestre* – a quintuple threat as choreographer, director, dancer, actor and singer, all of which specific talents he brought together to give an imperfect world the most perfect musical ever made.

Its inspiration was Hollywood during the years it first learned to talk, its achievement unique.

While *An American in Paris* was still in production, Arthur Freed decided to make a musical film using songs composed by himself and his partner Nacio Herb Brown in the same way that he had used Gershwin's songs for *An American in Paris*.

He had no idea what the story would be, and engaged Betty Comden and Adolph Green to think up a plot that would accommodate his catalogue of songs.

When Comden and Green arrived from New York they knew absolutely nothing about what Freed had in mind. They did not even know, they say, who the star of the picture was to be. Gene Kelly? Fred Astaire? Howard Keel?

From the outset, however, Gene insists that the film Freed had in mind was always meant to be a vehicle for himself, and cannot understand how Comden and Green were unaware of this, unless Freed failed to mention it – which is very unlikely. At any rate, Comden and Green suddenly found themselves with a blank piece of paper and a handful of Freed–Brown songs, which they and Roger Edens listened to in Freed's plushly furnished office suite on the third floor of the Irving Thalberg building ('the iron lung', as it was called) at MGM.

'The office was littered with Freed–Brown sheet music,' Betty Comden said, 'and as Roger worked his way through the songs in that Southern colonel's whisky baritone voice of his, we closed our eyes and tried to eke out a story suggested by the mood and flavour of the pieces.

'One of the very first songs Arthur wrote for MGM in 1929, when Irving Thalberg was still head of production, was an item for a chorus line called "The Wedding of the Painted Doll". Could that possibly provide the basis for a full-length musical? We couldn't somehow visualise it. And what about "The Broadway Melody" or "You Were Meant For Me"? What did they suggest? Initially, nothing.'

Then, as Roger Edens continued to play through the pile of songs at his side, Comden and Green could not help being struck by their uncanny evocation of the late twenties and early thirties (which was when the songs had been written), and the potent way they reflected the era of early talkies. There was something in the *atmosphere* of a song like 'You Are My Lucky Star', or 'All I Do Is Dream Of You', which took them back twenty years and conjured up the charleston, bobbed hair, the shimmy, Rudolph Valentino, the Model T Ford, and other figures and appurtenances of the era. It would not be possible to place these songs, they realised, in any context other than the one in which they were written. And as most of them had been featured in a handful of the earliest sound musicals why not, it occurred to them, set the story between 1927 and 1931 using Hollywood as its main locale and the awkward, tentative transition from silent pictures to sound as its basis? Both Comden and Green loved the period, knew its madcap vagaries intimately and claimed to be authorities on silent movies.

So it was decided then. Arthur Freed's new musical, which still did not have a title, would be about the film industry – and Comden and Green began work on a story-line which, in spite of their familiarity with the subject, gave them immense problems.

During an 'agonising' month, in which they tried to solve their problems, they found themselves with a series of beginnings, but no middle and no ending. 'We thought we'd open the picture in New York at a big silent movie première; show a phoney interview with the star; cut to a scene from the movie being premièred; then have the star meeting a young actress in New York, losing her and returning to Hollywood, etc., etc. It all seemed such a mess in which the darn thing never got off the ground, and after a month of this torture we were both prepared to hurl the whole thing in and give the studio back what they'd paid us so far. We were that despondent.'

It was Betty Comden's husband, Steve Kyle, who suggested they use *all* their openings in one lengthy sequence – and take it from there. Which is exactly what they did, but instead of having the première in New York, they decided to set the whole thing in Hollywood.

As most people are probably aware, *Singin' in the Rain* is the story of a matinée-idol called Don Lockwood, and a movie extra called Kathy Selden, who meet by accident when Don, to escape his clamouring fans after a film première at Grauman's Chinese Theatre, literally jumps into her open jalopy from atop a moving trolley-car. Pretty soon a romance develops between them, much to the chagrin of Don's glamorous but vacuous leading lady, Lina Lamont. With the arrival of talkies, however, Miss Lamont, who cannot string two syllables together without sounding like a grinding gear, is forced to accept Kathy, when Don points out to her that Kathy has a lovely voice and can dub her dialogue and songs for her. This works well enough at first. But soon Lina begins to make a nuisance of herself, and Don decides the time has come to reveal to the public the *real* owner of the voice they have all loved and enjoyed. Lina's career is ruined; Kathy's is just beginning. And at the final fade, she and Don find what they've been looking for all their lives – each other.

As soon as the script was completed, Betty Comden and Adolph Green showed it to Arthur Freed, who read it and passed it onto Gene and Stanley Donen, who were to co-direct it. Gene and Donen loved what they read, and began to work with Comden and Green on rewrites and changes almost immediately.

Only at this point were they actually given a title – *Singin' in the Rain*. For some reason Freed had always wanted to make a film called *Singin' in the Rain* – probably because it had been his and Brown's biggest hit – and this, Comden and Green were informed, was to be it. They both thought it ridiculous; so did Gene and Donen. After all, what did it mean? But Freed was the boss and they were stuck with it.

As soon as their rewrites were completed to everyone's satisfaction, Comden and Green returned to New York and began work on a Broadway show. Apart from the occasional 'phone call from Gene – who respected writers having once tried to be one himself, and who would not alter a line without their consent – their active association with the film ended as soon as the final draft of their screenplay was accepted.

The project was now the property of the Freed Unit whose combined skills were about to create a little miracle.

But first, as always, casting. For the role of Kathy Selden, the *ingénue*, Freed wanted someone fresh and innocent. But who? Kathryn Grayson wasn't young enough; Pier Angeli (who'd recently been put under contract) had altogether the wrong quality; June Allyson was a big girl now and Jane Powell's voice was too operatic. The only other girl MGM had under contract at the time was Debbie Reynolds, who was seventeen years old, and had briefly appeared as Helen Kane in *Three Little Words* as well as in three other minor musicals, *The Daughter of Rosie O'Grady*, *Two Weeks With Love* and *Mr Imperium* and who, by her own admission, would really have preferred to have been a gym mistress than an actress.

'I got a call from Louis B. Mayer, who was still head of the studio in 1950,' Debbie said. 'He told me to come and see him in his office. Then he sat me down and casually said he'd like to put me in a musical with Gene Kelly called *Singin' in the Rain* and how did I feel about it? I swallowed hard and said, "Gee that's great, Mr Mayer, what would you like me to do in the movie?" And he said: "I want you to play the lead opposite Gene Kelly . . ." Well, I was aghast, because up till then my experience of dancing had been the waltz, clog and the time-step. I was certainly no great dancer by any means, or no great *anything* for that matter. I'd only been dancing for about a year and anyone who's only danced for a year knows *nothing* about dancing, believe me! One, two, three, click your heels and that was my lot.

'Well, Gene Kelly was called in at that point, and Mayer told him I was to be his leading lady. Well, when he got up off the floor, he said he was shocked, amazed, and not at all pleasantly surprised because he'd hardly heard of me. "But what's she done?" he said to Mayer, who replied, "It's not what she's done but what she's *going* to do that matters. We want to make her a star."

'Well Gene was decidedly unhappy. And he said to me, "Can you do a Maxi Ford?" And I looked at him blankly and said, "What kind of a car is that?" Well, that *really* pleased him! Then he said, "Can you at least do a *time*-step? You *do* know what a time-step is?" I said, "Yes, sir, I do." And did one for him. Well, he still wasn't happy about the idea. But Mayer's word was law, and Gene was lumbered with me.'

Gene remembers the story somewhat differently. 'I wanted Debbie to do the part as soon as I saw her sing "The Aba Daba Honeymoon" from *Two Weeks With Love*,' he said. 'No one else at the studio could have touched it. I *insisted* she be used, and *never* had *any* meeting with Mayer concerning *Singin' In the Rain*.'

But whatever the circumstances, both Debbie and Gene agree on one point: her dancing was almost non-existent, and everything she did in the picture had to be taught to her from scratch. 'Gene would put me in a rehearsal studio,' she said, 'with either Carol Haney or Jeannie Coyne, his assistants, and a tap teacher called Ernie Flatt (who now choreographs the Carol Burnett Show), and he wouldn't let me leave until I was step perfect. Sometimes I danced for eight to ten hours a day and, perfectionist that he is, he'd come in and say, "Okay, show me what you've learned." And I was so petrified of him because of the temper I knew he had, that whenever he came in, I'd do everything wrong, and he'd say "Back!" and slam the door again. He would work me so hard that at times my feet bled – literally. But I wanted to prove to him that I could do it, so I just worked and worked. He makes you feel you're capable of more than you are, and I didn't want to let him down. Well, this torture went on for months, and I remember, Fred Astaire was in the rehearsal room next to mine, (where he was making *The Belle of New York*), and he would come in and pacify me. "It'll all work out," he'd say. "So don't get so discouraged." And I'd burst into tears and say, "But I'll *never* learn to dance. Never!" And he'd say,

"Debbie, if you want to be a great dancer, you'll have to keep trying and sweat it out for as long as it takes. It's the only way." And he was right. It *was* the only way. But it was sheer agony for me. Everyone else seemed to be having lots of fun but me. I had too much to learn, and in too short a period. There was just no time for fun. To be thrown into the Gene Kelly type of class was too formidable for fun.'

Donald O'Connor who, unlike Debbie Reynolds had been dancing in films since he was twelve years old, was chosen to play Cosmo Brown, Gene's best friend in the film. Millard Mitchell was cast as R. F. Simpson, the studio boss, Douglas Fowley was Roscoe Dexter, the demonstrative director, and Jean Hagen was the glamorous but vocally fractured Lina Lamont.

'We wanted Lina to be a combination Mae Murray and Judy Holliday in *Born Yesterday*,' Gene said, 'and as Jean had played in *Born Yesterday* on the road, we tested her and she was just perfect. The character was actually modelled on Judy Holliday's particular dumb blonde, and when Betty and Adolph were writing the script, they had Judy in mind because they used to work with her in their Revuers Act. I can't remember whether Judy Holliday was ever approached to do the role in *Singin' in the Rain*, but we were perfectly happy with what we got. I just told Jean to act Judy acting Billie Dawn in *Born Yesterday* – and it was easy after that.'

In fact, *Singin' in the Rain* is a compendium of borrowings whose inspiration is drawn from a variety of real-life sources and personalities. The entire scene on the sound stage with Jean Hagen desperately trying to 'speak into the bush' where the microphone has been hidden, has its origins in fact. Douglas Shearer, head of MGM's sound department, was consulted regularly about the hazards of early sound recording, and most of the tribulations suffered by the artists and technicians in *Singin' in the Rain*'s reconstruction of those times, actually happened. Rarely has a musical been so accurately researched.

Roscoe Dexter, the director in that scene, was modelled on Busby Berkeley, who liked to demonstrate everything in a most expansive manner, while R. F. Simpson, the studio boss, was inspired by Arthur Freed, who was a rather clumsy man whom Judy Garland used to refer to as 'the tank'; and the scene in which he trips over the cables in the film studio and brings poor Jean Hagen crashing down onto the floor, was just the sort of thing Freed might have done. But Gene and Donen were afraid to go too far with Freed who was, after all, their boss! – just as MGM were afraid of sending up Louella Parsons in the opening scene, for the character of Dora Bailey, played by Madge Blake was obviously meant to be Louella who, at that stage, could do a lot of damage if something or someone offended her. 'I personally was never bothered by either Hedda or Louella,' Gene said, 'or any other gossip columnists around the place. But one was never sure with those ladies, and we knew in *Singin' in the Rain*, that we were all taking a chance. Fortunately Louella adored it, and only said flattering things about us.'

Where Arthur Freed was concerned though, they were a bit more circumspect and apart from the cable incident, the only other characteristic Freed trait they brought into the picture was having R. F. Simpson unable to visualise the Broadway ballet after it has been described to him; a situation which often occurred with Freed. Gene would sometimes spend hours explaining an idea to him, but Freed always said he would have to see it on the screen first. The same applied to Dore Schary. In a sense, therefore, it was a little 'in' joke, which they never expected anyone else but themselves to appreciate.

Finally, the character of Kathy Selden was conceived as an *ingénue* June Allyson, 'full of saccharine'. But according to Gene, Debbie's own naïveté took care of everything. 'She didn't know what the hell was going on half the time, which was just the right quality we wanted, and she was marvellous. Just marvellous.'

Gene himself was a composite of several matinée-idols, but only where his 'public' image in the picture was concerned. For the rest he relied on his own personality entirely. Only Donald O'Connor was free of derivation. He was uniquely himself, inspired by no one.

Apart from the 'Moses Supposes' number, which Gene and O'Connor do together in their diction coach's studio, and which was specially written for the picture by Roger Edens, the only other new number in the score is 'Make 'Em Laugh' – which gave O'Connor a chance to shine in a way that he had never done before or since. The song, written the night before rehearsals for it began, is inexplicably similar in tune and sentiment to Cole Porter's 'Be A Clown' from *The Pirate*. No one has managed to discover why. Gene prefers not to think about the similarity, while Betty Comden and Adolph Green advanced the theory that Freed wrote it without realising he'd once produced a picture with so similar a song in it. 'Such accidents do happen,' Betty Comden said. 'And it must have been an accident, for what possible purpose could Arthur have had in deliberately stealing one of Cole's songs? Arthur himself wrote so many wonderful songs, he must have subconsciously thought he was dipping into something he'd composed years ago.'

All the other numbers, with the exception of 'Fit As A Fiddle', the sort of thing Gene and his brother Fred might have done while playing the cloops in Chicago, were featured in earlier movies. 'All I Do Is Dream Of You' was first heard in *A Night at the Opera*; 'Should I?' was featured in *Lord Byron of Broadway*; 'Singin' in the Rain' came from *Hollywood Revue of 1929*, *Hi Beautiful* and *Little Nellie Kelly*; 'I've Got a Feelin' You're Foolin'' from *Broadway Melody of 1936*; 'The Wedding of the Painted Doll' from *Broadway Melody*; 'You Were Meant For Me' from *Hollywood Revue*, *Broadway Melody*; 'Would You?' from *San Francisco*; 'You Are My Lucky Star' from *Babes in Arms* and *Broadway Melody of 1936*; 'Good Morning' from *Babes in Arms*; 'Beautiful Girl' from *Going Hollywood* and 'Broadway Rhythm' from *Babes in Arms*, *Broadway Melody of 1936*, *Broadway Melody of 1938* and *Broadway Rhythm*.

A ballet was planned for *Singin' in the Rain*, but as with *An American in Paris*, when shooting began, a synopsis had still to be thought of. All Gene knew was that it would come in the middle of the picture and that it would feature himself and Donald O'Connor. In the meantime, he had other things on his mind, not least of which was putting Debbie Reynolds through her paces so that she wouldn't let him or O'Connor down in their numbers together.

'Fortunately Debbie was as strong as an ox,' Gene said, 'and unlike Leslie Caron could work for hours. Also she was a great copyist, and could pick up the most complicated routines without too much difficulty.' 'Gene taught me discipline,' Debbie said, 'and he taught me how to slave. And today, if I don't drop dead from exhaustion after a rehearsal, I feel I haven't accomplished a thing. And this I got directly from Gene. He taught me how to be a perfectionist. For which I'm grateful. But at the time I could have done without his perfection. And his temper. It's a very short-lived temper, but when it breaks it's like a giant explosion and all hell is let loose.

'Fortunately he never blew up at me, but he did at a lot of other people, mostly through frustration at himself. One of the things I remember most vividly about Gene was that he never liked to be proved wrong. On the 'Good Morning' number, we were all doing a step around a stool at the bar counter, and suddenly Gene stopped and insisted that Donald was doing it wrong. In fact, Donald was doing it right and Gene was the one who was wrong. And both Donald and I *knew* Gene was wrong. But all Donald did was to say he was sorry. Well, Gene became very angry and said, "You should know this by now. We've worked long enough on it." I looked at Donald, because I expected Donald to say something back, but he didn't. He adored and worshipped Gene Kelly and wouldn't have dared answer back. Besides, Donald was younger than Gene, and being the very respectful type of person he is, he just kept quiet. So we did it again and again. Finally Gene stopped and said, "*I'm* doing it wrong! Why the hell didn't you tell me?!" Then he was madder than ever at us for not pointing it out to him. And I said to him, "But Gene, you can't win for losing with you." Which made him furious. But not as furious as he got with me while we were doing "You Were Meant For Me", which took place on a sound stage. I was on a ladder, and Gene was standing below me and singing up to me. Then he turned his head and leaned romantically up against the ladder. Well, just before the "take" began, I'd forgotten to remove a large piece of chewing gum from my mouth, and at the last minute, I stuck it under the ladder, so when Gene leaned back, his head somehow caught the chewing gum, and when he straightened up, he left a nice clump of hair behind. Well, he let out a yell and I just turned pale. There was a loud shout of "cut" from the floor, and that was the end of my, chewing gum days. And very nearly the end of me.'

Although the title on the shooting script read *Singin' in the Rain*

Gene had still not decided where, or how, to introduce the number into the picture. 'Freed and Roger Edens came to my office one day,' Gene said, 'and asked me what I'd thought up for the 'Singin' in the Rain' number. Well, I said rather vaguely, it's got to be raining, and I'm going to be singing. I'm going to have a glorious feeling, and I'm going to be happy again. What else? They knew I hadn't come up with an idea, but I told them not to worry, that I'd think of something. Then a couple of days later I was running through the lyrics of the song to see if they suggested anything other than the obvious when, at the end of the first chorus, I suddenly added the word 'dancing' to the lyric – so that it now ran 'I'm singing' and *dancin'* in the rain'. Instead of just singing the number, I'd dance it as well. Suddenly the mist began to clear, because a dance tagged onto a song suggested a positive and joyous emotion. Then I went through the script to find out at what point I was at my happiest, and decided my moment of greatest exhilaration came in the scene outside Kathy's house after we decided not to be beaten by talkies and to turn *The Duelling Cavalier*, the picture we were working on, into *The Dancing Cavalier*, a musical; and after I kissed her, and realised I loved her. From then on everything slotted beautifully into place. Roger Edens began the number using an expanded introductory 'vamp', and all that was left for me to do was to provide a routine that expressed the good mood I was in. And to help me with this I thought of the fun children have splashing about in rain puddles and decided to become a kid again during the number. Having decided that, the rest of the choreography was simple. What wasn't so simple was co-ordinating my umbrella with the beats of the music, and not falling down in the water and breaking every bone in my body. I was also a bit concerned that I'd catch pneumonia with all that water pouring down on me, particularly as the day we began to shoot the number I had a very bad cold, and kept rushing out into the sun to keep warm whenever I could.'

The set used for the 'Singin' in the Rain' number was a street on the MGM back-lot which was completely covered by a black tarpaulin in order to give the impression of night. The studio did not want to pay its crew double time by actually shooting at night; as Gene and Stanley preferred not to under-expose the scene, thereby shooting day for night (they also needed more space than the average interior studio provided), the only solution was to devise an exterior daytime set that excluded sunlight. So, using almost as much tarpaulin as ingenuity, the set on the back-lot was finally prepared. Next came the problem of fixing special rain pipes along the length and breadth of the street, and after that there was the further problem of lighting the set. As Technicolor film stock still required a great deal of light, the giant arc lamps or 'brutes' made it impossible for the rain to be seen when lit full on, so Harold Rossen, the cameraman, had to light it from behind. However, once all these technical problems were solved, the number itself went smoothly and was completed in one and a half days.

Far more troublesome in every respect was the Broadway ballet. Gene's original idea was to choreograph a ballet which would feature himself and Donald O'Connor. But because shooting on *Singin' in the Rain* began a few weeks later than planned, O'Connor, who was committed to doing a TV show for the Colgate Comedy Hour, was unable to take part in the ballet. Gene suddenly found himself without a story-line and without a partner. There was no way in which he could use Debbie, as she was just not a good enough dancer and would need more training than there was time for. So he decided to take a chance on a young dancer called Cyd Charisse, who had done several roles in MGM musicals, but nothing really notable, and who, from the age of fifteen, had been with the Ballet Russe de Monte Carlo. He had never worked with Charisse before, but believed she had the technique to adapt her own style to whatever demands he made on her. But she had just had a baby and had to get in shape and lose some of the excess poundage around her hips.

While she went on a diet and began to limber up for work, Gene started to play around with a few ideas, and again devised a libretto by returning to the source of the subject for his inspiration – in this instance a combination of two of Arthur Freed's and Nacio Herb Brown's songs, 'Broadway Melody' and 'Broadway Rhythm'. Obviously there could be no question where the ballet would be set.

What, he now asked himself, does Broadway conjure up to the

average person? Show-biz? Bright lights? Glamour? Young hopefuls arriving from out of town to seek fame and fortune? Damon Runyon and a shady underworld of gangsters and their molls?

Gradually from these disparate elements, a story began to take shape – a story about a young hoofer who arrives on 'The Great White Way' with a suitcase full of his dreams. As he goes from audition to audition, he is rejected. Then finally he lands himself a job at a night-club where he meets a beautiful girl and dances passionately with her. But the girl loses interest in him when a gangster offers her a diamond bracelet. Time passes. The hoofer hits the big time in show-business, becomes a star and finally meets the girl again. In his imagination, he sees himself dancing with her in some idyllic setting, far away from Broadway, but in reality she spurns him once more. The ballet ends as it began – in Times Square – with the arrival of another out-of-town hoofer determined to conquer Broadway . . .

At first Cyd Charisse, whose dancing was classically orientated, had difficulty adapting to Gene's particular style, and contrary to his belief that she would find the steps he gave her perfectly straightforward, she needed a great deal of rehearsing. 'I wanted to get her to look like a transformed ballet-dancer,' Gene said, 'and between Carol Haney and myself, eventually we did.'

One of the highlights of the ballet is what Gene calls the 'Crazy Veil' dance, in which Cyd Charisse dances with a fifty-foot piece of voile. 'It started off as a sort of scarf dance,' he said, 'something that Isadora Duncan might have done. But there was nothing especially new about that, and my concern was to devise a scarf dance that *was* new, and that could only work in the cinema. So, first of all, I decided an ordinary scarf wasn't any good. Mine would have to be at least fifty feet long – and it would be part of Cyd's costume. Well, the only thing you can do with a piece of material that size without tripping over it, is to keep it moving. But how? The answer seemed to be to use a wind machine. But the normal wind machine wasn't powerful enough to control the veil the way we wanted it controlled, so I finished up using three aeroplane motors. That's when our problems really began because how to use them without blowing Cyd clean off the set? We had to experiment for days before we discovered that by pointing the machines down on the ground, we could make the veil shoot up, or by pointing them straight at Cyd and lowering the velocity, we could get it to fly back or ruffle slightly. I can honestly say the shooting of that particular dance was about as complicated as anything I've ever done – including the "alter ego" and the squeaky board numbers, because we had to get that veil to move on a certain beat and not just haphazardly. Without Jeannie Coyne and Carol Haney, who operated the machines and counted every bar of music in order to get it right, I would never have got the number to work.'

The rest of the ballet was straightforward enough. It was shot on Stage 27, and to accommodate its vast sets, an adjoining stage was used as well so that finally, the two biggest stages in the studio became a stylised Times Square, replete with dazzling neon signs and hundreds of extras.

Like the rest of *Singin' in the Rain*, the ballet drew its inspiration from the movies and satirised many aspects of the early years of sound pictures. A gangster flicking a coin is an obvious send-up of George Raft, Cyd Charisse was made up to look like Louise Brooks, while the young hoofer with his straw hat and cane is a nod in the direction of Harry Richman. The scene in which the screen fills with people rushing towards the camera and waving their hands, echoes King Vidor's *Hallelujah* and there is also a homage to the evergreen cliché of depicting a young performer's rise to stardom by having him repeat his favourite routine first in Burlesque, then in Vaudeville, and finally at The Follies.

The Broadway ballet runs twelve minutes – not as long as the *An American in Paris* ballet, but possibly too long for what it is.

'I'd have liked to trim three minutes out of it,' Gene said, 'but I just didn't know where. I didn't want to remove any of Cyd's stuff because she needed as much time as possible on the screen to establish herself.'

Two numbers were, however, removed from the final print. In one Debbie Reynolds sang 'You Are My Lucky Star', now reduced to one verse at the very end of the film, and a reprise of 'All I Do Is Dream Of You', which had Gene dancing around his bedroom on the night he first meets Kathy Selden. Of all the numbers Gene forfeited to the cutting room floor, this one pains him the most, for he regards it as one of the best he has ever done. But it slowed down the narrative, and 'for the good of the show' had to be abandoned.

Apart from the length of the Broadway ballet and its rather tenuous link with the rest of the film, *Singin' in the Rain* remains Gene's undoubted masterpiece, and the most enduring film musical to have come out of Hollywood. In twenty-two years not a frame of it has dated; it still retains all its freshness and sparkle. If the test of a good musical is that you can see it over and over again without longing for the dialogue to end and the musical numbers to begin, then *Singin' in the Rain* passes *victor cum laude*. If anything, it is more popular in today's nostalgia-addicted world than it was when it was first seen in 1952. Television has given a generation a taste for the old Hollywood; and the movies of the thirties and forties, and what twenty-two years ago were rather obscure 'in' jokes, are now in the public domain. But even to those customers who do not possess a television set or buy books and magazines about the movies, *Singin' in the Rain* remains an invigorating musical, perfect in its reconstruction of a world gone forever, and unforgettable if only for Gene's joyous dancing in the title number, as he abandons himself to a Californian cloudburst, kicks and stamps at a gutterful of water, swings his umbrella around and around in an infectious display of good spirits, climbs half-way up a lamp-post, arms outstretched, water pouring onto his face, as he defies adversity. The number is the apotheosis of his art and the climax of an adventurous career. And although the Broadway ballet and the *American in Paris* ballet contain better dancing from him, nothing he has ever done before or since matches, for sheer exuberance, and what Betty Comden and Adolph Green have called an 'irrepressible ode to optimism', his jubilant cavortings in this, his most famous dance.

Though the rest of *Singin' in the Rain* never quite equals the magic of those five minutes of Gene dancing into the night, every number is still light years ahead of what was being seen in other screen musicals of the time. Donald O'Connor has never been as good again, and in his famous 'Make 'Em Laugh' routine, dances, clowns, and sings as if his artistic life depended on the success of it. Every trick in his repertoire is aired afresh and the cumulative effect is devastating in its virtuosity.

And for all Debbie Reynolds' misgivings about her abilities, she too has never worked as well. Her dancing in 'Good Morning' in no way betrays her inexperience, and she is the perfect partner (chewing gum notwithstanding!) in the lyrical 'You Were Meant For Me', into which Gene attempts to inject the perfect romantic atmosphere on a sound stage through the auspices of five hundred kilowatts of stardust, and a soft summer breeze.

It was the third time he had used this device – first in *Anchors Aweigh* where, on a real sound stage at a film studio, he placed Kathryn Grayson in an imaginary Spanish courtyard and tangoed his way into her heart; and next in *Summer Stock*, where he wooed Judy Garland in a barn transformed into a more appropriately romantic setting by soft lights and sweet music. But 'You Were Meant For Me' is better than both its predecessors for it is less contrived, and is ideally placed in the film between the 'Beautiful Girl' production number (which glorifies the American girl via Busby Berkeley) and the zany 'Moses Supposes'.

Singin' in the Rain, which was released in April 1952 on the heels of *An American in Paris*, did not receive the glowing reviews of the Gershwin film, nor were the box-office returns as healthy. Over the years, however, it has surpassed *An American in Paris* in popularity and is now recognised as one of the 'all time greats', though even at the time there were a handful of people who realised this.

On the night before the film was released, Betty Comden and Adolph Green recalled being at a party given for Charles Chaplin and his wife, Oona. They had never met Chaplin, but in the course of the evening they got chatting, and Chaplin suddenly described a picture he had seen the previous night at Samuel Goldwyn's house, which he said was quite wonderful – one of the best he'd ever seen. It was called *Singin' in the Rain*, and he asked Comden and Green whether they'd ever heard of it. 'Heard of it?' they blurted out in the sort of moment every writer dreams of, 'We wrote it!' Similarly at a party in Paris several years later, they were introduced to François Truffaut, the French director, whom they greatly admired and who disarmed them completely by confessing that he had seen *Chansons sous la Pluie* more times than he could remember, and knew every frame of it by heart. It was praise indeed, and one more indication, if any further indication was needed, that *Singin' in the Rain* had become a classic of the genre. Truffaut has since acknowledged that it was *Singin' in the Rain* and its humorous look at film-making which gave him the idea to make his own '*hommage*' to the cinema—*La Nuit Américaine*.

For Gene, however, the years that followed *Singin' in the Rain* were to be something of an anticlimax. It was as if he had reached the very zenith of his creative powers with that picture, and there was only one direction left to go – down.

Part Five

In December 1951, the United States Congress passed a law which stipulated that any American citizen who had spent seventeen months out of eighteen away from home would be exempt from paying income tax during that time. It was an incentive to American oil workers and key defence men to leave the comforts of their homes for the far-flung uncertainties of Alaska or the Middle East, and proved so popular that, in Hollywood, Gene's powerful agent, Lew Wasserman of MCA (whose agency Gene joined in 1946 when Leland Hayward became a producer), decided that what was good for the oil men was just as good for his clients, and made a deal with MGM in which twenty-five of the studio's stars would be sent abroad to make pictures. Salaries would be paid in dollars, in America – without tax deductions, and the capital gains would be enormous.

It was an opportunity too good to miss, and before you could say Wasserman, there was a sizeable exodus from the film capital to Britain, particularly as studios with 'frozen' funds – profits which could not leave the country – agreed to use the itinerant stars in pictures made either in Britain itself or on location in Europe.

It was a most felicitous arrangement. The studios would be putting their 'frozen' pounds (hopefully) to profitable use while the stars themselves would be earning more money than ever before. Gene, whose weekly salary from MGM in 1952 was 2,500 dollars, was the first to take advantage of the attractive windfall offered by Congress and within weeks of the law being passed, he and Betsy decided to rent out their home in North Rodeo, and spend the next eighteen months of their life in London.

Gene, however, arrived in Europe a couple of months ahead of Betsy and in January 1952 he checked into the Bayerischer Hof Hotel in Munich. His first project abroad was a thriller called *The Devil Makes Three*. Its setting was Germany in 1947, at a time when the CID division of the army was hard at work ferreting out smugglers, black marketeers and ambitious members of the defunct Nazi party. In theory, at any rate, it sounded like a good idea, and Gene was anxious to return to a 'straight' dramatic part after his successful run in musicals.

His role was that of Jeff Eliot, a captain who returns to Germany after the war to see the family which had once saved his life by giving him food and shelter after he had escaped from a prison camp. He discovers, however, that they were all killed in an air-raid, except for Wilhelmina, their daughter whom he meets, and who prevails on him to drive her to and from Salzburg in a dangerous smuggling operation.

Pier Angeli was signed to play Wilhelmina.

Shortly before shooting began, Gene had his appendix removed at the Clinique de Belle Feuille in Paris. He spent the next couple of weeks recuperating at the Hotel Lancastaire and at the ski resort of Klosters near Zurich. As soon as he was well enough, he took a train to Munich where work on the film had already commenced.

On March 5th, Betsy, Kerry, Gene's secretary Lois and Jeannie Coyne, his assistant, left New York on the *Isle de France*, and arrived at Le Havre five days later. They stayed in Paris overnight, then took a train to Munich.

The script of *The Devil Makes Three* was written by Jerry Davis and from the outset Gene was well aware that it was inadequate. He knew it was little more than a 'B' feature which would do his reputation no good, especially after the success of *An American in Paris* (*Singin' in the Rain* had not yet been released).

As shooting progressed in conditions of extreme cold and heavy snow, the quality of the script deteriorated still further, and in desperation he called Lew Wasserman and insisted that he fly out to Munich to see what could be done to salvage the mess. Jerry Davis, Gene told Wasserman, had missed on this one, and unless MGM sent along a replacement, they would all make idiots of themselves.

MGM, however, was interested only in unfreezing the Deutschmark regardless of the manner in which it did so, and failed to respond to Gene's and Wasserman's SOS.

So Gene did what he always did in such circumstances. He made the best of the situation and had some fun, wandering off to the local beer gardens and drowning his anxieties in goodly quantities of Steinheger. 'We were shooting on location most of the time, in Salzburg, Munich and Berchtesgaden,' he said, 'and I rationalised that at least I was seeing some of Austria and Bavaria, so what the hell? The only way to treat it all was as a paid holiday.' Which is exactly what he did. At weekends, or whenever he wasn't required on the set, he and his family took off to see some of Ludwig II's castles and generally have as pleasant and informative a time as possible.

One night he even managed to get into a fight with a couple of American ex-GI's in a Munich beer cellar. Kerry recalled the incident: 'The Americans,' she said, 'made some derogatory remarks about the Germans, which Gene took exception to, and lost his temper. He must have been going through a terrible crisis of conscience because, after all, only a few years ago we were at war with the Germans, and in that sense he didn't want to take their side against an American. Yet, at the same time, his sense of fair play which, after all, had nothing to do with the war, got the better of him – or the worse – and a fight broke out. I remember it was a very painful thing for him to punch an American over a German – but he did.'

A punch-up was one way of working out his aggression over the dissatisfaction he felt for *The Devil Makes Three*. Unfortunately, the director, Andrew Marton (who directed the spectacular chariot race in *Ben Hur*), had no similar recourse and had to suffer it through. 'If the picture was a catastrophe,' Gene said, 'Andrew would be blamed. Yet there was no way the picture could succeed, and he knew it. And when you're that sure of failure, there's no point in continuing. It's exactly like living on borrowed time.'

During the filming of *The Devil Makes Three*, Gene heard that he had won an Academy Award for his 'extreme versatility as an actor, singer, director and dancer, but specifically for his brilliant achievement in the art of choreography on film'. *An American in Paris* received the Oscar for Best Picture against such competition as *Decision Before Dawn*, *A Place in the Sun*, *A Streetcar Named Desire* and *Quo Vadis*, and also won awards for Walter Plunkett, Orry Kelly and Irene Sharaff, Alan Jay Lerner, Cedric Gibbons and Preston Ames (for their sets), Alfred Gilks and John Alton (for their photography), and Saul Chaplin and Johnny Green for the best scoring in a musical picture. Arthur Freed received the Irving Thalberg Award as producer of the year.

The news thrilled Gene, and at the same time depressed him. For, having attained the heights on one side of the Atlantic, it threw into sharp focus the realisation that the picture he was working on on the other side was a disaster which no amount of beer-drinking, castle-gazing or fist-fighting could conceal. It was a monument to mediocrity and as far as Gene was concerned, an indelible blot on a career which seemed in the ascendant. Short of inspiration from some hitherto unforthcoming muse, *The Devil Makes Three* would bring discredit to all those unfortunate enough to have been associated with it.

Alas, no miracle occurred, and the film was the failure Gene always knew it would be.

On his return to London, he, Betsy and Kerry checked in to the Dorchester Hotel in Park Lane where they stayed for a couple of weeks. Then they moved to the Savoy for the next two months although, by this time, Betsy had found a job in Paris as dialogue coach with the director Anatole Litvak, and commuted between the two cities.

Kerry adored living at the Savoy where she was royally treated by the staff and fussed over by the many celebrities staying in the hotel – including Danny Kaye who, learning that she had gone down with a bout of flu, visited her every evening and entertained her until she was well again.

During her stay in England Kerry went to the Royal Ballet School, having already been taught by Carmelita Marachi in California. Gene's prominence as a dancer initially filled Kerry with all the obvious complexes, which she gradually overcame, only to be told by a ballet mistress at the Royal Ballet School that she would never be a ballerina because the arch of her foot was not high enough.

When Gene heard about this, he was disappointed and immediately took off his shoes and socks and compared his arch with hers. They were identical. 'No daughter of his,' said Betsy, 'was going to be criticised for not conforming to stereotype. Gene hated that kind of rigidity.

High enough arch or not, Kerry decided, after all, not to pursue her dancing, so the judgement passed on her by the mistress at the Royal Ballet School is hypothetical. But it does reveal Gene's attitude towards personal criticism (for he felt, indirectly, that judgement had also been passed on him), as well as his distaste for conventional rules where dancing was concerned.

In the summer of 1952, Gene began work on the second of the three pictures he made during his eighteen months away from Hollywood – a full-length ballet film called *Invitation to the Dance*, which he persuaded Arthur Freed to allow him to direct and choreograph. It was to be a specialised but popular film in four separate parts, utilising the talents of some of Europe's and America's greatest dancers, the idea behind it being to show the world that there were other dancers around apart from Gene Kelly and Fred Astaire. 'Of course, this wasn't news to people in the more sophisticated cities. But what about audiences in the provinces of Vietnam? or Senegal? or Indonesia? or Central Africa? – who'd never seen a ballet company in their lives? Or even people nearer home – in Dubuque or Hackensack? It was to them I wanted *Invitation to the Dance* to appeal.'

So he rented a house, called Moulin de la Roche, from a well-to-do French family in a small village six miles from Chartres, and he and Kerry as well as his assistants Jeannie Coyne and Carol Haney and his secretary Lois, moved to France for the summer. Betsy, who was still working in Paris, joined them at weekends.

The working conditions were idyllic and with Jeannie and Carol around, Gene was able to 'block out' his choreography with the two dancers 'trying each new step for size' as he went along. For Gene it was the perfect creative set-up, and he and his entourage spent a blissful couple of months preparing a picture which he hoped would contain the synthesis of his art.

The four ballets Gene devised for *Invitation to the Dance* could not be more varied in character.

The first, 'Circus', would be a semi-classical piece about a lovesick pierrot in white-face, who falls to his death from a high-wire trapeze while trying to impress the girl he loves. It was to feature Igor Youskevitch and Claire Sombert (whom Gene had first spotted at a dancing academy in Paris) with music by Jacques Ibert.

The second, 'Ring Around the Rosy', composed by André Previn, would be a *La Ronde*-type story which traces the history of a bracelet given by a doting husband to his wife, who gives it to an artist who, in turn, gives it to a model, whence it passes to a crook, a night-club siren, a crooner, a hat-check girl, a sailor, a whore, and, finally, back again to the husband. For this section Gene wanted the Russian ballerina Tamara Toumanova, American dancer Tommy Rall, Claude Bessy, a French ballerina, Diane Adams, from the New York City Ballet, Igor Youskevitch and, from Britain, Paddy Stone and Irving Davies.

Item no. 3 would have Gene and the rest of the dancers interpreting through dance a dozen popular songs, such as the 'Whippenpoof Song', 'Just One of Those Things', 'St Louis Blues', 'Orange Coloured Sky', 'I Feel A Song Coming On' and 'On The Sunny Side of The Street'.

The finale was to be a version of 'Sinbad the Sailor' using the music of Rimsky-Korsakov's *Scheherazade*. As in the Jerry Mouse sequence in *Anchors Aweigh*, it would also combine live action with animated cartoon, and feature young David Kasday as a genie and Carol Haney as Scheherazade.

Initially, Gene had no intention of appearing in the film himself, but MGM had other views on the matter and insisted that he be starred, for without his participation in front of the cameras, they assured him the film would certainly fail.

So, reluctantly, Gene cast himself in all four ballets, and in the autumn of 1952 work commenced at the MGM studios in Boreham Wood, Elstree.

The shooting of *Invitation to the Dance* was inundated with difficulties, the main one being the unavailability of the dancers, whose various commitments made it impossible for them all to assemble at the same time, so that Gene was forced to shoot in bits and pieces according to their various schedules. This was further aggravated by the crew assigned to Gene at Boreham Wood who, though willing, were unable to utilise a camera crane to his satisfaction. As well as this, some of the more sophisticated requirements he asked of them, which would have been commonplace in Hollywood, took ages to accomplish. Nor were most of his performers able to adjust to dancing for the camera. They were, after all, stage artists with little or no knowledge of film technique. Youskevitch recalled that, although Gene was extremely helpful and gave him as much guidance as he could, he was also extremely demanding. 'There were times, I think, when he overdid things,' he said. 'He rehearsed us all so rigidly – and on cement floors! – that it required superhuman energy not to collapse. I remember one day he wanted me to do five double turns in a row and always land exactly on the same spot. He didn't want the camera to move at all, which meant that after each turn I had to remain totally in frame. Well, as any dancer will tell you, it's very hard to land on the same identical spot each time, and what would happen was that I'd do three double turns, and on my fourth my hand would be slightly out of the frame, and the whole thing would have to be done all over again. He worked me for an hour on this, until finally I injured my knee and he realised he was wrong. A couple of days later, when I was able to continue working, he agreed to move the camera slightly for me to keep me in the frame. Which he did, though in the picture you can hardly notice it.'

Apart from having to adapt to a foreign medium, Youskevitch

also had to cope with what he called the 'exaggerated respect' Gene somehow induced in people who worked with him. 'Of course, the ballet world has *premier danseurs* of its own, but somehow things are more democratic. In the Hollywood milieu, I discovered that the star is God. I remember there was a moment in our ballet when Gene had to fall off a tight-rope and die, beautifully, on a red cloak. Well, just before we made the scene, the atmosphere in the studio was quite unbelievable. Everyone spoke in whispers as though the most momentous event in the history of art was about to take place. The reverence was out of all proportion to what we were doing, and after Gene "fell", Claire Sombert and myself were suddenly struck by the phoniness of the whole situation in the studio, and we both burst out laughing and continued to laugh uncontrollably. To his eternal credit, Gene kept his notorious temper, though on this occasion he had every right to lose it. We had ruined his death scene and it had to be done all over again!'

Tamara Toumanova, a beautiful and most accomplished ballerina, was another who had immense difficulty in adapting her classical training to the uniquely American, altogether freer approach Gene had in mind in 'Ring Around the Rosy', and the limited time she could devote to the film added to Gene's increasing frustration.

'Tamara was a terrific dancer,' he said, 'but there were certain things she was just not able to do in modern dance. It wasn't her fault. Her orientation was completely different. I worked as hard as I could in the time available, and she was a marvellous sport, anxious to learn. But it was all too new for her. I just couldn't cut together what I'd shot and the result was disappointing. With more time maybe, I could have got it to work.'

The time factor was crucial also to Claude Bessy who, during the day was filming *Invitation to the Dance* and on certain nights was dancing at the Paris Opera. Once, heavy fog closed Heathrow airport and Jeannie Coyne had to take a boat-train to Paris to collect a couple of tutus from Mademoiselle Bessy's costumier, which were needed for the next day's shooting. Fortunately she did not have a performance at the Opera House that night, for she would most certainly have missed it. It was imperative, however, that the tutus arrived. They were specially made by a designer, who alone knew the secret of making Claude's rather muscular thighs a little less so, and had Jeannie not made the trip over and brought them back with her, Claude would have refused to work the next day.

When the first three ballets were completed, Gene decided that the cartoon work required on the fourth was far too complicated to be done at Boreham Wood, and would have to be completed at some later date in Hollywood.

By now it was the winter of 1952 and Gene, Betsy and Kerry left their house in Chapel Street that they had rented since the autumn and, together with Lois and Jeannie Coyne, spent Christmas at Klosters. It was a depressing time for Gene, who learned during his stay in Switzerland, that MGM had decided to drop the 'popular songs' item. Gene believed the studio had suddenly lost faith in the picture, and as he still had the intricate and expensive cartoon segment to complete, he felt dejected and worried. *Invitation to the Dance* was, after all, his brainchild. It *had* to succeed. But unless MGM promoted it with the full weight of its publicity machine, it wouldn't stand a chance. And if there was no enthusiasm for the project at executive level, no money would be spent on selling it.

Gene's doubts were not unfounded. *Invitation to the Dance* wasn't released until 1956, four years after it was made, and although it did not cost more than six hundred thousand dollars (half of which went on filming the cartoon), it lost money. A 'commercial art film' is a contradiction in terms, and it pleased neither the layman nor the connoisseur.

Today the film is rarely seen, which is a pity as it does have a few unforgettable moments, and a substantial amount of good ones. The *pas de deux* in 'Ring Around the Rosy', danced by Youskevitch and Claude Bessy (while she bites into a sandwich and washes it down with a glass of milk!), is extremely effective; and also in 'Ring Around the Rosy', Irving Davies, who plays a night-club crooner, does a marvellous dance with Diane Adams. In the same ballet there is a deliciously choreographed party scene depicting the 'social set' at its most obnoxiously snobbish, and Tommy Rall performs a spirited, invigorating piece of tap. In fact, the entire second ballet is consistently entertaining with thanks, in no small measure, to André Previn's witty score. Its history is worth relating.

Originally, the score for 'Ring Around the Rosy' was composed by the British composer Malcolm Arnold, but shortly after Gene began to shoot the sequence, he decided that Arnold's score was not suitable, and assigned the job of rewriting the score to André Previn, who until then had done no large-scale composing. Previn recalled the circumstances vividly: 'Gene asked me to write him a score for piano and orchestra which was to be about half an hour long. I jumped at the chance for here, at last, was an opportunity to write music that wouldn't be lost under pages of dialogue – and also because I had an enormous fondness and respect for Gene.

'What he didn't tell me, was that he had already shot the ballet and that I would be presented with thirty minutes of silent film to which I'd have to put appropriate music! Some of the ballet, I discovered, had, in fact, been shot to Malcolm Arnold's music, some of it to Carol Haney and Jeannie Coyne counting beats off camera, but most of it to nothing. So I said to Gene, "How do I know whether what they're dancing is meant to be a bridge passage, or a waltz, out of tempo, in tempo, or what?" Well, he gave me Carol Haney, and together we sat in a claustrophobic little viewing theatre in the music department which had all sorts of sophisticated knobs that allowed you to stop the film, or make it go up or down, or backwards or sideways – frame by frame – and between the two of us, sitting in that terrible little room from 9 am to midnight for three long weeks – during which time Carol tried to remember the tempi and the ideas behind the moves Gene had choreographed – I finally managed to chart down some sort of musical framework for myself, so that not once during the whole of 'Ring Around the Rosy' was I able to develop an idea without considering the restrictions imposed by the film; and since the ballet had already been shot, I couldn't even say to Gene "give me another extra beat here or a half a bar there to finish the phrase." And as I've never been much good at jigsaw puzzles, the whole thing was a nightmare.'

The least successful ballet is the first, which in spite of its splendid *pas de deux* is relentlessly mannered and pretentious. In it, Gene strives towards being the sort of classical dancer he patently is not, and the strain shows.

The 'Sinbad' sequence, arranged by Roger Edens, is most adroitly animated and charmingly performed by Gene and young David Kasday. But it is too long, and soon loses its charm.

Still, *Invitation to the Dance* was something Gene needed to squeeze out of his system. But by shelving it for as long as they did, MGM lost its potential audience. By 1956 TV had become part of the world's furniture, and the great dancers Gene hoped to introduce to small-town America had already been seen on TV programmes. The novelty value of his film was irretrievably lost. Yet *Invitation to the Dance* provided Gene with his first solo directorial credit, and continued to stretch his range as a choreographer. 'If,' said Igor Youskevitch, 'Gene had decided to abandon Hollywood and concentrate on stage work, there is no doubt in my mind he could have become a most distinguished and important choreographer. Some of the things he did in "Circus" are evidence of that. And where his own dancing is concerned, although he does not quite have the noble bearing for a Prince Siegfried in *Swan Lake*, if he had continued to work in the field of serious dance, he would surely have been one of the finest character performers in contemporary ballet. It is true, Gene is not an ideal classical dancer. He does not have the proper training. His technique is not good enough. But in dancing that calls for a freer, less restricted technique than classical roles – and I'm talking about the stage – he could have been outstanding.'

After their few weeks at Klosters, Gene returned to London with his family and stayed at the late Robert Donat's house at No. 3 King's Yard in Mayfair. He then began work on his third and final film in London. It was an Anglo-American propaganda story for the Boulting Brothers, called *Seagulls Over Sorrento* (retitled *Crest of the Wave* in America), in which he played an American seaman. The film was about a group of servicemen isolated on an island not far from the mainland of Scapa Flow, and the personal sacrifices they are obliged to make to propagate peace. It was originally a play by Hugh Hastings (which opened at the Apollo Theatre in London on June 4th, 1950), and starred Ronald Shiner, John Gregson, Nigel Stock and Bernard Lee. The play's mixture of humour and melodrama was palatable to West End audiences who enjoyed its overtly British flavour. When it transferred to Broadway, however, it flopped dismally.

If possible, *Seagulls Over Sorrento*, which, in its film incarnation, also starred Sidney James, John Justin, Bernard Lee and Jeff Richards, was an even worse film than *The Devil Makes Three*. Gene knew it hadn't succeeded on Broadway, but he thought the Boultings, who were 'champs' at this sort of thing, would get it to work as a picture. He was wrong.

From the outset, Gene wasn't happy with the property, and he found the Boultings' working methods alien to his own. 'They had every shot carefully worked out beforehand,' he said, 'so that when the actors got onto the set there was no interchange of ideas, no creative rehearsals. We were rigidly told what to do and the scene was shot. Solid preparation, which I believe in, is one thing – but one must allow for some flexibility, otherwise it becomes a technical exercise having very little to do with acting.'

Seagulls Over Sorrento offered Gene no creative stimulation, and the contrast between the work he was doing on it and the work he had just done on *Invitation to the Dance* was immense. The experience was not unpleasant, but whatever enjoyment he had during the shooting came from his fellow actors whom he liked and admired. Everyone, he remembered, was more concerned about a series of cricket test matches between England and Australia than the film itself; and the Boultings, he swore, lost weight not over anything as unimportant as their film, but through worrying about England's chances of victory!

When *Seagulls Over Sorrento* finally arrived in America, it was so irredeemably British that MGM returned it with thanks and ordered large sections of it to be dubbed into accents understandable to people not born within the sound of Bow Bells.

But removing the offending patois was no help at all, and the film was a disaster both artistically and at the box-office. About its subject-matter Gene had no qualms. 'I still think it was a nice idea to make a picture about England and America staying friends in peacetime and doing great things together. But the humour in it didn't work in the States, where it was torpedoed and sunk without trace.'

Gene tried not to think too seriously about the film and its failure, and continued instead to make the best of his stay in London. He found the English warm and considerate, enjoyed the atmosphere of the pubs, hired a boat and took Kerry on a ten-day trip up the Thames to Oxford, cooking lunch over a small primus stove in the pouring rain; and at night booked into whatever riverside inn or hotel was most convenient. Betsy, who never did respond to the healthy, outdoor life, would meet them at the end of the day, spend the night with them and motor back to London the following morning. They stayed at the Compleat Angler in Marlow and at the Bell at Hurley. The Bell, in fact, became one of Gene's chief weekend pleasures, and every Sunday morning he, Betsy and a few of their friends would converge on the place, order a couple of rounds of Bloody Marys to help them overcome their Saturday night hangovers, and walk around the immaculately manicured lawns nibbling away at some smoked salmon. After lunch they would take a walk down to the river and spend what remained of the afternoon relaxing in the sun.

If the weekend weather wasn't conducive to a country outing, Gene might stroll across Hyde Park Corner to the Star – a pub frequented on Sunday mornings mainly by theatre people. He would usually be joined by Robert Taylor or Errol Flynn – two more actors hoping to benefit from the tax laws – and, after closing time at two o'clock, John Mills, who owned Les Ambassadeurs Club off Park Lane, the chief hangout for expatriate Americans, would drive them out to 'an illegitimate watering hole' on the outskirts of London, where they would spend the rest of the afternoon drinking and chatting away in some mysterious back room.

Humphrey Bogart was also in England at the time and he, his wife Lauren Bacall and Gene and Betsy would invariably meet every night at Les Ambassadeurs and generally 'lower the tone' of the place. Once, Gene recalls introducing Bogart to Margaret Leighton. Bogart immediately slapped the great actress's behind, and congratulated her: 'You've got a beautiful ass, baby.' Miss Leighton leaned over, gave him a kiss on his forehead, and complimented him on his taste.

One of the highlights of the Kelly trip was the Coronation of Queen Elizabeth in June 1953. Gene and his family were invited by Jules Stein of MCA to breakfast with him and his family and watch the main part of the procession from his balcony window. When the day arrived, they awoke at 7.30 am hoping to avoid the crowds. But they might as well not have bothered, for the streets were jammed solid with people who had gathered overnight. It had been raining and the air was cold. Gene began to grumble about the almighty effort it had taken to heave himself out of bed so early.

'The constabulary were out in full force,' he said, 'and I didn't think they'd let us pass through the crowds to where we wanted to get. The sky was a heavy grey and as it was beginning to mist over, I pulled my coat collar up, bundled Kerry and Betsy into their raincoats and started to think of the best way to get to the MCA building a few blocks away. Suddenly, over the loudspeaker system, a man who had been keeping everyone informed about what was happening, said: "Now ladies and gentlemen, I'd like you all to join Gene Kelly in 'Singin' in the Rain' and on came my record. A few seconds later, thousands of lovely, cold, wet, shivering Englishmen and women started to sing. It was the biggest thrill of my life. It beat anything I'd ever known – the opening of *Pal Joey*, my Academy Award – you name it. It was a once-in-a-lifetime experience, and I felt if I never achieved another thing – which was the way things seemed to be going! – I'd have justified my existence. Suddenly the English could do no wrong.'

Until his eighteen-month trip to Europe, Gene, being staunchly Irish, had always nurtured an ingrown prejudice against England, which had been planted in him years ago by his father, who had never overcome the Irishman's distrust of the English. 'So much so,' said Gene, 'that until he had positive proof of Hitler's persecution of the Jews, he wanted Germany to win the war. Once he realised what Hitler was doing, he changed his mind, of course. And I'm embarrassed to admit it, but I too, for no particular reason, felt hostile towards the "limeys" when I first visited England in 1947. But I realised I was wrong. My eighteen months in London convinced me of that.'

In July 1953 Gene came to the end of his tax-free sojourn abroad and returned to California with his family. But by then Congress had changed its mind about the tax windfall. The mass exodus from Hollywood during the past year and a half had upset the unions who were complaining bitterly. Their complaints were taken seriously, and a year after it was introduced the law was repealed. All that Gene was able to keep was the first thirty-five thousand dollars of his earnings which, as an American earning money abroad, he would have been allowed to keep anyway. The rest was taxable in the usual way. So the windfall he and others hoped to make turned out to be little more than a tantalising mirage. Still, thirty-five thousand dollars clear of tax was not to be scorned and, as much as he had enjoyed his stay in England despite the pitiful outcome of *The Devil Makes Three* and *Seagulls Over Sorrento*, as well as the disappointments he had had to endure on *Invitation to the Dance*, he was glad to get home.

While Gene was abroad, life at MGM under its new boss, Dore Schary (who had replaced Louis B. Mayer as head of the studio in November 1951) was vastly different from what it had been in 'the good old days'. The immense financial overheads of the studio was Schary's most persistent concern, and as he was once head of MGM's 'B' picture department, he prided himself on his ability to make pictures 'for spit' as he put it. Schary had an eye for economy which went against the grain of the studio executives, who did not like to be made to feel the economic pinch. Nor was his penchant for making films with social content, in contrast to films of sheer escapism, popular. Schary, said his detractors, would sell his soul for a pot of message.

When Schary became the overlord of MGM, the studio was serviced by some four thousand employees working on an output of between twenty-five to thirty pictures a year. As money was scarce in 1951, it was not possible to increase production. Besides, there were no longer captive audiences who would indiscriminately swallow anything and everything that was offered to them. Television had made quite sure of that. Millions of homes in America were equipped with this entertainment miracle, and apart from the cost of the set, it was all free.

Schary had no choice but to cut production and production costs drastically. He gave writers more status at the studio, hoping that his faith in them would result in an assortment of quality scripts which could be made economically and without loss of entertainment value. As far as musicals were concerned, Schary sent a directive to his three major producers that they were, in future, to be 'less indulgent' and not shoot expensive sequences they had no intention of using. Before being appointed head of the studio, Schary had heard of instances where elaborate production numbers were shot by a producer to pacify stars like Judy Garland and Frank Sinatra, although these numbers were never used, nor even intended to be used. Money was not to be squandered on unnecessary footage, said Schary. If, at a preview, it was apparent that extra material was required, only then would he give his permission to shoot it. Whims he absolutely refused to pander to.

It was to this climate of frugality and extreme caution that the empiricist Gene, who relied on experimentation as part of his mode of expression (and whom Schary admired for 'his protean talent') returned in 1953. Almost at once he, Arthur Freed and Vincente Minnelli became victims of Schary's economy drive, when it was decided that the studio's version of *Brigadoon*, which Freed was to produce (with Gene starring and Minnelli directing), would not be made abroad on location. It would, however, be made in Cinemascope.

In 1954, the film industry was chasing its tail in some desperate attempt to attract audiences back to the cinema – not with quality films, but with technical innovations such as Cinemascope and 3-D, both in their infancy, and both of which contaminated rather than improved whatever they touched. Original ideas suffered at the expense of gimmicks, and although there were a few notable exceptions (*Brigadoon* was not one of them), producers failed to realise in their fright, that a property which in itself is nothing becomes plenty of nothing in Cinemascope. They had hoped that the novelty of the big screen compared to the eighteen-inch tube was an end in itself, and would provide the incentive for audiences to rediscover the joys of the silver screen.

While in Britain, Gene and Arthur Freed had travelled to Scotland in search of suitable locations, only to be told that the picture would have to be shot in California instead, possibly at Carmel, on the coast. But in time even that idea was quashed, and Gene and Minnelli found themselves confined to a studio, which they were trying to avoid, as neither had worked in Cinemascope before, and neither fancied the idea of shooting a basically out-of-doors story – in a new process – indoors. But Schary informed them there wasn't sufficient money for location work of any kind, and that was that.

Thus Gene's hopes of seeing the gathering of the clans – with hundreds of extras materialising over the mountain-tops from the north and the south and the east and west – went for nothing. 'It could have been magical,' Gene said, 'and in the old days, it would have been.'

All the same, he could not really blame Dore Schary, who, he realised, had taken over the running of the studio at the most impossible time in its history. Schary, as one executive put it, 'became Mayer while Rome burned.' 'He was trying to save MGM from ruin,' said Gene, 'and doing it in the only way he knew how. Unlike Louis B. Mayer, who spent the last ten years of his tenure at Metro breeding race horses, Schary was really concerned with what was going on in the studio and in the industry. Maybe that's why he was never particularly liked and why he was always considered an outsider. He was too intelligent for the job. And he had integrity. He had a job of work he called "trimming the fat", and that's what he tried to do.'

Schary's decision to confine *Brigadoon* to a sound stage was, unfortunately, a bad one, and the film never recovered from it. Lerner and Loewe's whimsical fantasy in which two Americans from Manhattan stumble across the fairy-tale village of *Brigadoon* while out grouse-shooting one day and learn that it only materialises out of the highland mist once every hundred years, needed the conventional confines of the theatre or the spaciousness of the real outdoors to contain it – not the compromise offered by MGM. The awkward dimensions of the Cinemascope screen only accentuated the staginess of Cedric Gibbons' and Preston Ames' sets and, as in *The Pirate*, Minnelli's direction was claustrophobic and airless. Gene and Van Johnson were cast as the two Americans and Cyd Charisse played Fiona, the beautiful Scottish lass with whom Gene falls in love, and who forces him to choose between her and his fiancée back home in Manhattan.

Apart from Charisse's duet with Gene in 'The Heather On The Hill', Gene's solo dance to 'Almost Like Being In Love', and the hybrid tap-dance the ensemble energetically rattle out to 'Go Home With Bonnie Jean', *Brigadoon* offers very few pleasures. Van Johnson's dancing, even in the simple soft-shoe he does with Gene, looks ponderous; Cyd Charisse moves exquisitely, but is rather colourless, while Gene himself, instead of playing against the whimsy of the piece, tends to squeeze every groan out of this bag-pipe of a musical. Minnelli's direction is undistinctive, and even his use of colour in this instance disappoints.

After *The Devil Makes Three* and *Seagulls Over Sorrento*, and the obscurity into which *Invitation to the Dance* sank, the charmless version of *Brigadoon*, which totally misses the element of fantasy so necessary to its success, was another severe blow to Gene's ailing career. But what could he do? The creative atmosphere which produced his greatest musicals no longer existed. It was a period of upheaval and change; Gene, whose reputation was solidly established on the foundation of the old order, when studios had money to burn was, alas, one of its victims. Also, having made *On the Town*, *An American in Paris* and *Singin' in the Rain*, could it be that there was nothing left for him to achieve? Had every target on which he'd set his sights been bull's-eyed?

All except Cinemascope. He had still not mastered that.

As soon as *Brigadoon* was completed, Gene teamed up with his brother Fred for a spot in Stanley Donen's starry musical biography of Sigmund Romberg called *Deep in My Heart*. The number they did together was a straight bit of vaudeville hoofing called 'I Love To Go Swimmin' With Wimmen'; the kind of routine both had done together in the mid-thirties in Pittsburgh. It is an entertaining item in a 'biopic', whose musical sequences are far jollier than the screenplay (by Leonard Spiegelgass) – and the only occasion in which Gene and his brother appeared together on film.

Over the years, Fred had kept working. After the war, he went to New York and involved himself in television, directing the first Steve Allen and Kay Kaiser shows. He settled down with his wife and three children in New Jersey, where he opened a dance school of his own and which he still runs.

In Pittsburgh, Louise, who had married, continued to run the school her mother and brother had founded, but changed its name to the Bailey School of Dancing, as she ran it with her husband,

William Bailey. Jim had moved to California, Jay was still a school-teacher, and Mr and Mrs Kelly were both retired.

After Gene completed his bit in *Deep in My Heart*, he went on a skiing holiday to Klosters in Switzerland, where he 'holed up' and isolated himself from the hassle of Hollywood. Betsy, meanwhile, had been offered a leading role opposite Ernest Borgnine in *Marty*, and in view of her hitherto unimpressive track record in pictures, she accepted without hesitation.

Since their eighteen months in London, their lives seemed to be developing quite independently of each other. They travelled together only occasionally, and were no longer inseparable.

The fun, with which their marriage was once shot through like an electric current, had disappeared.

Gene's next film, the last he made for Arthur Freed, was a conscious, all-out attempt to recapture some of his former glory, and also to bully the hateful medium of Cinemascope into submission. It was called *It's Always Fair Weather*, and was written by Betty Comden and Adolph Green, with music by André Previn. Gene and Michael Kidd did the choreography, and both co-starred with Dan Dailey, Dolores Gray and Cyd Charisse.

It was also the last time Gene was to work with Stanley Donen, who recollects the making of it as one of the most wretched experiences of his life. The two men rarely saw eye to eye on matters of artistic policy, and an incompatibility developed between them. What, according to Donen, had once been a workable and productive partnership had, by 1955, irrevocably deteriorated.

The idea for *It's Always Fair Weather* came from Comden and Green, who had for some time been thinking about a sequel to *On the Town* for presentation on Broadway. But when they mentioned it to Gene, he let out a whoop of excitement and said it was exactly what he had been searching for during the last few years. The possibilities inherent in a story, which reunited the original three sailors from *On the Town* after the war, were endless, and he persuaded Comden and Green to develop the idea into a full-scale screen musical for himself, Frank Sinatra and Jules Munshin.

Sinatra, however, had by this time won an Academy Award for

his performance in *From Here to Eternity*, and did not feel he wanted to return to his nautical pranks. So he turned the idea down. Without Sinatra there was little point in doing *On the Town* revisited, and instead Gene decided to cast Michael Kidd in Sinatra's role and Dan Dailey in place of Jules Munshin, and do a musical in which all three leading men were dancers capable of handling dance routines which would have been beyond the range of Sinatra and Munshin. And instead of three sailors, they were all to be soldiers.

The story is simple enough. Three wartime buddies decide to meet by arrangement at a spot, ten years after demobilisation, and see how each is coping with the rigours of civilian life. Time and the pursuit of their individuality have inevitably changed their wartime personalities and when, reluctantly and grudgingly, they arrive at the prearranged bar, all three realise that they no longer have anything in common. Still, for old time's sake they feign a *bonhomie* and make an effort to recapture the spirit of *camaraderie* that brought them together in the first place. But it is no use. Yet, though the reunion is a disaster, the three men stick together for the rest of the day and, as in *On the Town*, the following twenty-four hours' time-span provides the musical with its story-line.

It's Always Fair Weather does not have the expensive MGM look of *An American in Paris* or *Singin' in the Rain*. Its budget was drastically reduced as is visible in the rather cheap sets and the frugality of the production numbers. Again Gene found himself working in conditions of austerity. Schary was still in the process of 'trimming the fat', and the sort of money which once allowed talented people to turn commonplace ideas into masterpieces was no longer available. None the less *It's Always Fair Weather* has more than its quota of originality and bright ideas, and has improved with the years.

Its use of Cinemascope is especially striking. After his experiences on *Brigadoon*, Gene realised that the long piece of ribbon within which he had to work was totally unsuited to solo dancing, as the gaps on either side became large areas of waste-land. Not only did this look bad, but it diminished the stature of the dancer. Then there was the problem of the close-up. How do you achieve any intimacy with a face that stretches the length and breadth of the Grand Canyon? The problem is partially solved in one of the best moments in the film, when the three 'buddies' get together and, to a revamped version of 'The Blue Danube', voice their thoughts about the mistake they have all just made in getting together.

As each man stares balefully into the middle distance wondering why the hell he came, the camera closes in on their faces, one at a time and masks out the other two, so that the effect is of a normal-sized close-up albeit on the wide screen.

Masking within the frame – by no means a technique new to the cinema – was common practice as far back as D. W. Griffith. But it had never been done before in Cinemascope. Similarly, the split screen technique, which Gene and Donen also incorporated into *It's Always Fair Weather* and which could show several scenes happening concurrently, wasn't entirely new either. As long ago as 1926, Abel Gance used it in his film *Napoleon*. But, again, it was the first time it had been attempted in Cinemascope.

Technical difficulties abounded. The three cameras used in the split screen sequence had to move at exactly the same speeds, so that the figures in the frame wouldn't appear to be jumping all over the place. As in the 'alter ego' number in *Cover Girl*, timing was of the essence and Gene and Donen and Michael Kidd had to make quite sure they counted the music beats correctly, for the cameras were controlled by the speed of the music. Also, the height and width of the frame had to be carefully measured in order to keep the figures within the lens area. It was precise, exacting work with very little margin for error allowed. One of the most imaginative uses of Cinemascope in *It's Always Fair Weather* comes at the end of the film, during a climacteric fight sequence, which takes place in a TV studio. In one highly original shot, the bulk of the fight is shown through the Cinemascope-shaped windows in the TV control room – while, at the same time, three TV monitors above the window show three additional views of the fight simultaneously.

Technicalities aside, *It's Always Fair Weather* is an interesting musical for several other reasons. Its theme dealing, albeit light-heartedly, with the incompatibility of three men who, a decade earlier would have died for one another, is treated by Comden and Green in a manner more cynical and hard-hitting than we have come to expect from them, and the satirical swipes the film takes at television which, at the time *It's Always Fair Weather* was being made, was responsible for the industry's encroaching malaise, leave a sting far more painful than the affectionate ribbing the same authors gave the early talkies in *Singin' in the Rain*.

The musical numbers are effective too (though several of them have little or nothing to do with the plot), most memorable of which is Gene's solo song-and-dance which he performs on roller-skates – and which not only keeps him moving around the elongated Cinemascope screen, but is also most strikingly performed. It is Gene's emphatic return to form, and a reminder after three years in the artistic doldrums, of his capabilities.

Cyd Charisse, as a lady sports fanatic, does an energetic number in Sillman's gym, accompanied by a dozen or so prize fighters which, in the parlance of that particular item, is a knockout; and Messrs Kelly, Dailey and Kidd have some effective moments dancing with the lids of three garbage bins attached to their feet.

When *It's Always Fair Weather* was first previewed, it was a disaster. Gene hadn't bothered to check that the projection equipment in the particular theatre was suitable for Cinemascope (he naturally assumed it was), and only found out once the film began that it was not. The result was that the intricate work he, Donen and Michael Kidd had done was completely ruined. And, today, television gets its revenge on the film by severing the dancers' feet and lopping off the carefully composed frames on either side.

It's Always Fair Weather did fairly well at the box-office, though it in no way equalled the success of *An American in Paris* or *Singin' in the Rain*, and Gene and Donen were disappointed with its reception. An 'all right' success, Gene said, never made him happy. 'It had to be a smash, or nothing. I work too hard on a picture to be satisfied with anything other than an out-and-out hit. If I worked exclusively in television, maybe I'd be less demanding. But not in pictures.'

But Gene was to continue finding the sort of success with which he had been associated in the early part of his career more and more elusive. MGM no longer flooded him with scripts, and he felt much the same as he had felt fourteen years before, at the beginning of his Hollywood career, when Selznick first put him under contract but failed to use him. Except that those years, at least, were fun. Now even that was gone.

He was offered several roles verbally, but they never materialised.

This first happened early on in his career, when Elia Kazan sent him the script of *Death of a Salesman*, and said he wanted him to play Biff on Broadway, which Gene would have loved to do. But that was the last he heard about it. The next time Kazan contacted him was about a part he said he wanted him to do in the film of Tennessee Williams' *Camino Real*. But he read the play, didn't like it and turned it down. The film was never made. Gene was also offered *Teahouse of the August Moon*, yet, for some 'inexplicable' reason, it was taken away from him and given to Marlon Brando.

But the biggest disappointment of his career, was MGM's refusal to allow him to play Sky Masterson in *Guys and Dolls* for Samuel Goldwyn. 'A part like Sky comes along once or twice in a lifetime, he said. 'It happened to me with *Pal Joey*, and miracle of miracles, Goldwyn was about to make it happen a second time. I was born to play Sky the way Gable was born to play Rhett Butler. But the bastards at MGM refused to loan me out.'

In desperation he and his agent Lew Wasserman flew to New York 'like a couple of anxious schoolboys' to see Nicholas Schenck, the financial controller of MGM, and begged him to allow Gene to do the film. Nothing was pencilled in for him at the time, and there was no reason why he shouldn't be loaned out to Goldwyn. Schenck listened patiently while the two men pleaded – as if for their lives – then calmly admitted that he was angry with Goldwyn over some past indiscretion, and wasn't about to do him a favour. Wasserman tried to persuade him to look on it as doing Gene, rather than Goldwyn, a favour, but Schenck would not be swayed and refused.

Gene and Wasserman took the next plane back to Los Angeles, defeated and disappointed. Goldwyn, however, was convinced that in the end he would get Gene – just as Harry Cohn had been over *Pal Joey* ten years earlier. He told Gene he was prepared to wait two months to see if anything further developed. Nothing did. Schenck would not be persuaded, and eventually Goldwyn cast Brando in the role. Gene was distraught and the incident directly motivated his decision to leave Metro. There were only two other roles he had wanted to play as much: *Pal Joey* for Columbia and *Cyrano de Bergerac*. On both occasions MGM had refused him.

By the beginning of 1956, Gene found his position at MGM

untenable. The studio's lack of faith in *Invitation to the Dance* and the bad feeling Nicholas Schenck had created by using Gene as a pawn in his vendetta with Samuel Goldwyn, made it impossible for him to feel any loyalty towards the studio and this, plus the deceleration of the production of musical films, gave him no alternative but to ask for a release from his contract which, in 1950, had been renewed for a further seven years, and which still had several months to run.

Schenck, however, refused to let him go. So Gene talked to Arthur Loew senior, one of MGM's chief executives who compromised, and after discussing the matter with Schenck, said he would release Gene on condition that he did two more pictures for them, and gave MGM first refusal on a property called *The Happy Road*, which Gene was preparing just then and hoped to release as an independent production. Gene had little option but to agree.

In the midst of his professional upheavals, Gene's private life was also causing him pain. His and Betsy's respective careers continued to keep them apart and months would go by without their seeing each other. What had been a perfect marriage for ten years was deteriorating fast. As the fun deserted Hollywood, so their relationship crumbled. The social life at North Rodeo had lost its glitter, and the tensions that had developed in Gene's career, plus Betsy's own determination (especially after winning the Best Actress Award at Cannes in 1955 for her performance in *Marty*) to pursue her own career even at the expense of her marriage, hardly made for smooth-running domesticity. Betsy also found that she and Gene were no longer compatible. The rather paternal attitude he tended to adopt towards her, and to which she once responded, she now no longer wanted or needed. This caused her as much dissatisfaction and heart ache as it did him.

'For quite some time,' she said, 'I felt I should leave Gene. But somehow I just couldn't. It's very difficult being married to a well-known film-star because wherever you go, there are pictures and posters of him. His presence is always felt. I remember seeing *Singin' in the Rain* a couple of years after it was released, at a point when our marriage was becoming pretty shaky, and at the end of the Broadway ballet, there was this enormous close-up of a smiling Gene which came sailing out of the screen, and I realised I was *never* going to escape him. And not only could I never escape him, but he would always be larger than life. So, when the situation became intolerable, I decided to go to an analyst and see if he could help me. He did. He made me face the reality that the only way out was divorce.'

After *It's Always Fair Weather*, Gene began work on *The Happy Road*, a simple story written by his friend Harry Kurnitz with Joe Morhaim and Arthur Julian, about two youngsters – a boy and a girl, played by Bobby Clark and Brigitte Fossey – who run away from their Swiss school and head for Paris. The adventures they have form the basis of the story, with additional romantic interest supplied by their parents – Gene as a rich American widower and Barbara Laage as a French divorcée – who join forces to search for their missing children and, predictably, fall in love.

It was Gene's first picture as an independent producer, and his total budget was not to exceed a half a million dollars.

Principal shooting took place in the Haute Savoie and in the Burgundy wine country and was plagued by six weeks of almost constant rain – which added another hundred thousand dollars to the budget, making impossible the four hundred thousand dollar target he was aiming at. Gene not only produced and starred in the film, but directed it as well. He found the experience exhausting and vowed he would never take on all three roles single-handed again.

During *The Happy Road*, Gene once again hired Moulin de la Roche, where in the summer of 1952 he had worked on *Invitation to the Dance*, and it was there, one weekend, that he and Betsy finally decided to get a divorce. Kerry, who was fourteen, was present at the time and recalled the effect it had on her.

'As soon as they told me,' she said, 'I ran away and locked myself in my bedroom for twenty-four hours without speaking to anyone. Through the closed door Gene asked me whether it would help if he called Jeannie in California. I said yes, and they did. A day or so later, she arrived. Ever since I can remember, Jeannie had been like a second mother to me.'

'For Gene,' Kerry said, 'the whole experience was shattering. He was utterly helpless, couldn't cope with the situation, and was no use to anybody. In some ways I don't think he has ever recovered. I don't mean that he still carries a torch for Betsy, but that he's never quite regained his unassailable self-confidence. He's never felt as obviously *sure* of himself since the divorce. He became much more reflective and down to earth. He developed a sense of reality about life which he never had before.'

Apart from a few professional setbacks in his career, Gene's divorce was the first time he had cause to admit failure in his private life, and for someone as determined to succeed as Gene, whether at volley-ball, in his career, or in his home as a father and husband, the shock to his system was incalculable, and it left him stunned and confused.

Kerry was equally shaken, and one of the reasons she took it so badly was that, until the moment it happened, she had had no indication that anything was wrong between them.

'I knew my mother and father were rarely at home at the same time,' she said, 'but I believed this was because of their work, and nothing more. Everything had always been so consistent in our home, with Betsy coming and going, and Gene doing the same, I naturally assumed when they weren't together the reason was professional. They're both very private people, and they never let on what was happening. Certainly not to me. And even in what must have been their worst time together, just before the divorce, they behaved as well as they always did. Which was good in one respect and bad in another – because when they were divorced it came as a terrible shock.'

Because Betsy was aware what the failure of their marriage would mean to Gene, she felt guilty about having to go through with the divorce. But equally she knew it would do neither of them any good if she renegued. She also felt bad that their break-up coincided with the virtual disappearance of the screen musical. Now there wasn't even that to which he could cling. Nor did he have any really deep friendships. 'For all the scores of people he surrounded himself with,' Betsy said, 'he was a very private man.

People liked, respected and enjoyed him. But few people understood him. I always thought this was a pity, and never more so than after the divorce when, apart from Kerry, the only other person he could turn to was Jeannie. But he had no real close male friends. After Dick Dwenger, his best friend, was killed in the war, I tried desperately to introduce him to people I thought he might develop a real friendship with. I felt, in a romantic sort of way that, after Dick died, he should have another "best friend". I even introduced him to Paddy Chayefsky, who wrote *Marty*, because I knew that politically they were on the same side of the fence and should have a lot in common. But it didn't happen. After fifteen years of marriage and hundreds of people passing through our lives, I had to face the fact that Gene was a loner and was somehow going to have to get through the divorce on his own.'

Gene's main concern at the time was, he insists, for Kerry. 'I think that if it wasn't for her, Betsy and I would probably have gone our separate ways much sooner than we did. But to divorce when you know it could harm a child who loves you both dearly, isn't so easy. Kerry took it much harder than we thought. Somehow she had fooled us into believing that she was more grown up than she really was.'

While *The Happy Road* was being made, James Kelly died in Pittsburgh. Shooting was temporarily halted and Gene flew to the States for the funeral. A week later he returned to Europe and completed the film. What should have been a delightful experience for him became a chore. The technical problems were overwhelming, the weather was impossible, and his heart and soul, understandably, hardly matched the mood of the story.

Under the circumstances, it is not surprising that *The Happy Road* is not the success Gene had hoped it would be. Although the two children – particularly little Brigitte Fossey – are not without charm, the story puts them through a series of predictable situations which their limited talent cannot overcome. Also, Gene himself seems uneasy and strained, as if he has sacrificed his own performance in order to concentrate on the children as well as on the other aspects of the production. But far more crucial to the film is the failure of its central idea: to show the French through American eyes and vice versa, to pinpoint the fundamental difference in the two cultures, and to highlight the misunderstandings and confusion that arise when people who cannot speak the same language are thrown together. But as the entire film is in English, the joke is lost. What emerges, instead, is a folksy view of the French through American eyes – a view not unlike Gene's and Vincente Minnelli's in *An American in Paris*.

After *The Happy Road* (which was financially only a moderate success) was completed, Gene returned to California to settle the divorce. The next six months, between September 1956 and March 1957, were, Betsy recalled, extremely difficult for both of them as she continued to live at North Rodeo until the divorce was through· 'It was an awkward period all round, because although at one point Gene moved in with Saul Chaplin, our friends never knew whether to invite us out separately or together. We generally would go out together, but only if we were sure there'd be a few other people as well.'

On one occasion, she and Gene were out with Adolph Green and his wife. Jeannie Coyne came along as well, and Betsy noticed that whenever Adolph Green cracked a joke, Jeannie would put her head on Gene's shoulder and laugh. It was, she said, one of the first indications she had that Jeannie wasn't just fond of him, but in love with him. 'Jeannie had been around for so long – as part of the furniture almost – that it never occurred to me she could have also been in love with Gene. On the contrary, while most of the women who ever worked with Gene seemed to adore him unquestioningly, Jeannie, for all her sweetness, was often rather sharp and curt with him, and would think nothing of deflating him if she thought he needed it. But more to the point, I never guessed she was in love with Gene because she never flirted with him while our marriage was still working. She wasn't that sort of woman. On the same night we'd all gone out with Adolph Green and his wife,' Betsy said, 'I had a heart-to-heart talk with Jeannie much later, after everyone had gone home. We were sitting in my car, and we chatted away for about four hours or so. I remember asking her whether she'd been waiting all these years to marry Gene – and whether she was really serious about him. She said she was. I told her I thought that was great, but that it would never work unless he got himself analysed. "He'll just treat you like a child – like he did me," I said.

'But, of course, she was right and I was completely wrong because she didn't care about that. She didn't have to establish her grown up self. She had already established it. But in my case, I never had a chance to be "grown up" until I left.

'I didn't have anything against Gene – except that with him, I couldn't grow up.'

On April 3rd, 1957, thirty-three-year-old Betsy Blair ended her fifteen-year marriage to Gene in Las Vegas when she obtained an uncontested divorce on charges of mental cruelty. Newspaper reports at the time stated that she received a settlement of $500,000, which was not the case. She received $180,000 over a period of ten years, and waived any alimony claims. Kerry was placed in joint custody with her school holidays to be divided between her mother (who, in 1963, married film director Karel Reisz) and her father.

It wasn't long after Betsy moved out of North Rodeo, that Jeannie Coyne (unofficially) moved in.

Part Six

Shortly after his divorce, Gene returned to London, and at Les Ambassadeurs one evening, he received a long-distance call from Benny Thau, who at the beginning of 1957 was put in charge of MGM, after Dore Schary was dismissed with a million-dollar handshake. The studio, said Thau, had bought the screen rights of a successful Broadway comedy called *The Tunnel of Love*, and he wanted Gene to direct it. It was a 'package deal', which meant it came together with its stars – Doris Day and Richard Widmark, and producers Marty Melcher (Doris Day's husband) and Joe Fields. Thau also told Gene that if he agreed to direct it, he would write it off as one of his two remaining commitments – *The Happy Road* having been the first, and Gene agreed. The play, adapted by Peter de Vries from his novel, was being presented in London at the time, and the following night Gene went to see it. He enjoyed it enormously, laughed a great deal and returned to California a couple of days later to commence work on it. The object of the exercise for everyone concerned was to make as much money for as little outlay as was humanly possible. The film – about a childless couple who wish to adopt a baby but find it isn't as easy as they thought – was completed in three weeks. It was made in black and white for a few hundred thousand dollars, virtually all shot on one set, and in no way extended the talents of its stars or its director. It was a pleasant, efficient comedy with a few good lines and precious little else, and for Gene noteworthy only as a statistic: it was the first feature film he directed but did not appear in as well.

His last film for MGM, indeed the last major musical he was to star in, was *Les Girls*, produced by Sol C. Siegel and directed by George Cukor. Jack Cole, with whom Gene had never worked before, was the choreographer, as Gene did not wish to star in the film and handle the dance direction as well.

Les Girls is not a Gene Kelly musical in the strictest sense of the phrase. Its accent, as the title proclaims, is on the female of the species (hence the studio's choice of Cukor, whose reputation for directing women was well known), represented on this not too noteworthy occasion by Kay Kendall, Mitzi Gaynor and Taina Elg. The words and music are by Cole Porter, who was extremely ill and needed the invaluable assistance of Saul Chaplin to enable him to complete the score – and the screenplay is by John Patrick.

In a London courtroom, Lady Wren, played by Kay Kendall, a former show girl who had been part of an act called 'Les Girls', is facing a libel action as a result of her recently published memoirs. For, in those memoirs, she recounts certain incidents involving her boss (Kelly) and the two other show girls who were part of his act. Lady Wren's confessions, however, seem to be at variance with the stories her colleagues have to relate, and as each woman takes the witness stand, we are given a veritable Rashomon-style handling of the truth.

It is a perfectly workable idea which unfortunately became confused in the telling. To put it bluntly, *Les Girls* is a shambles. John Patrick, who wrote *The Teahouse of the August Moon*, contributes a screen-play the sum of whose three parts fails to balance, and Cole Porter's score is not only his last but in quality his least. Even Gene's dancing seems to do battle with the numbers Jack Cole choreographed for him before he – Cole – fell ill with hepatitis and left the picture.

'I tried,' said Cole, 'in one or two instances, to stage some things that wouldn't be typically Gene Kelly. I wanted Gene to take on a more sophisticated, less bravura look. After all, on paper, *Les Girls* was the essence of chic. But I knew it wouldn't be any good. Even Jeannie Coyne, who worked as Gene's assistant on the picture, told me to forget it, that there was no way Gene was about to change his style at this late stage in his career. The thing about Gene,' he said, 'is that he is far more interested in the staging of a number than in the actual dancing of it and that, I guess, is where we are different and wrong for each other.'

The differences of opinion between Gene and Cole over the choreography did not extend into the body of the picture, and Gene's relationship with Cukor was warm and cordial. All three women responded to Cukor and Gene could see why he had acquired a reputation for being a woman's director. 'He'd think nothing of spending a couple of hours going over a scene which needed no explanation at all,' Gene said. 'I'm pretty conscientious myself, but there's a limit as to how long you can go on discussing a line, and every once in a while, as much as I loved him, I'd find myself interrupting and saying: "For Christ's sake, George, let's just *shoot* the goddam thing!" Then we'd all laugh and everything would be fine. Then we'd do the same bit the next time. But the women loved it, and in a way there's a canny method to his madness, because by the time he's through explaining what he wants out of a scene, you feel you know everything there is to know about it, and you go out and play it with confidence. It's a luxurious way of working – but too damn time-consuming for me.'

The only one of the three women to have had misgivings, in spite of Cukor's guidance, was Kay Kendall, who was petrified at the thought of having to sing and dance and was, initially, promised she would not have to do either. As it turned out, she had two numbers in the film, one with Gene and one with the two other girls. 'She came to me in a state of shock,' said Jack Cole, 'and was ready to quit when she heard she'd have to do a number with Gene. And I told her not to be a fool and to get out there and just be her divine self. "Be Kay Kendall, and I'll do the rest," I said. "Who the hell cares whether you can dance or not?" And I gave her my assurance that she wouldn't make a fool of herself. The result was that whenever she was on the screen, you couldn't take your eyes off her. And she was right, of course. She couldn't dance. And she couldn't sing. But in the 'Ladies in Waiting' routine, her presence was so stunning she took the number clean away from Mitzi Gaynor and Taina Elg – neither of whom had her star quality which, in this business, is all that counts.'

Apart from Kay Kendall, the other good thing about *Les Girls* is a musical parody of Marlon Brando's 1953 film *The Wild Ones* in which Gene appears clad from head to foot in shiny black leather. Mitzi Gaynor is his moll. The number, called 'Why Am I So Gone About That Girl', is played out against a red bar-room background and, with a chorus of caricature Brando-types to lend support to the two principals, it is a delightful moment in a show woefully and conspicuously devoid of sparkle. Sadly, it was the last musical number Gene was to do at MGM, and although it hardly provided a stunning climax to his variegated fifteen years at that studio, it was the best thing in the film.

After a slow start at the box-office, *Les Girls* not only recouped its costs but actually made some money – particularly in Europe where it proved to be more popular than in the States. It was fitting that Gene's last film for the studio was not a commercial failure.

During the summer of 1957, Gene, Kerry, his secretary Lois and Jeannie Coyne, took a house in Malibu which Gene had rented from Raquel Torres, the Mexican actress who had made a name for herself in the twenties. Though idyllically situated not twenty yards from the ocean, it had a swimming pool in a large courtyard, which so impressed Gene, who had hitherto refused to install one in his own home in North Rodeo, claiming he could always use his neighbours' pools if he wanted to – that he immediately had one built for himself. 'He suddenly woke up to the fact it would be rather nice to be able to have a swim first thing in the morning or last thing at night, as his whim decreed, and without having to go next door,' said Kerry. 'It had nothing to do with his keeping fit, because he never consciously exercised. After all the years of living without one, a swimming pool suddenly became a fun thing to have. It also gave the house a new "toy" which in no way could be related to Betsy.'

During his summer in Malibu, Gene signed with Warner Brothers to star opposite Natalie Wood in an adaptation of Herman Wouk's best-seller *Marjorie Morningstar*, to be filmed in Hollywood and on location in Scroon Lake in upper New York State.

Wouk's novel describes how the young daughter of a respectable,

Gene Kelly and Vera-Ellen dance "Slaughter on 10th Avenue" from *Words and Music*.

(Opposite page) Gene Kelly, Frank Sinatra, and Jules Munshin deciding how to spend their twenty-four hours in New York in *On the Town*.
(Above) Alice Pearce, Frank Sinatra, Betty Garrett, Gene Kelly, Ann Miller, and Jules Munshin in *On the Town*.
(Below) Phil Silvers and Gene Kelly as hillbillies rest between takes in *Summer Stock*.

(Opposite page) Judy Garland and Gene Kelly take a break during rehearsals for *Summer Stock*.
(Above) Gene Kelly and fellow artist in a scene from *An American in Paris*.

Gene Kelly in his most famous number—*Singin' in the Rain.*

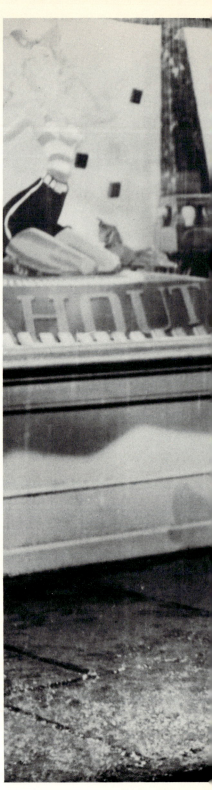

(Top right) Gene Kelly, Debbie Reynolds, and Donald O'Connor film the opening sequence of *Singin' in the Rain*.
(Bottom) Cyd Charisse doing the "crazy veil" dance from *Singin' in the Rain*.
(Opposite page) Gene Kelly and Debbie Reynolds in *Singin' in the Rain*.

(Top) Gene Kelly and Pier Angeli in a scene from *The Devil Makes Three*.
(Bottom) John Justin and Gene Kelly in *Crest of the Wave*.

(Top) Van Johnson, Cyd Charisse, and Gene Kelly in *Brigadoon*.
(Bottom) Fred and Gene Kelly sing and dance "I Love to Go Swimmin' with
Wimmen" from *Deep in My Heart*.

(Top) Taina Elg, Mitzi Gaynor, and Kay Kendall rehearse a number from *Les Girls* with Gene Kelly.
(Bottom) *The Tunnel of Love* line-up: Doris Day, Gig Young, Elizabeth Fraser, and director Gene Kelly.
(Opposite page) Gene Kelly and Natalie Wood in *Marjorie Morningstar*.

(Opposite page) Yves Montand learns how to dance from Gene Kelly as Marilyn Monroe looks on between takes of *Let's Make Love*.
(Top) Gene Kelly directs Diane Gardner in a scene from *Gigot*.
(Bottom) James Stewart, Henry Fonda, and director Gene Kelly in a recording session on *The Cheyenne Social Club*.

(Opposite page) Gene Kelly and Binnie Barnes in *40 Carats*.
(Top) Gene Kelly and his two assistants, Jeannie Coyne (left) and Carol Haney, rehearsing for *Invitation to the Dance*.
(Bottom left) Donald O'Connor, Carol Lawrence, and Gene Kelly recording a TV special for NBC.
(Bottom right) Gene Kelly as Father O'Malley in the "Going My Way" TV series.

(Top) Gene Kelly and company take a call after the first performance at the Paris Opera of *Pas de Dieux*.
(Bottom) Gene Kelly and sportsmen Sugar Ray Robinson, Mickey Mantle, and Dave Sime in *Dancing: A Man's Game*.

(Top left) The young Liza Minnelli and Gene Kelly take a break from record-
ing a Gene Kelly special for CBS.
(Top right) Kerry Kelly and Liza Minnelli on a visit to their respective parents
during the filming of *The Pirate*.
(Bottom) M. Julien, director of the Paris Opera, awarding Gene Kelly the
Chevalier of the Legion of Honour.

(Opposite page) Gene Kelly dances with Danny Kaye on TV.
(Top) The Kelly family at home: Bridget, Gene, Timothy, and Jeannie.
(Bottom) Gene Kelly at the wedding of his daughter Kerry to
Dr. John Novick in London.
(Overleaf) Gene Kelly, Jackie Gleason, and Brigitte Bardot on
the set of *Gigot* in Paris.

Gene Kelly "immortalised" at Hollywood's Grauman's Chinese Theatre with wife Jeannie and their two children, Bridget and Timothy, looking on.

middle-class Jewish family from New York becomes attracted by the glamour of show-business, and falls in love with a carefree, easygoing producer of a resident summer theatrical company at a lakeside holiday resort. Gene was cast as the producer, Noel Airman, and Natalie Wood as Marjorie Morgenstern (later Morningstar), who fancies both him and her chances of stardom.

It was a fine opportunity for Gene to establish himself as an actor of quality, and although over-earnest at times, he did an excellent job of work in the film, despite the screenplay's insistence on soft-pedalling the Jewish aspect of the story and characterisations – thus filleting the soul out of the subject.

The part of Noel Airman was originally offered to Danny Kaye, who turned it down as he was 'insecure' about the Semitic aspect of it, after which Jack Warner decided to underplay the Jewishness completely by casting non-Jews in the leading roles. 'If it were made today,' Gene said, 'they'd probably star Barbra Streisand and Dustin Hoffman in it – which would be perfect casting. But in 1957 Hollywood's commitment to authenticity was non-existent and, as a result, the picture suffered.'

Ed Wynn, who *was* Jewish, played Marjorie's eccentric old uncle, to whom she goes for comfort when things go wrong – and if at times Gene's performance was too serious in tone, Wynn's was far too comical, and instead of simply providing the light relief, he threw the film out of focus whenever he appeared.

In the end, *Marjorie Morningstar* is remembered, if that is not too strong a term, by its theme song, 'A Very Special Love', which tugs persistently and irritatingly at the sound-track.

In December of 1957, Gene and Jeannie flew to Switzerland where they were joined by Kerry who, in the autumn, had enrolled at the International School in Geneva. Together the three of them went to St Moritz in search of snow and wound up spending Christmas at the Hotel Chesa Grischuna. They were joined by Betsy, who flew over from Paris to see Kerry, Harry Kurnitz the playwright, and Anatole Litvak.

For the next few months Gene travelled between Switzerland, Paris, London and New York, and spent Easter, again with Kerry and Jeannie, skiing in Zermatt with a group of Olympic champions in much the same way as he had played hockey with men twice his age as a youngster in Pittsburgh. He was pretty good and fast, but obviously not in their league, and after taking in a couple of slopes with them each day, was exhausted. 'One day,' he said, 'I was on my way back eager to get to the hotel and soak my feet in a nice hot bath, because those guys had really taken it out of me, when I hit some slush, fell, and somehow managed to rip my cartilage apart. I staggered in agony for about a quarter of a mile to the hospital, and the doctor there took one look at my knee and wanted to operate. But I was advised by one of the skiers to wait until I got to Zürich or Geneva. In the meantime I had some treatment and hobbled around with a bandaged knee until I got the damn thing properly seen to after Kerry's holiday was over and she'd gone back to school. If I'd allowed that quack to cut me up, I'd probably never have danced again. As it happened I've never worked as well since that accident. That was really the end of serious dancing for me.'

In the winter of 1957, Gene was on one of his frequent visits to London when he received a 'phone call from Oscar Hammerstein, who was staying at Claridges. Hammerstein wanted to talk to him about a show he and Richard Rodgers were writing, and invited him to his hotel for a drink.

'Oscar sat on the edge of his bed,' Gene recalled, 'and I took a seat near the window. Then he told me about a show called *Flower Drum Song* and asked me whether I'd be interested in directing it for Broadway. It was about Old World and New World Chinese customs in San Francisco's Chinatown, and the whole thing sounded charming. Also, as I'd never directed a full-scale Broadway musical before, the challenge appealed and I agreed. After seventeen years in the picture business, it would make a nice change.'

So, in May 1958, Gene began work on *Flower Drum Song* which Hammerstein described as a Chinese *Life With Father*, because its story dealt with two Oriental fathers and the problems they faced controlling their modern families. It was to be produced by Rodgers and Hammerstein in association with Joe Fields (with whom Gene had worked on *Tunnel of Love*), and Carol Haney was engaged to do the choreography. The sets were by Oliver Smith, who had designed *My Fair Lady* a couple of years earlier, and the costumes by Irene Sharaff. The casting was left to Gene who, with Carol Haney and Jeannie Coyne, spent quite a bit of time in San Francisco and Hawaii scouting around for Orientals who could sing and dance. The two leading roles went to Pat Suzuki and Myoshi Umeki, with other parts being taken by Juanita Hall, Jack Soo (whom Gene spotted in San Francisco), Arabella Hong and Keye Luke.

On August 29th, Gene, Jeannie and Lois flew from California to New York and moved into Milton Berle's apartment in Park Avenue. The Berles, meanwhile, had flown to Los Angeles and were living in North Rodeo. Rehearsals for *Flower Drum Song* began on September 1st.

'It wasn't one of Rodgers and Hammerstein's best shows,' Gene said, 'but it had a warmth about it and a sweet sentimentality. And it somehow didn't matter that the quality of the score wasn't up to *South Pacific* or *Oklahoma!* I knew that as long as I crammed the show brim-full of every joke and gimmick in the book, I could get it to work. It was what was known as an "audience" show rather than a critic's show. That much was obvious from the start.'

While *Flower Drum Song* was still in the preparation stages, Gene visited Hammerstein at his farm in Bucks County, Pennsylvania, to discuss various aspects of the musical and generally to thrash out some of the problems that had arisen. Once rehearsals commenced, however, Hammerstein took ill and was hospitalised. 'I hadn't realised how ill he really was,' Gene said, 'because he never ever complained about not feeling well. I was sure they'd postpone the show until he felt well enough to get back to work, but to my surprise Rodgers and Joe Fields went ahead without him. They'd already got an opening date set for the St James's Theatre and Oscar, apparently, was insistent that there should be no postponements. Both Dick and Oscar, I discovered, were extremely strong-willed men. If they had a show scheduled for production, they'd allow nothing to stand in its way. They were fighters, both of them, and I admired this quality tremendously.'

While *Flower Drum Song* was trying out in Boston, illness struck

Joe Fields as well. He had a heart-attack and returned to New York to recuperate.

For Gene, however, the assignment was relatively uncomplicated, and the out-of-town traumas usually associated with Broadway-bound shows were kept to an absolute minimum. 'Obviously there were things wrong with the show that had to be put right, and there were times when I was out-voted on some production point or other and just had to compromise. And only on one occasion did we have to replace one actor with another. In this instance it was particularly unfortunate as our replacement, Larry Blyden, was in the throes of being divorced from Carol Haney. I'm sure they both found it difficult working with each other under the circumstances, but they braved it out magnificently and there were no problems.'

Flower Drum Song opened on Broadway on December 1st, 1958, and received lukewarm to poor reviews from the seven major New York critics. The show was unfavourably compared to *The King and I*, and the score was skewered for not having the immediate appeal of *Carousel*.

But, as Gene predicted, audiences adored it and before the show even opened, the advance bookings had reached a staggering one and a half million dollars; thus ensuring a long run and rendering it impervious to the critical cat-calls it received. In all, *Flower Drum Song* ran for six hundred performances on Broadway, and as Gene was on a percentage of the gross, he had no cause for complaint. He had done the best job he could on what was no more than a moderately entertaining musical, and his direction hit the right note exactly.

As Richard Rodgers put it: '*Flower Drum Song* required the sure-fire touch of an experienced professional to spark it all off, and in Gene Kelly we got a man who was not only experienced and professional to the very marrow of his bones, but hard-working and inspired. Without him, who knows how it all would have turned out.'

Within days of *Flower Drum Song*'s Broadway opening, Gene undertook his first major television show. Apart from an appearance in a

TV Playhouse 90 in 1956, he had always resisted any serious involvement with the medium. But it had now become too big and profitable an institution to be resisted. Besides, with the film industry in its present state, it offered employment, a factor which could no longer be ignored. So when Alistair Cooke, the master of ceremonies on NBC TV's popular *Omnibus* series invited Gene to do a show on dancing, he immediately accepted. The programme was called *Dancing: A Man's Game* and in it Gene tried to eliminate the stigma of effeminacy that has always clung to the art of the dance. It was an old hobby-horse of his, and he took the opportunity of selling it to a mass audience for all it was worth.

To prove that dancing is, indeed, a man's game, he gathered together some of America's greatest sportsmen and set out to show that each dance step has its physical counterpart in one sport or another (as he had done years before when he was a camp counsellor in Pittsburgh). He then went on to demonstrate how, for example, Mickey Mantle, going for a line drive, was the epitome of grace. No movement, Gene insisted, was more balletic than Johnny Unitas fading back to throw a pass, or basket-ball star Bob Cousy guarding his man, or Sugar Ray Robinson throwing a punch. The programme stated Gene's belief that the only difference between sport and dancing is that one is competitive and the other creative. 'Any man,' he maintained, 'who looks sissy while dancing is just a lousy dancer. A good dancer simply takes the physical movements of sport, exaggerates them, extends them and distorts them in order to show what he wants to say more clearly and more strongly. There's very little difference between a footballer warming up for the game and a modern dancer going through his paces before the show. It's only a matter of intention.'

In one hour of riveting television, Gene was at last able to articulate a philosophy that informed everything he did as a dancer. It underlined the reason for his athletic style, and went a long way in explaining the genesis of the Kelly persona. Yet, at the same time, by revealing his *idée fixe* in so clear-cut a manner, and by explaining so lucidly his thesis, something of the magic of Gene, the performer, got tarnished in the process. It was as if by dotting the i's and crossing the t's of his trade, he had been too generous with himself. To see so clearly what one had always felt instinctively about his work was rather in the nature of a magician giving away some of his best tricks. Yes, it is interesting to know how it is done – but can the effect ever be the same again?

Dancing: A Man's Game was enthusiastically received by the critics and the public, and received *Dance Magazine*'s annual TV Award. It was also nominated for the best choreography for television by the National Academy of Television Arts and Sciences.

In September 1958, a week after rehearsals for *Flower Drum Song* began, Gene took a few days off and flew to London to discuss a £500,000 film project with the Rank Organisation, which he was to star in as well as choreograph and direct. The film, a period musical set in Edwardian England and called *Gentleman's Gentleman*, was destined (if all went well) to be the most 'super colossal' British musical ever made, and was to star Moira Shearer, the actress cum ballerina, and the French actress Noelle Adam. The producer was Benny Fisz, who hoped to gain world prestige with the picture and, at the same time, give Britain 'a potent weapon in the battle for screen supremacy'. But a few months later, while Gene was spending Christmas in Klosters with Kerry and Jeannie, he received a call from London telling him the project was off. The decision to cancel the film came as a result of a readjustment of Pinewood Studios production plans for 1959. Or, as Connery Chappel, Pinewood Studio's assistant executive producer put it: 'We merely came to the conclusion that the film was not likely to be right for our programme.'

Gene flew to London a couple of days later to see what could be salvaged, but Pinewood's chief Earl St John confirmed the decision that it was irrevocably off.

After a short stop-over in Paris, the one place he loved almost as much as California, Gene returned to New York to begin work on the first of two TV Specials for Pontiac.

But he very nearly didn't make it. The Boeing 707 jet-airliner on which he and a hundred and fourteen other passengers were travelling – including several prominent fashion writers returning to New York from a show in Paris – suddenly dropped thirty thousand feet over the dark North Atlantic on a freezing winter's night.

'The plane,' said Gene, 'was spinning as it plunged and there was a shattering noise. I felt as if all the blood was being drained out of my body, and my lungs were tearing to shreds. The pressure pinned me to my seat, but people who were moving around were thrown to the floor. My first thought was, should I pray or not, and I decided I wouldn't because I hadn't been in a church or prayed for several years, and the last thing I wanted to be was a death-bed Catholic and a coward. Then, having made up my mind there were to be no prayers, my next thought was whether I'd paid my insurance and whether Kerry would be sufficiently provided for. After that, I just settled back, said to myself: "This is it. You've had it", and tried to make conversation with Harry Kurnitz who was sitting behind me, only to discover that he had had a mild heart-attack. It was about the most unpleasant experience of my life.'

In the ensuing panic, the passengers were ordered to take out their life-jackets, and stewardesses prepared life-rafts. Then, just as the crew and passengers had resigned themselves to their fate, the plane levelled out at six thousand feet and was flown manually by its pilot to Gander, Newfoundland.

What had happened was that the aircraft, which was cruising on 'automatic pilot' while the captain was mingling with the passengers, had developed a fault in the 'trimming' component. In Gander it was learned that two of the flight stewardesses had made a pilgrimage to Lourdes and were taking bottles of Holy water back to America with them. Prudence Clark, a fashion expert and one of the passengers on the 707, admitted afterwards that, although she was not religious, she couldn't help feeling that everyone on board the plane had been 'touched by a miracle'.

Five hours later, the hundred and fourteen passengers were picked up by a second Boeing 707 headed for New York. A few minutes before landing at what was then still Idlewild Airport, disaster almost struck again when the Boeing narrowly avoided colliding with another plane over the East River. Ironically, a plane *had* crashed into the East River earlier that day and when Jeannie Coyne, who had arranged to meet Gene at the airport, heard about it, she was convinced he had been killed. The fact that he wasn't was, indeed, a miracle.

There were, however, to be no miracles in his career that year, although the first of the two TV Specials for Pontiac, in April, sent the TV critic of the *New York Daily News* into raptures. He described it as 'blithe as the air of the springtime, swift as shadows on the summer grass, a merry mélange of talk, song and hoofing.' The guest stars were three European ballerinas; the poet Carl Sandburg, who read a piece written for the occasion called 'A Poem to be Danced To', with Gene providing the dancing, and a five-year-old Chinese girl who sang and danced. The music was by Henry Mancini.

It also introduced to American audiences a thirteen-year-old girl called Liza Minnelli. Over the years Gene had watched Liza grow up, and one night, at Ira Gershwin's home, Roger Edens sat her down at a piano and got her to sing a song. Liza was enchanting. 'So much so,' said Gene, 'that I said to Vincente, who had brought her along, that I thought it would be a great idea to introduce Liza to the public on a TV Special I was doing. What I had had in mind was to stage a medley of numbers I'd already done with some of my leading ladies, and I thought it would be just marvellous to do 'For Me And My Gal', which, of course, I'd done with Judy. Vincente said he liked the idea, but thought I'd better discuss it with Judy and see how she felt. So I went to see Judy the next day, and told her what I had in mind. She said it sounded fine, but she wanted to see what Liza would do with the number. So we 'auditioned' Liza, and it all went beautifully. Judy said great, go ahead. But, when we came to recording the number on the night, I suddenly got terribly worried that Liza would hit a clinker and that Judy would scold the hell out of her – and me! But, as it happened, Liza was spectacular. She kept as cool as a cucumber, and it was I who was as nervous as a cat. I remember quivering like a leaf. Anyway, it was a great success, and people adored her. Just as they do now.'

Prior to the Pontiac show, Gene was invited to sit on the jury of the Cannes Film Festival and, during the summer of 1959, he and Kerry accepted an invitation from a family of Greek shipowners they had met in Klosters, to spend some time with them on one of the islands off the mainland of Greece.

It was in Greece that Gene received a note from Stanley Kramer asking him whether he would like to appear in his film version of *Inherit the Wind*. His role, Kramer warned, wasn't to be either of the two leads, but it was a good, showy part – and he said he felt Gene would be ideal for it.

Gene had seen the play in New York and enjoyed it. It was based on the famous John Scopes 'Monkey' Trial, in which a young schoolteacher in Dayton, Tennessee, was charged with violating the State Law by teaching Darwin's theory of evolution; most of it took place in a courtroom. The protagonists, though called by different names, were clearly meant to be Clarence Darrow and William Jennings Bryan.

Gene asked Kramer whom he had cast in the two leading roles. 'Spencer Tracy in the Darrow role,' Kramer said, 'and Fredric March in the other.'

As Gene had a healthy admiration and respect for both these actors – especially Tracy – he accepted Kramer's offer without hesitation. Whatever part he was meant to play was immaterial. What mattered was that he was at last being given a chance to appear with these two formidable talents. The theme of the film appealed to him too: that all men should be allowed the right to think for themselves.

A week later he was back in Hollywood ready for wardrobe fittings. The role assigned to Gene in *Inherit the Wind* was of a nimble newspaper reporter called E. K. Hornbeck or, in actuality, H. L. Mencken – one of America's greatest journalists who, as Tracy put it in the film, 'never pushed a noun against a verb except to blow up something.' Though subsidiary to the two main roles, it was, as Kramer had promised, 'showy' and Gene excelled in it. It is a beautifully observed performance, solid in conviction and in no way eclipsed by the two heavyweights on either side of him.

As Gene was convinced he was never any good as a straight actor, he tried to learn as much as he could about style and technique from Tracy and March. In many ways, he felt that he and Fredric March, who were both stage-orientated (despite their enormous success in films) were not all that dissimilar. 'I could understand and see what Fred was doing,' he said. 'He was like Olivier. A wonderful technician. You could *see* the characterisation taking shape – the cogs and wheels beginning to turn. If you studied his methods closely, it was all there, like an open book. But with Spence it was just the reverse. He'd play a scene with you, and you'd think nothing much was happening. Then, when you saw the rushes, there it all was – pouring out of his face. He was quite amazing. The embodiment of the art that conceals art. It was impossible to learn anything from Spence, because everything he did came deep down from some inner part of himself which, to an outsider anxious to learn, was totally inaccessible. All you could do was watch the magic, and be amazed. He was also one of the most thoroughly professional men in the business. I never knew him to fluff his lines or come late. And he would remain on the set doing things his stand-in could easily have done for him. The only thing he insisted on, and which he even had written into his contract, was that he was to be given two hours off at lunch time. It wasn't for make-up purposes because he never wore any. I guess he just wanted to rest. All I learned from Spence was that no matter what I did, I'd never be as good as he was.'

If Tracy and March were the most impressive actors with whom he had ever co-starred, Stanley Kramer was by far the most provocative director – and, after so many inferior 'black and white' films with which Gene's career had been strewn, *Inherit the Wind* was a refreshing change.

The commercial success of the play was not, alas, to be repeated by the film, and in Britain, particularly, it hardly did any business at all. Nor did it do a great deal for Gene's flagging career, and he returned to TV with a second Pontiac Special, this time with Donald O'Connor and Carol Lawrence as guest stars. It went out on a Saturday night at prime viewing time, and was cosy and well liked. But it broke no new ground, and the most popular items were a Spanish number which he danced with Carol Lawrence, and a vaudeville medley. Until something more challenging was to come along, Gene, the erstwhile innovator who had taken the movie musical by the scruff of its neck and shaken it free of cobwebs, seemed content now to spend his time appearing in lucrative specials, more or less recapping his career in musicals for the benefit of a new generation of Americans too young to have remembered him in his heyday.

The following year, however, something more challenging did come along. The Ballet Company of the Paris Opera, aware that their unempirical adherence to the traditional classical ballet was in danger of keeping them wedged into an unadventurous rut, invited Gene to choreograph a modern ballet for them, and Gene arrived in Paris in April 1960 with Jeannie Coyne who, ever since his divorce, had been his constant companion. Initially, Gene was far more concerned about teaching the French company some of the rudiments of American dance styles than developing a libretto. That would come later. He knew his dancers would have to be drilled until they were as slick as a Broadway chorus line, and that if his experiences on *Invitation to the Dance* were indicative of what he could expect, it would be a battle for him to attain the sort of rhythmic precision he was after, a precision which did not come easily to European dancers. 'No matter how hard they try,' he said, 'they somehow can't quite bring it off. They can't capture the jazz in the background. They remind me of a little girl who tries on her mother's clothes in front of a mirror.'

As he had done in *An American in Paris*, Gene turned to the music of Gershwin and chose the 'Concerto in F'. The story of the ballet, he finally decided, would be a sophisticated bedroom farce in which the goddess Aphrodite descends to earth for one last marital fling. Claude Bessy was cast as Aphrodite.

For three arduous months Gene worked on the company, rehearsing them to the point of total fatigue. While the majority of the dancers found his slave-driving stimulating and his ideas refreshing, a handful resented his intrusion into a long-established tradition and complained bitterly. 'They resented that, after they'd spent years cultivating a classic "line", here was I trying to rub it out. It was only natural they should feel uncomfortable. But in the end there were only a couple of dancers who still resisted what I was doing. Most of the company found the work exciting.'

The title Gene finally settled on for his ballet was *Pas de Dieux*. 'I thought the French would appreciate the pun,' he said. 'But for some reason it passed without much comment.'

Fortunately, the ballet which opened on July 6th, 1960, did not. As the *New York Times* described the event: 'American dancer Gene Kelly invaded the musty confines of the Paris Opera with a leggy, sexy, modern ballet that shook the crystal chandeliers. Nothing like it had ever been seen on the stage where ballet is treated with fragile care.' And if *Pas de Dieux* wasn't exactly a repeat performance of the historic first night of the *Rite of Spring* some fifty years before at the Theatre des Champs-Elysées, the enthusiasm generated by its approving audience certainly gave the Paris Ballet one of its most memorable nights in years. However, the ballet critic in *Le Monde*, the following morning, was less enthusiastic than either the audience the night before or the *New York Times*.

'Ballet audiences,' ran the notice, 'are more tolerant than those of the opera. If *Lucia*, *Tosca* or *Samson* had been presented in the state of unpreparation that *Pas de Dieux*, the new ballet by M. Gene Kelly, was, there would have been a riot in the stalls as well as in the gallery. Dreadful noises behind the curtain between the 2nd and 3rd scenes and vociferous shouts and hammer blows obliged the conductor, M. Richard Blareau, to interrupt the prelude to the 3rd movement of Gershwin's concerto and wait with arms crossed as the din swelled and the audience amused themselves. A colleague's falsetto behind me accused the scene-shifters. On the contrary, what is miraculous is that these athletes of the décor, of whom one asks a super-human effort, didn't hurl the whole lot down on the stage. My bravos go to them as well as a large bravo to the corps de ballet who were not made to look ridiculous, but appeared to be delirious with joy at being able to dance to Gershwin. The only person responsible for the scenic chaos is M. Gene Kelly himself. He had three months to rehearse his ballet. If he did not have the time to try out the stage and costumes more than once, then it is his fault.

'It was a bad idea' (the review continued) 'to insist pompously on evening dress for the opening. To have been at one with the other side of the footlights last night, we should have come in jeans.

'No doubt, M. Gene Kelly will rectify everything before tomorrow evening's performance and that *Pas de Dieux* (what a title!) will be inscribed as the most modern and least conventional work in our old repertoire.'

The work itself, which had war chariots descending from the heavens, beds floating around in the air, as well as large street-lights directing traffic and flashing red, yellow and green – depending on Aphrodite's moods – 'held the audience in a state of divine disbelief' – as another observer put it – and despite *Le Monde*'s reservations was received with a fifteen-minute ovation and twenty-seven curtain calls. Gene was called out of the audience and onto the stage and responded to the cries of '*auteur*' with tears and smiles. A few days later he was made a Knight of the Legion of Honour by Monsieur A. M. Julien, the Director-General of the Opera.

Gene had always been popular in France. Even before *An American in Paris*, his French admirers were hailing him as the saviour of the American musical. *On the Town* was regarded as a masterpiece among the pundits of the erudite Cahiers du Cinéma and the yard-stick against which all other musicals must be measured. The French were also appreciative that, in *An American in Paris* Gene (and Vincente Minnelli, of course) avoided the cliché of incorpor-ating into the arrangements of Gershwin's songs the ubiquitous French accordion, which the majority of American musicals set in Paris could not do without. The elimination of the accordion was an example of what they considered to be a stroke of daring and originality – the two qualities most respected by French cinephiles.

But what was really responsible for Gene's prestige in France was, quite simply, that he happened to be a brilliant dancer. And being a nation where dance and film play such an important part in their culture, he became a natural and obvious hero. Even Jean-Luc Godard, the most *avant-garde* of the French *nouvelle vague* directors, paid homage to him and to *An American in Paris* in his delightful comedy, *Une Femme est Une Femme*. In fact, Godard was so taken with Gene and his work, that he suggested they collaborate on a musical. 'And I would have,' Gene said, 'except that we didn't have a script. Naturally that didn't bother Jean, because he likes to work from day to day. But it's not my style at all. He didn't seem to realise that you can't get in front of a camera and improvise a dance and hope to get the same results as we got in *On the Town* or *Singin' in the Rain*. So nothing came of it. But it was an interesting thought.'

The following year, the French honoured him still further when

Jean Cocteau presented him with an award on behalf of the Cinémateque Française. Only two other foreigners, Alfred Hitchcock and Fred Zinnemann, have been recipients of this award.

During his three months in Paris, Gene and Jeannie stayed in an expensive apartment on the Avenue Foch, a luxury, he claims, that cost him every franc he earned that spring. It was an enormous apartment, far too large for just the two of them, but he adopted a 'what the hell' attitude (of which his mother would not have approved!) and enjoyed himself.

One of his nightly rituals in Paris was walking to the Invalides and into a near-by bar for a beer and a few games of pinball. Like most things Gene did, the pinball games were competitive and he and Jeannie played against each other to win. 'I usually won,' Gene said, 'because I used to cheat outrageously. I knew how far I could tilt the machine without actually forfeiting the game, which is a skill acquired through years of hustling. Well, one night Jeannie and I were playing, and a stranger came over to watch us. All of a sudden he turned on Jeannie and started to call her the foulest names in the French language – of which, I think, the nicest was 'whore'. So naturally, I slugged him. He fell, and when he staggered up, the bar-tender came over and broke it up and threw the guy out, because he'd heard the names he was calling Jeannie.

'On our way back to the apartment I said to Jeannie, "Now why would the dirty son of a bitch, for no reason at all, want to call you such terrible things? Was he just anti-American and wanted to pick a fight?" And very guiltily she looked at me and said, "But he did have a reason. I kicked him in the groin."

'What had happened was that I was cheating as usual, and she took a kick at my shins. She was trying to do it surreptitiously but she missed me and caught the other guy in the groin. Well, naturally, he was furious – and who can blame him? I asked her why she didn't say something at the time, but she said she was too ashamed. And stunned, of course. Anyway, the story has a happy ending. A few weeks later we passed the man on the street, and I apologised and invited him for a conciliatory drink with us and to play a few games of pinball. It so happened he was an expert at the game and beat the hell out of me.'

From Paris Gene and Jeannie went to Yugoslavia for a much-needed rest, and on the advice of Barry Berenson (the father of the actress Marisa Berenson and consul in Belgrade at the time), they hired a Russian-built car called a Zim – similar to an American Buick – plus a chauffeur, as they were not allowed to drive it themselves, and motored to Dubrovnik. A few weeks later they returned to America where Gene made a brief guest appearance with Milton Berle and Bing Crosby in *Let's Make Love*, teaching Yves Montand how to dance – and in August 1960 he finally decided to ask Jeannie to marry him.

Jeannie had been in love with Gene ever since her dancing-school days in Pittsburgh. But to Gene she was little more than a good friend and, when she first arrived in California in 1942, an invaluable assistant. It was only after his divorce in 1957 that he began to take a romantic interest in her. 'Until then,' he said, 'she'd been around so long I took her for granted. Besides, before the divorce there was no reason for me to fall in love with her. I was still very happy with Betsy. And if anyone had told me that one day I'd be marrying Jeannie, I'd have laughed at them.'

From 1946 to 1948 Jeannie and Lois lived with the Kellys in the 'guest quarters' at North Rodeo, and the two of them became very much a part of the Kelly *ménage*. (Nor were they the only other residents. Invariably the Kellys were playing hosts to visitors from abroad or New York and, as Kerry recalled, there was hardly a night that passed without the dinner-table being laid for at least ten people.)

In 1948, however, Jeannie married Stanley Donen and shortly after Carol Haney married singer Dorian Johnson. Jeannie's marriage was not at all successful and it soon began to deteriorate. So did Jeannie who, eighteen months later, had lost several stone in weight, and was down to seventy-five pounds. It was the emotional black-spot of her life, and after she and Stanley were divorced, Betsy took her off to Europe in the winter of 1949 for a 'giggly schoolgirl's holiday', very Cornelia Otis Skinner, doing mad crazy things, in order to revive her spirit which her marriage had totally destroyed.

'Jeannie's marriage to Stanley,' Gene said, 'was doomed from the start. Because every time Stanley looked at Jeannie, he saw Betsy, whom he loved; and every time Jeannie looked at Stanley, I guess she saw me. One way and another it was all pretty incestuous.'

'The whole group,' said Kerry, 'was full of intrigue, counter-intrigue and unconscious connections.'

Until the day he proposed to Jeannie, Gene believed, or thought he believed, that Kerry was unaware of their affair. It was, she said, the only occasion she knew him to be unrealistic about something. 'For three years he tried to fool me about what was going on,' she said, 'and for three years Jeannie and I were hoping that he'd ask her to marry him. Then, just as we were beginning to despair, it finally happened. One morning, at two o'clock, Gene knocked on my door very quietly and wanted to know whether I was asleep because, he said, he needed to have a talk with me. He came in, sat down on the corner of my bed, and asked me what I thought about his marrying Jeannie. Well, I played it very straight and said: "What a wonderful idea dad. *How* did you ever think of it?"

'The next day he slept late, and kept managing to avoid proposing to Jeannie. Naturally, I was on tenterhooks, waiting for the big moment. But nothing happened, and by four o'clock in the after-noon, he still hadn't proposed to her. It was all terribly frustrating! I kept leaving them alone, then coming back a little while later to see what had happened. Finally I heard a screech from Jeannie's bedroom window. At last he'd plucked up the courage. And, of course, she was overjoyed. It was a very happy moment with hugs and kisses all round.'

Gene, who was forty-eight, and Jeannie, who was thirty-seven, married on August 6th, 1960, in the County Court House, at Tonapah, Nevada. They had planned to marry in secrecy because Gene felt that by underplaying the marriage he was protecting Kerry, whom he did not want involved with reporters. But the news leaked out, and after they returned to Los Angeles and stepped out of the plane, they were met by a battalion of photographers, 'Which was rather embarrassing,' Gene said, 'because it was a sweltering day, and we'd just driven a couple of hundred miles through the desert from Las Vegas to Tonapah and back, and were all looking terribly dishevelled and in no way ready to have a set of wedding pictures taken! It proved one thing to me, as if I still needed proof: there is no such thing as a secret in Hollywood. It's a contradiction in terms.'

Though Jeannie was almost the same age as Betsy, and in appearance wasn't all that dissimilar – both had reddish hair and blue eyes – temperamentally they could not have been less alike. There was not the slightest trace of ambition in Jeannie, except to marry Gene, and the day she did, she renounced show-business completely, and refused even to read the scripts Gene was sent. Where Betsy was peripatetic and hard to pin down, Jeannie was sedentary, a homebody bereft of ego, whose priorities centred around her husband and his well-being. And unlike Betsy, who in her daily intercourse with life was disorganised, unpunctual, irresponsible, capricious, flighty and undependable (qualities which seemed to endear her to her friends but irritated her family), Jeannie was practical, considerate, totally reliable and more than a little puritanical. The only quality germane to both of them was charm. Also, Jeannie was not in the least bit interested in politics and, on the occasions she attended political meetings with Betsy, it was more to keep her company than out of any inner conviction.

If she had any fault at all it was, according to Kerry, a neurotic denial of her own intelligence. 'She believed a married woman's place was in her home, with her husband and children, to the exclusion of all else. She and Gene reinforced the conscientious sides of their natures past the point where they needed to be reinforced. The result was that they both became more serious than ever before. She had an image of "family life" and what it meant to her, and she was intent in turning that image into a reality even if it meant suppressing her actual intelligence in the process.'

After Gene's marriage to Jeannie, their life-style changed dramatically. Despite the number of *soirées* she had attended at North Rodeo on those famous Saturday nights between 1946 and 1953, Jeannie basically disliked large social get-togethers, and, by 1960, the Kelly residence was no longer the open house it used to be. Once a year there would be a large gathering the day after Christmas, when the Kellys would invite their friends and their friends' children. An early dinner for the children was prepared, after which they would be taken home. Their parents returned and the party would then continue early into the morning.

The golden age of game-playing, volley-ball and impromptu entertainment by the world's greatest performers was a thing of the past – as was the golden age of Hollywood itself. Indeed, the next few years of Gene's career were to be, professionally, the leanest in his life, though, privately, the happiest.

In February of 1961, Gene signed with Seven Arts Productions to direct two non-musical films for them. The first was to be a melodrama called *Gigot* – from an original story by Jackie Gleason, who would also star in the film; and the second was a modern version of the romantic drama *One Way Passage*.

Gigot was to be shot in France, and if the schedule permitted, Gene also hoped to be able to accept an offer which Sam Spiegel had made to him to appear in a cameo role in *Lawrence of Arabia*. At the same time, Gene was also on the lookout for a *Roman Holiday*-type story that would lend itself to musical treatment and become a possible subject for Brigitte Bardot. On *paper*, at any rate, the future was full of promise.

Gigot is a grubby and unshaven Parisian deaf-mute hobo who lives all alone in a basement in Montmartre. Because he cannot communicate other than by eccentric pantomimic gestures, he is taunted and reviled by his neighbours and becomes the butt of practical jokers. His only friend in life is an alley-cat who visits him in the morning in return for a bowl of milk. The plot thickens when one night, during a rainstorm, Gigot finds a prostitute and her child, both in need of care and attention, and takes them back to his hovel to look after them. In time, he falls in love with the little girl.

Apart from Gleason and Diane Gardner as the girl, the rest of the cast were entirely French, and it was in French that Gene directed them.

The film took six months to shoot and edit, and when it was completed, Gene and Gleason were convinced they had a minor classic on their hands. 'It wasn't *The Birth of a Nation*, or even *Gone With the Wind*,' he said, 'but it was something special just the same, and we were rubbing our hands with glee. It had really worked, and Jackie gave the performance of his life. I was a very proud and happy man.'

But he was not to remain proud and happy for long. After *Gigot* was selected for exhibition at the Radio City Music Hall in New York, someone (it was never discovered who) re-edited it prior to its release, and without Gene's knowledge removed most of the scenes in which Gleason did not appear. The result was that the shortened version had Gleason following himself in scene after scene without much variation, and instead of the delicate, Chaplinesque pathos Gene was after (for the story is nothing if not a silent-screen melodrama), he was lumbered with a top-heavy weepy in which the heart-strings were shamelessly tugged at without relief. And ninety-five minutes of Gleason unrelieved was more than audiences and critics could take. The film was a mawkish disaster and the reviews left Gene and Gleason heartbroken.

After the lack of consideration towards him on *Gigot*, there was no question that he should work for Seven Arts again, and he abandoned all ideas of doing *One Way Passage*. Nor was he able to appear in *Lawrence of Arabia* due to the timing of the project and his own commitments.

While *Gigot* was being made in Paris, Jeannie became pregnant and informed Gene of the fact by sending him a birthday card which simply told him that she had his present inside her. She returned to Los Angeles from Paris in September, and their first baby, a boy whom they called Timothy, was born on March 3rd, 1962.

Also during the making of *Gigot*, Gene was offered the role of Father O'Malley in a TV series based on Bing Crosby's 1944 award-winning film *Going My Way*. A script was sent to him from Hollywood, and although he liked it and found it charming, he felt he did not want to commit himself to a twenty-six-week series. But when he learned that Jeannie was pregnant, he changed his mind. The series, which was to be made at Universal Studios, guaranteed his being at home when his baby was due to be born, and besides, the money he was offered was far too tempting to refuse, so he agreed, and in February 1962, he and his co-stars, Leo G. Carroll and Dick York reported to ABC TV for work.

As it was the first TV series in which he had appeared, Gene found the pace and the weight of the lines he was expected to learn sheer drudgery. The shooting schedule was extremely tight (each story had to be completed in four days, leaving a fifth day free for reading the next script and the weekend to commit lines to memory), and when it came to an end, he was glad to move onto something which did not invite the same rigid routine. He was also unhappy about the passive nature of the part for, what with the numerous restrictions imposed on the series by the Church and the network, the stories were much too tame to be stimulating. Once the writers tried to introduce some red corpuscles into the series by devising a story in which a young girl, seeking an abortion, comes to Father O'Malley for advice: the network balked in terror and scotched it completely. In twenty-six weeks, the most provocative thing Gene was called on to do was dance a jig.

When *Going My Way* first appeared it competed against the popular *Beverly Hillbillies* and was not strong enough to lure viewers away from that family's eccentric carryings-on. So ABC changed the slot. They need not have bothered though, for it stubbornly refused to attract audiences, and although two of its four sponsors – William Morris cigarettes and Breck Shampoo – were willing to risk a second series, the programme was dropped. However, it was extremely popular in Catholic countries abroad, and although not the success Gene had hoped it would be in the States, it was an interesting experience he does not regret having undertaken. Which was more than can be said for his next venture.

Early in 1963 Frank Sinatra formed a company and made a three-picture deal with Warner Brothers. Gene, who accepted Sinatra's offer to become part of the company, would produce the first film, appear in the second and direct the third. Sinatra, it was agreed, would appear in all three.

Their first project was to be a spoof of the prohibition days in Chicago called *Robin and the Seven Hoods*, with lyrics by Sammy Cahn and music by Jimmy van Heusen. Gordon Douglas was chosen to direct, and apart from Sinatra, the cast included Bing Crosby, Dean Martin and Sammy Davis, Jun. It was a formidable line-up of talent, and Gene was anxious to begin work on it. More anxious, however, than Sinatra who, for some reason, kept delaying his departure from New York to the coast, where the film was being made. 'If he'd told me to postpone rehearsals for whatever reason he had for not showing, I'd have done so,' Gene said, 'but he kept telling Howard Koch, who was his right-hand man (and has since been the head of Paramount Pictures), that he'd be arriving the next day, then the day after that and so on, until I decided the tension and the waiting wasn't doing any of us any good, and I told Jack Warner I was quitting. Warner kept reminding me how friendly I was with Frank, to which I replied that I was more than friendly. I really loved him and that was the reason I was walking out because it was my intention to remain friendly with him, and that if I stayed on as a kind of paid labourer our relationship would be over. I told Warner to call his public-relations man and release the story that I wanted nothing more to do with the set-up, but I stressed to him that I didn't want Frank to come out of it badly. They could tell the Press we had a difference of opinion and leave it at that. Which is exactly what they did, and I quietly withdrew. Most of the other fellows remained on except Saul Chaplin, who was doing the music. He left as well.'

Eventually Sinatra showed up and the film was made. 'I didn't speak to Frank while it was being shot,' Gene said, 'and our first contact with each other after it was completed, took place at Mike Romanoff's place a few months later. We had a fine time together with no hard feelings on either side. And when he asked me why I walked out on him, I told him the conditions he imposed didn't suit my temperament, which he must have known anyway since we'd done several pictures together, and he knew my working methods and the professional approach I expected everyone around me to have. I was perfectly honest with him and he took my point without any malice. Today we're just as friendly as we were, if not more so.'

Not long after Gene's abortive association with *Robin and the Seven Hoods* he moved into Universal Pictures. The move was instigated by Lew Wasserman at MCA as MCA had just bought Universal.

Ed Muhl and Mel Tucker were, however, still in charge of production at the studio and resented Gene's presence as they had no say in the conditions of his employment. The next two years were to prove extremely frustrating and, in terms of creative output, the most impoverished in Gene's career.

His first project at Universal was a version of *Beau Geste* which he and writer Millard Kaufman scripted. It was to be a prestige production, or at least so Gene hoped. But six weeks after the script was submitted, he learned that it was to be made on a shoestring with left-over footage from an earlier Rock Hudson programmer called *Bengal Brigade* – and decided he wanted no part of it.

A similar fate overtook his second project there, which was a comedy called *Send Me No Flowers*, based on the Broadway play of the same name. Gene wanted to shoot it with Warren Beatty, but the studio offered him Bobby Darin instead. Again he withdrew.

Career-wise nothing, it seemed, would go right for him. Everything he touched curdled or lost money. The last film with which he was connected and which had made money had been *Marjorie Morningstar*, and that was nearly six years ago. In a profession where a man is considered to be as good as his last couple of films, Gene's recent form – regardless of circumstances – was anything but inspiring. It was high time he had a lucky break.

Towards the end of the year, Gene was asked by the State Department whether he would undertake a six-week propaganda tour of Central Africa. Many of the old French colonies and also Ghana had just gained their independence from France, and now that they were on their own, the Russians were sending in musicians and ballet companies in an attempt to establish amicable relations with equatorial Africa in the hope they, in turn, would trade with them. As the US State Department claimed it did not have enough money to despatch their own entertainers into the bush, the idea was that Gene should 'make friends for America' by hawking around Africa a thirty-five-minute film compilation of some of his most famous dance numbers. While all his expenses would be paid, he himself was to receive no payment.

Carrying a can of film under his arm, he arrived in Dakar on

January 4th, 1964, and together with a projectionist who was travelling with him, began his tour of the local schools, orphanages, hospitals and any other place in which people showed a willingness to watch.

'Sometimes I'd play to an audience of five, other times five thousand,' he said, 'depending on where we were. For six weeks I bummed around visiting places as remote as Ouagadougou, or as sophisticated as Abidjan, the French-speaking capital of the Ivory Coast where, being French, the people there knew more about pictures than I did. And in townships where they had never heard of me, it didn't matter because Africans love the universal language of dancing, and they responded so well to the film clips that after I was through showing the picture, we'd exchange dance steps. It was a marvellous mixing of two very distinct types of culture and a pretty exciting adventure for me, though at the time it was more like hard work than anything else, especially as I wasn't used to living in the bush and was terrified by every mosquito that came within biting distance of me.'

Gene returned to California and 'civilisation' and in February signed with 20th Century Fox to appear in one of the half-dozen stories that comprised a comedy called *What a Way to Go*. Three years earlier, Gene had taken an option on the property (it was then called *The Richest Girl in the World*), which he sold to Arthur Jacobs and John Springer, two publicists turned would-be producers who saw it as a vehicle for Marilyn Monroe. Monroe was approached and promised she'd do it if they could find a suitable director. Which was easier suggested than done, for Monroe had a reputation for being 'awkward', and most of the directors Jacobs and Springer had short-listed put their health and state of mind before their careers and said no. The rest were already committed to other projects. Finally they signed J. Lee Thompson, a workmanlike though uninspired British director (whose most successful film had been *The Guns of Navarone*), and a production date was set. Then, in August 1962, news reached Jacobs and Springer that Monroe had been found dead, at which point Springer decided he had had enough of the vicissitudes of film production and went back to being the highly successful publicist he is. Arthur Jacobs, however, persevered, and after trying to acquire the services of Elizabeth Taylor and then Kim Novak, finally settled for Shirley MacLaine. In 1964, the film was made under the title of *What a Way to Go*, with a screenplay by Betty Comden and Adolph Green.

The idea of *What a Way to Go* had Miss MacLaine as a basically simple country girl whose sad fate in life was to marry a succession of millionaires, all of whom were doomed to meet a sorry demise. End of idea.

The men were played by Robert Mitchum, Bob Cummings, Dick van Dyke, Dean Martin, Paul Newman and Gene Kelly. It is of little consequence how each died, thereby leaving Miss MacLaine a few million dollars richer; for the record, Gene (in top-hat and tails) played a night-club hoofer who is trampled to death when a horde of adoring fans overpower him as soon as he becomes a famous star.

The story required the lightness of a Lubitsch or a René Clair to give it some buoyancy, but under J. Lee Thompson's suet-pudding direction (and with scant assistance from Comden and Green's screenplay), it remained immobile and resisted laughter – except of the derisive variety. Of Gene's performance there is little to say other than that he could have played it in his sleep – and probably did.

A far happier occasion, that year, was the arrival of Gene and Jeannie's second baby, a girl they called Bridget, which was the name Gene originally wanted to call Kerry twenty-two years ago before being dissuaded from doing so by Betsy.

Gene recalled the occasion: 'I was in the Cedars of Lebanon hospital waiting for Jeannie to give birth, when I received a 'phone call from a well-known newspaper columnist who congratulated me on becoming a father again and what, he wanted to know, did I have to say for myself? Well, I had no idea Jeannie had already delivered, and wondered how the hell the guy had heard before me! I knew it was impossible to keep a secret in Hollywood, but this, I thought, was ridiculous. What apparently had happened was, that after Jeannie had given birth, one of the doctors' surgical instruments went missing, and they thought they may have left it inside

Jeannie. But before they did anything drastic, they had a thorough ten-minute search around the operating theatre and, thank God, they found it. But while they were searching, word had got out that Jeannie had had a little baby girl, and a "spy" employed by the newspaper, and whose job in life was to hang around maternity hospitals waiting for the wives of the famous to deliver, rushed to the 'phone and called his office. I couldn't believe it, but that's Hollywood. Even in its death throes the old town wasn't going to miss a story – no matter how unimportant.' So, at the age of fifty-two, Gene became a father for the third time.

Although Gene had always been a most attentive father to Kerry, his career was just as important to him as his family, and only his end-less supply of energy made it possible for him to combine the two. No matter how busy he was, he had always found time for Kerry. And as Kerry was as cosmopolitan, as adaptable to new environ-ments, and as well-travelled as both her parents, she spent the majority of her school holidays accompanying them on their various trips around the world. Only after the divorce did she feel betrayed and neglected and withdrew her affections. But her animosity was short-lived, and today she remembers Gene as a most painstaking and conscientious father, with boundless enthusiasm for whatever they did together.

Gene, however, is still convinced he could have devoted more time to Kerry and, when Timothy and Bridget were born, made up his mind that he would give as much of himself to them as he could.

In the forties and fifties he would sometimes make dozens of trips a year. If he had a couple of days off, he'd fly to New York or Paris and back to see a show and think nothing of it. He would just get on a plane with one small suitcase, as he has always believed in travelling light: a suit, a tie, a few shirts and an all-weather coat from Aquascutum, and that was it. But when Timothy and Bridget were born, he decided to stop gallivanting around, because he did not want to be away as they were growing up. This was driven home to him very forcibly in 1967, when he was asked by Jacques Demy, who had just made a successful French musical called *The Umbrellas of Cherbourg* whether he would like to appear in his next film, a musical called *The Young Girls of Rochefort*. 'The film was to have much more dancing than the earlier one,' Gene said, 'and as I hadn't done a musical for some time, and as it only meant being away from home for six weeks, I said okay. Well, when I returned to California, my kids looked as though they were twenty years older. In six weeks they had changed enough for me to feel resentful that I had missed out on some vital part of their development, and I made up my mind never to spend any time away from home unless I could take them with me. Twenty, or even ten years earlier I wouldn't have given it a thought.'

Unfortunately after a bleak 1965 and 1966, *The Young Girls of Rochefort* which starred Catherine Deneuve and her sister, Françoise Dorleac, with music by Michel Legrand, was another soggy entertainment, as effete as it was boring, and it hardly gave Gene's ailing career the boost it so badly needed. It was also the first film in which his singing voice was dubbed. For the last couple of years he had devoted his energies to a handful of TV specials, including one with Britain's Tommy Steele and another called *New York, New York*, as well as an ambitious version of *Jack and the Beanstalk* (which again combined live action with cartoon animation). But nothing Gene was attempting during those lustreless years stretched his talent. At fifty-five it was unrealistic, of course, to expect the sort of dancing from him which gave *Singin' in the Rain* its special distinction, but even as a director his critics looked in vain for the sort of energy, drive and originality that informed every frame of, say, *On the Town*. Having reached the very summit of his art in 1952, by 1967 his decline was becoming almost as spectacular as his rise had been. True, the kind of film in which he had made his name was no longer a part of Hollywood in the sixties; the only musicals in production were such solid Broadway hits as *Funny Girl* with Barbra Streisand. The original screen musical was a thing of the past, and Gene's acceptance of this seemed, at the same time, to vitiate his own creative processes.

Whatever one says about *The Young Girls of Rochefort*, and there is a great deal to say about it (mostly unkind), it was at least an original idea, and it was this plus Gene's romance with France and admiration for Jacques Demy, that were the reasons for his agreeing to appear in the film. He also realised, after shooting the film, that his 'skiing knee' was never going to get any better and that the combination of his accident and the added years meant he'd never dance with the same energy and ability he used to have.

The story of *The Young Girls of Rochefort* told of two girls who run a ballet school and who pine to meet their ideal men. Gene, who played a concert pianist, and his co-star, Jacques Perrin, were pining to meet *their* ideal women, and you did not have to be Nostrodamus to predict the outcome.

Jacques Demy requisitioned the entire town of Rochefort-sur-Mer, gave it a pastel paint job from top to bottom, and set out to make a lyrical musical which would also capture something of the dynamism of the Hollywood musical's golden age. But it did not work out that way. Michel Legrand's score tinkles away to little effect, the choreographer, a young Irishman called Norman Maen had not yet learned to choreograph with the camera, so the routines are haphazardly cut together, without a sense of rhythm or movement; and Françoise Dorleac and Catherine Deneuve were incapable, between them, of breathing life into the numbers (that neither could sing nor dance hardly helped matters). As for Gene, he was not employed for himself but for his image, and to provide the film with an authentic face from the classic Kelly musicals it was paying homage to. *The Young Girls of Rochefort* also shows that, seventeen years after *On the Town*, admiration for that film was as strong as ever, and Demy uses the sailor suit as an aesthetic motif which will always be associated with Gene. And although as a film it is a very sad occasion indeed, it is at least proof of the continuing legend Gene created for himself in the fifties. But it was now 1967, and the very last thing Gene wanted was to be wedged into a past decade.

At a time when fewer films were being made in Hollywood than ever before – except, possibly, for the present time – Gene's decision to remain in Beverly Hills with his family, even if it meant turning down work abroad or on location elsewhere in America, was his first positive step towards finally 'settling down'. It was a decision which, over the next few years, was to cost him a fair amount of money and prestige in the work he refused. But he was happy with his young family, and that, finally, was what mattered most to him.

In 1967, after a half a dozen years of stillborn projects, mediocre films and rent-paying TV specials, Gene was asked by producer Frank McCarthy, who had been with Universal Pictures with Gene between 1962 and 1963, whether he would like to direct a comedy called *A Guide for the Married Man*. It was to be made at 20th Century Fox where, in 1965, Gene had taken an office and begun work (again to no avail) with Alfred Hayes on an abortive musical set during World War One. Therefore, when McCarthy offered him a picture definitely scheduled for production, he was happy to accept.

Coming as it did just prior to the new 'permissive' cinema, its subject, which advances the theory that it is perfectly feasible to be a good husband *and* have affairs on the side, as long as you don't get caught, was considered quite daring for its time, especially as the film consisted of a series of vignettes setting out to demonstrate the various ways a man can cheat on his wife.

'Two years earlier,' said Frank McCarthy, 'we couldn't have made it. But with the introduction of the new adult classification, I knew we could get away with it with an "A" or adults only classification. So I took the screenplay, which was by Frank Tarloff, to Richard Zanuck, then head of the studio, who read it and liked it, but wasn't sure who could direct it. I told him there was only one person: Gene Kelly. Well, Zanuck wasn't convinced. "Why Kelly?" he asked, and reminded me that *Gigot*, which Fox had released didn't do any business at all. "Look," I told him, "the subject-matter is so delicate that unless it's done with impeccable taste and perfect judgement, we'll have one helluvan embarrassing and vulgar picture on our hands. And Gene", I said, "has the necessary discretion to pull it off." Well, Zanuck still wasn't convinced and started suggesting a half dozen other directors. He had nothing personal against Gene, he said, it was just, like everyone else, he tended to think of him as a performer. But I persisted and finally Zanuck let me have my way.

'Apart from Gene's innate good taste,' said McCarthy, 'there was another reason why I wanted him. My idea was to cast practically every available comedian in Hollywood in small cameo parts throughout the picture, and the only guy I knew who was popular enough, and who was sufficiently highly respected in the business to get them to say yes, was Gene. I mean, you couldn't send out a casting director and expect him to come back with Lucille Ball and Jack Benny and Carl Reiner and Terry-Thomas and Hal March and Art Carney and Joey Bishop and Jayne Mansfield and Polly Bergen – all of whom were in the film. But Gene could get them, and he did. He even managed to talk Walter Matthau, who had recently had a heart-attack, into making a come-back and playing one of the two leads (the other was Robert Morse) – which was quite an achievement.'

Matthau remembers Gene calling him one day and telling him about this script he had. 'I said to him, okay, send it along and I'll read it. He said no, he'd prefer to talk to me about it personally, because I may not *like* the script. I said, okay, so start talking. He said, "Not over the 'phone. Can I come out and see you?" Now I was living in Upstate New York, which is one helluva 'shlep' from Beverly Hills, and I told him he'd never find it. "You have to take an aeroplane," I said, "and a train, and a car, and a mule; then you have to swim through crocodile-infested waters, so why don't you just send me the script?" So he sent me the script – and he was right. I didn't like it. It was pretty bad. Without one redeeming feature as far as I was concerned. It was of such low quality that I didn't want to have anything to do with it. Not that I hadn't done "drek" before, but this was the bottom and I told Gene so.

'Well, I must say, he listened patiently to what I had to say, then he told me about McCarthy's idea to have a lot of famous comedians in small parts. I said to him it would probably make him a successful picture but not, I repeated, one which I wanted to be part of. Well, the Irish not only have tempers, I discovered, they have persistence as well, and he kept calling me and nagging me to change my mind. And I kept saying no.

'Then one night I was talking to Billy Wilder about it and describing the two leading parts; and with that unerring instinct for what is right, Wilder said it would work if the roles were switched – and that the part originally intended for Robert Morse went to me, and vice versa. So when Gene called for the thirty-fifth time, I finally said okay, I'd do it, on condition that the parts were switched; so instead of me playing the smart, wise-cracking sophisticated member of the duo, I played the schnook. Gene liked the idea, and said fine – and that's how he got me, and I'm happy to say it was a most pleasant experience. He's an easy person to work with, comfortable and relaxed, with a definite flair for comedy and directing comedy. The film was full of pretty girls whose breasts and bums bounced pertly, and a lot of Jew comics. An impeccable formula for success.'

Lloyds of London insured Matthau in case he had another heart-attack, and shooting began.

Gene worked extremely hard on the script with Frank Tarloff, for he, too, like Matthau, was aware of its lapses in taste, and the last thing he wanted to direct was a load of vulgarity. It also gave him an opportunity to experiment with various techniques – such as conversations overlapping from one scene into the next, playing around with continuity, and jump-cutting from sequence to sequence with a daring refreshingly new to him. At times he seemed to choreograph the film along the lines of a fast-paced modern dance, often shouting out the desired rhythms he wanted as if he were a ballet-master.

He was, McCarthy recalled, extremely money-conscious, and totally committed to bringing the film in on time and on budget. 'With Gene, certainly at this stage in his life, there were no temperaments, no traumas, and no tantrums. He had a job of work to do and he did it with a professionalism almost unique in my experience of the industry. His touch,' he observed, 'was so light with actors that he almost danced behind the camera. He allowed each of the guest stars to "do their thing" yet he managed very subtly, quietly and diplomatically, to make them fit the structure of the story. And having been an actor himself, he knew just how to talk to other actors; how to greet them in the morning in a way that put them in a good mood for the rest of the day, and he knew how to cater to their whims, while at the same time being firm. It was a joy and an experience to watch him work.'

The only person with whom Gene did not see eye to eye was Robert Morse, who was giving the same characterisation he had given in the Broadway musical *How to Succeed in Business Without Really Trying*, which first brought him recognition.

'Morse was so contained in that performance,' McCarthy said, 'that he wanted to go on playing it rather than the one Tarloff had written. And to watch Gene slowly coaxing him out of the one into the other was a work of art. And it wasn't easy because at the beginning Morse took it very hard, and would disappear into his dressing-room and weep or make a bee-line for me demanding to know why Gene wasn't allowing him to do the things he did best.

'With Matthau, on the other hand, there was no trouble at all. He is ten times the actor Morse will ever be, and he took direction perfectly.'

McCarthy observed that, in between set-ups, rather than retreat to his dressing-room cum office, Gene would spend all the time he wasn't required on the set in the cutting-room, or in the sound department listening to tracks, generally learning every facet of film production he felt he had not yet mastered. 'I never saw anyone as anxious to improve his skills as Gene,' he said, 'even at his age and with his immense experience. His overwhelming desire to be master of every situation he found himself in, sent him rushing off, trying to absorb as much as he could, as often as he could – and in an industry awash with complacency and mediocrity it's a very refreshing approach indeed.'

A Guide for the Married Man was the big break Gene had been waiting for during the last fifteen years. With it, he proved he was every bit as contemporary as some of his younger colleagues, and in the eyes of the 20th Century Fox hierarchy, it firmly established him as a viable commercial proposition. The film was justifiably well reviewed and praised for its 'impudent candour and freedom from leer'. More important, it made the studio a great deal of money and restored Gene's faith in himself and his ability – if, indeed, he had ever despaired of having lost either. And it was the first film with which he had been associated during that decade that unmistakably belonged to the sixties – not, like *Gigot*, *What a Way to Go* and *The Young Girls of Rochefort*, a faint echo of the twenties, thirties and forties.

After *A Guide for the Married Man* had established itself as one of the studio's big money-makers for 1967, Zanuck called Gene and Frank McCarthy into his office and asked them whether they'd like to join forces once again on a mammoth film the studio were planning of Victor Appleton's *Tom Swift and his Wizard Airship*, whose main production value was to be, as its title suggests, a wizard airship. Both Gene and McCarthy liked the idea, particularly Gene, who still maintained a child's wonderment in matters fantastical, and although a script was already in existence, it was jettisoned and a new one started from scratch. Aerodynamic experts were hired to give technical advice on the creation of the fabulous machine, and no expense was spared to ensure a dirigible of a wondrousness no schoolboy, or his dad, could possibly resist.

Then one morning, Zanuck called Gene into his office and told him that he had finally decided to make a start on a property the studio had bought in 1964 called *Hello Dolly!*, a musical that was still running on Broadway, but which would no doubt be off by the time the film was completed. It was, Zanuck told him, to be a road-show and would have a budget in the vicinity of twenty million dollars, making it the most expensive musical ever made. Then he asked Gene whether he would like to shelve *Tom Swift* temporarily, and direct *Dolly* for them. Gene said he couldn't do that to Frank McCarthy. They'd both been working on *Tom Swift* and it just would not be fair. Zanuck asked him under what conditions he would do it. Only, said Gene, if McCarthy was immediately assigned to another picture, and that as soon as *Dolly* was completed, they could both return to *Tom Swift*. Zanuck agreed.

'There are very few people around today,' said McCarthy, 'who would have made those stipulations, and jeopardised a chance to direct as important a show as *Hello Dolly!* Gene is one of the few.'

The original play on which *Hello Dolly!* was based has a long and chequered history. In 1835, an Englishman called John Oxenford presented the first version of the story to London audiences in a piece called *A Day Well Spent*. Some years later, in 1842, a German adaptation by John Nestroy appeared in Vienna. Then, in 1938, Thornton Wilder, the distinguished American dramatist, best known for *Our Town*, followed up an idea by Max Reinhardt of adapting Nestroy's play for Broadway. The result was *The Merchant of Yonkers*, which starred Jane Cowl. But it was not a success. Wilder, however, was sufficiently enamoured of the story to adapt a second version of it, which he did fifteen years later, and which he called

The Matchmaker. This time it succeeded. It opened in London in 1954 with Ruth Gordon–excellent as the interfering Dolly Levi, and the following year David Merrick invited her to repeat her performance on Broadway, where it ran for four hundred and eighty-six performances. Paramount Pictures then filmed it with Shirley Booth as Dolly. Nine years later, David Merrick felt the subject would make an attractive musical comedy and commissioned Jerry Herman, whose one Broadway success had been *Milk and Honey* starring Molly Picon, to write the music and lyrics. Michael Stewart, who wrote *Bye Bye Birdie* was commissioned to write the book.

Hello Dolly! opened on Broadway on January 16th, 1964, at the St James's Theatre with Carol Channing in the title-role and David Burns as Horace Vandergelder. The show was an instant smash, became the hottest ticket in town and ran a total of 2,844 performances, making it the second longest running musical in Broadway history. (*Fiddler on the Roof* later outran it by three hundred and ninety-eight performances.)

Carol Channing left the cast after eighteen record-breaking months, to be followed by Ginger Rogers, Martha Raye, Phyllis Diller and Betty Grable. In 1967, Gower Champion, who staged and choreographed the show, hit on an idea worth a couple of million dollars of anybody's money, when he restaged *Hello Dolly!* with an all-black cast headed by Pearl Bailey and Cab Calloway. It was a stroke of genius that added two years to the run of the show, and made David Merrick and his angels a bonus fortune. Finally, Ethel Merman played Dolly Levi. This was right and proper, since the show had originally been written with her in mind; but she had turned it down in 1964, not wanting to involve herself in another long run as she had recently completed three triumphant years in *Gypsy*.

Shortly after *Hello Dolly!* opened on Broadway, 20th Century Fox, still riding high on the success of *The Sound of Music*, bought the film rights for two and a half million dollars plus a percentage of the gross (there was a clause from Merrick preventing the film being released while the show was still running on Broadway).

Set in Yonkers and New York City in the 1880s, the basic story of *Hello Dolly!* is about a matchmaker called Dolly Levi – a middle-aged widow who suddenly realises that life is passing her by and decides the time has come to find herself a second husband before it is too late. So, being an immensely practical woman, one who knows she isn't likely to fall in love again (at least not passionately as she did with her first husband Ephraim), she sets her sights on money. On Mr Horace Vandergelder, a wealthy 'hay and feed' merchant who lives outside New York in Yonkers.

Vandergelder, however, is, as he puts it, 'rich, friendless and mean, which is as low as you can get in America'. He is also the sort of man whose idea of a handsome gift is a box of unshelled chocolate-coated peanuts, and Dolly realises that wooing and winning Horace won't be easy, especially as he has his eye on Miss Irene Molloy, a milliner. But it's a challenge she is prepared to undertake. In the end, she wins, of course, but not before arranging romances for Horace's chief clerk Cornelius Hackl, a twenty-eight-year-old virgin, and his nineteen-year-old assistant Barnaby. The woman she has chosen for Cornelius is Irene Molloy, thus eliminating her competition where Horace is concerned, while for Barnaby she has decided on Irene's pretty assistant, Minne Fay. The whole candy-floss concoction takes place in one adventure-filled day – the day of the famous 14th Street parade in New York.

Richard Zanuck assigned the production of *Hello Dolly!* to Ernest Lehman, who had written the screenplays for *The Sound of Music* and *West Side Story*, both of which were huge money-makers; and who had just produced and written the screenplay for *Who's Afraid of Virginia Woolf*. Barbra Streisand, fresh from her success in *Funny Girl* and currently the hottest property in town, was chosen to play Dolly, and Walter Matthau, Vandergelder. Britain's Michael Crawford was cast as Cornelius Hackl and Danny Lockin was Barnaby. The rest of the cast included Marianne Mac-Andrew, Tommy Tune, E. J. Peaker, Joyce Ames and Judy Knaiz.

Barbra Streisand was not the studio's first choice for Dolly Levi. 'We wanted Carol Channing,' said Ernest Lehman, 'but the trouble was Carol didn't photograph too well; it had nothing to do with the fact that she wasn't as big a marquee name as Streisand.

'Frankly, I would have preferred Carol to Barbra. But after seeing *Thoroughly Modern Millie*, I honestly felt that I couldn't take a whole movie in which Carol was in practically every scene. Her personality is just too much for the cameras to contain.'

He then considered Julie Andrews, another 'hot' property, but decided she would be totally wrong, as wrong in fact as Elizabeth Taylor, who also wanted to play it. 'I talked to Elizabeth when we were on the final stages of *Virginia Woolf*,' he said, 'and casually asked her whether she'd ever thought of doing a musical. She got quite excited at the prospect, and a couple of years later, when I came to cast the picture, her agent rang me up and told me Elizabeth really wanted to play Dolly. And I must admit I felt very guilty at having ever mentioned it to her, because it was a thoroughly rotten notion of mine. At least I *think* it was. In this business you can never ever tell until after the event.'

Having finally decided on Streisand who, although far too young for the role, did at least have the right vocal quality for it, the next step was to find a suitable director. Gene was chosen, said Lehman, because there was no one else around whose knowledge of musicals was as wide and as varied as his. And as he would not be handling the choreography – Michael Kidd was given that particular job – Lehman felt that he would have the time to devote his energies to every other facet of the production – in terms of sheer size and expense a quite formidable task. Also *A Guide for the Married Man* was continuing to make the studio rich, which was recommendation enough. 'He too was a hot property,' Lehman said, 'and it seemed a smart move. *Was* a smart move.

'Gene had exactly the qualities we needed on the picture. Tremendous energy and vitality, and a maddening cheerfulness. Whether he *felt* all that cheerful as the production got under way and encountered certain difficulties, is another matter. But outwardly, at any rate, he always maintained a bright, confident attitude towards his work. He just doesn't believe in showing fear, anxiety, uncertainty, lack of confidence or pessimism. And if he felt any of these on *Dolly*, which he must have, he kept them very private.'

Right from the start there were problems in bringing *Hello Dolly!* to life on the screen, the main and most organic one being that Thornton Wilder's play *The Matchmaker* on which it is based, is not all that much about Dolly Levi. 'It devotes as much time to Cornelius and Barnaby and their two young women – all of whom are naïve and childish,' said Lehman, 'and nothing I could do made them any less childish. But that, I'm afraid, was the nature of the beast. In fact, *Hello Dolly!* is a pretty infantile story, and very early on in adapting it to the screen, I realised my biggest problem would be how to make it less silly. On the stage it was absolutely asinine. For example, on stage Horace Vandergelder was absolutely ridiculous – a real idiot. At least on the screen I think he made slightly more sense as a person. And the stage show was full of coincidences like the way Cornelius and Barnaby just wandered into the Irene Molloy's shop by accident. Well, I couldn't live with that, and I had Dolly Levi send them there deliberately. There were dozens of things like that I had to put right.'

Another problem was Barbra Streisand. 'I'd heard,' said Gene, 'that she was a difficult lady, so as soon as I agreed to do the picture, I flew to New York and met her with her agent David Begelman at the Oak Room in the Plaza Hotel, and I came straight out with it and said: "Barbra, is there any truth to all these stories that you don't want to rehearse and that you're difficult?" And to that she said no. All she needed, she said, was a director to guide her, and that she was dying to do the role, and that I could count on her. I told her she would have to work damn hard because the part called for a matron and she was still a young and blooming woman. She agreed with me and said she would.'

But a few weeks after signing with Fox, Barbra was suddenly overcome with insecurity and her enthusiasm for the role turned to fear as she realised that she was, indeed, far too young and did not know how to overcome this obstacle. For to have a Dolly Levi still in her twenties obviously did not make sense. And as the entire picture was to be built around her, the responsibility gave her sleepless nights. Ernest Lehman recalled that, on several occasions, she telephoned him in the middle of the night, to ask him what the hell she was doing in the picture, and insisting that she shouldn't be anywhere near it. How, she demanded to know, do you get Barbra Streisand to play Dolly Levi in a way that made sense of the woman? Unfortunately, Gene was unable to mould her excesses into a workable characterisation, and for this he takes full responsibility.

'If only there'd been more time,' Gene said, 'I'd have tried to help her work out a clear-cut characterisation, but we had a tight schedule and I left it up to her. With the result that she was being

Mae West one minute, Fanny Brice the other, and Barbra Streisand the next. Her accent varied as much as her mannerisms. She kept experimenting with new things out of sheer desperation, none of which really worked to her satisfaction. And as she's such a perfectionist, she became terribly neurotic and insecure.'

Because Gene was unable to help her find an acceptable interpretation of Dolly Levi, Barbra lost confidence in him almost as soon as shooting began and, Lehman said, got along with Gene 'very poorly'. 'They were just not meant to communicate on this earth,' he said. 'It was really a formidable task for Gene to have to take on Barbra at that particular point in her career, and just as difficult for Barbra to take on Gene. Gene expects people to regard him with a certain amount of respect, shall we say – to acknowledge who and what he is. And Barbra wasn't impressed. She knew he was Gene Kelly, that he wasn't twelve years old, that he was the director, and that he'd been in films for more years than she had – but she didn't make any of this particularly obvious to him. In other words, she wasn't showing him what he thought he deserved.

'Barbra, in turn, requires special handling as well. She wasn't a veteran, and because of her doubts about the part, was nervous of the way Gene was directing her. As a result I don't think they enjoyed being in each other's presence.' As Gene remembers it:

'Barbra made no secret of the fact that after she had signed to do Dolly Levi, she felt she was wrongly cast in the role. It wasn't exactly a director's dream to have the star walk into a movie not liking what she was going to do from the beginning. But she was a terribly good sport and did her best. As the picture progressed she tried very, very hard to make her characterisation work, and I have some fond memories of her *constructive* attitude . . . a side which is often ignored by other people. A couple of times, to try to get things on the right track, Barbra would work on the weekends with me. She would take her son, Jason, and I, my daughter, Bridget, and we would meet in the deserted, empty spaces of 20th Century Fox to work out problems while the children played together.

'During key rehearsals or at the end of "takes" I had a sign that I'd give to Barbra that she was getting it "on key" . . . it was the old British "thumbs up" signal. She would always look towards the camera at the end of the take and if she saw me giving her the "thumbs up" she thought she was doing well.

'At the end of the picture Barbra gave me a lovely memento. It was a large World War One poster "three-sheet size" done by James Montgomery Flagg . . . the one where Uncle Sam points his finger and says, "I WANT YOU!" . . . a real collector's item. On it she wrote, "To Gene, thumbs up, and thanks for everything. Love, Barbra."'

Barbra's problems with Gene were not, however, nearly as serious as her feud with Walter Matthau, who said he found it 'painful' to adjust to her personality, particularly as she made no attempt to adjust to his.

'The trouble with Barbra,' he said, 'is she became a star long before she became an actress. Which is a pity, because if she learned her trade properly she might become a competent actress instead of a freak attraction – like a boa constrictor. The thing about working with her was that you never knew what she was going to do next and were afraid she'd do it. I found it a most unpleasant picture to work on and, as most of my scenes were with her, extremely distasteful. I developed all kinds of symptoms. Pains in the lower abdomen, severe headaches, palpitations: I was in agony most of the time. I wish I could figure out exactly what happened to me, but I haven't been able to yet. All I remember and know is that I was appalled by every move she made. I was in a terrible fright and in a state of shock most of the time. Once I heard her tell Lennie Hayton, our musical director, that the flutes were coming in too soon, and that the first violins were too fast. Then she started telling Gene how she thought I should feed her lines. Gene, meantime, was trying to placate her and, like a good director, to keep the peace. He should, of course, have told her to mind her own business and do as she was told and not pay so much attention to other people as she had a lot to learn herself. And when she had twenty years more experience, then she should still shut up because she wasn't the director. The poor girl was corrupted by power in her second movie!

'Unfortunately,' he said, 'I'm rather slow to fight back. I'll adjust, assimilate and give ninety per cent in order to make something work. I will totally submerge myself or turn my back if someone needs the stage or the camera. And I hasten to add that I don't do this because I'm such a wonderful, self-sacrificing guy. It's sheer vanity on my part. I think I'm such a good actor, you see, it doesn't matter *what* the hell I do! At the same time I'm helping the other person in the picture or the play or whatever. But when the other person abuses this and takes it all as a sign of weakness, that's when I fight back and lose my temper. And the realisation, as *Hello Dolly!* progressed, that I'd agreed to take a supporting role to a beginner probably didn't help matters either.'

The feud between Walter Matthau and Streisand came to its head on the day Senator Robert Kennedy was assassinated. The unit was on location in Upstate New York and it was a hot, trying, muggy day. The set-ups between shots were interminable, and the mosquitoes which flew in from a near-by lake made life doubly difficult for everyone.

'As if contending with the elements were not enough,' Matthau said, 'Barbra kept asking Gene whether he didn't think it would be better if I did this on this line, and that on the other, etc., etc. – and I told her to stop directing the fucking picture, which she took exception to, and there was a blow-up in which I also told her she was a pip-squeak who didn't have the talent of a butterfly's fart. To which she replied that I was jealous because I wasn't as good as she was. I'm not the most diplomatic man in the world, and we began a slanging match like a couple of kids from the ghetto. I think Gene thought one of us was going to die of apoplexy or something, or that I'd belt her, or that maybe she'd scratch my eyes out – or worse, that we'd just walk off leaving twenty million dollars' worth of movie to go down the drain.'

By the end of the day a truce was called and both stars agreed that from henceforth, they would be civil towards one another. But the situation, if possible, got worse.

'We tried to be civil – that's why things got worse,' Matthau said. 'I'd come to work and say to myself, I'm going to be so nice to Barbra even if it kills me – until, in the end, the strain was too much. We just had to face the fact that the chemistry between us was wrong.'

Gene took a more sober view of the situation: 'Barbra wouldn't do anything to anyone deliberately,' he said. 'Whatever Walter claims she did, like stepping on his lines or telling him what to do, was done out of sheer ignorance and insecurity. She's not that kind of person. She's ingenuous and unsophisticated, and hard as it may be to believe, naïve. She is definitely not a girl who "does things" to people. Insecure is the best way to describe Barbra, and her problems with Walter sprang from her insecurity. I'm sure of that.'

Lehman also says it was difficult for Gene to work with Michael Kidd. Being a choreographer himself, Gene was naturally concerned with the way the dance routines looked, and although he tried to be as diplomatic as possible, the presence of another choreographer and dancer wasn't exactly the best set-up in the world. 'I'd often find Gene muttering away in the background about something he felt was wrong in the dance direction,' said Lehman, 'and I'd tell him to have a word with Michael on it. He said he couldn't and that I'd better do it. And, of course, I saw Gene's problem. He admired and respected Michael and didn't want to upset him or interfere. At the same time he was aware that a lot of people were going to assume the great Gene Kelly had given his approval to anything of a dancing nature in the picture, because his name is so inextricably linked with dancing.'

As a result, the relationship between Gene and Michael Kidd became, as Lehman put it, 'egg-shell time'; polite, friendly, but which the two of them negotiated with absolute caution. Kidd was also concerned that his choreography would be unfavourably compared with Gower Champion's original Broadway staging, and that he would be accused of copying it, with the result that he would often go against the mood of a number to avoid comparison.

'It was not, in retrospect,' said Lehman, 'a happy film. There were things going on that were terrible. The intrigues, the bitterness, the backbiting, the deceits, the misery, the gloom. Most unpleasant. It's quite amazing what people go through,' he said, 'to make something entertaining for others. I'm always shocked by it.'

He was also shocked by an incident involving the composer Jerry Herman during the shooting of the film.

Gene, Barbra, Roger Edens, the associate producer, and Ernest Lehman all felt the show needed a ballad to 'humanise' the character of Dolly Levi a bit more. It would come at a point in the film just after the big parade, and just before the famous 'Hello Dolly!'

number in the Harmonia Gardens. It was agreed, too, that an additional ballad sung by Barbra would help boost the sale of the sound-track recording. So Jerry Herman was called in and asked to provide a brand new song, which in due course he did. Roger Edens wrote a brief introductory passage to it, and the number 'Love Is Only Love', which in terms of its staging is the simplest in the film, was recorded and shot.

A few months later, Richard Zanuck was sitting next to Angela Lansbury on an aeroplane, when Miss Lansbury casually mentioned to him that the 'new' song Herman had been commissioned to write for Barbra was a reject from the original score of *Mame*, in which Miss Lansbury appeared on Broadway for a couple of years. 'Zanuck and Ernie Lehman were particularly angry about it,' said Gene, 'as Jerry Herman had got paid double for that song. He really hoodwinked us.' (During the Broadway run of *Hello Dolly!* Mack David, the composer of the song 'Sunflower', which was popular in the forties, claimed that Herman had 'stolen' his melody for the title song. The matter was finally settled with Herman paying costs of $250,000.)

By the time the cameras started turning on *Hello Dolly!* the cost, it was clear, would escalate way beyond its budget. Apart from the initial amount of money paid for the rights, and the high salaries all around, there was no way in which the art directors could 'do over' New York to give it an 1880s period look, so the whole of 14th Street had to be reconstructed for the film. But as Fox had already sold its back-lot, the main driveway into the studio was used instead. The result was a set as impressive as any seen on the screen since the silent days of D. W. Griffith – and as expensive. It was shown to its best advantage in the parade scene when it was filled with 3,782 men, women and children, including a band of a hundred and sixty, a cavalry troop of forty, fifty-six flag-waving 'Coronettes', forty bagpipers, a hundred-piece youth band, forty of Vandergelder's lodge marchers, fifty Civil War drummer boys, forty-one Civil War veterans, thirty-two suffragettes, eight clowns, five midgets, two banner carriers, three large floats, three fire engines and fifteen high-wheeled bicycles. Shooting lasted four days.

The other major set construction took place at Garrison, in

Yonkers, where a railway station, *circa* 1880, and several streets were built. The most expensive of the interior sets was the Harmonia Gardens, the opulent restaurant in which the show's famous title number takes place.

Because of Louis Armstrong's phenomenally successful recording of 'Hello Dolly!' he was asked to make a guest appearance and repeat his famous rendition of the song. For Lehman, no film of the show would be complete without it. He had also heard that during *Dolly*'s Broadway run, many out-of-towners were bitterly disappointed to find that Satchmo wasn't in the show, and was determined to avoid further disappointment when the film was released. 'Everyone thought it an excellent idea,' Lehman said, 'except Barbra, who was dead against it. She thought it was cheap and obvious, and accused us of exploiting him. But she changed her mind, and on the day we shot it, she was in a good mood and the sequence went very well.'

'Most of the sequences went well,' said Michael Crawford, who played Cornelius Hackl. 'I was always on the set, even when I wasn't on call, because it was the first musical I'd been in, and I wanted to learn as much as I could. And apart from Barbra arriving late, which she wouldn't have done had she only been given one hair-dresser instead of three, because all three insisted on fixing her hair, and that took time – everything went very smoothly. Gene always knew exactly what he wanted, and more important, he knew how to get it. He gave as much of himself to the film as was humanly possible, and didn't mind how hard he worked. If there was one destructive element in the whole project (apart from Walter's feud with Barbra, which was something personal between the two of them), it was Ernest Lehman, who walked around looking like an unhappy man all the time. But then anything Ernest does is bound to make him unhappy. He's that sort of person.

'Now with Gene it's just the reverse. He brings a joy and an ebullience to his work which is a fantastic morale booster for the cast. Nothing is too much trouble or effort for him. There were some weekends when he would 'phone me up and ask if he could come round because he'd thought of something new for me to do, and he'd jump into his car and come all the way just to give me a new inflection on a word! Then he'd get back into his car and drive home again. That's how conscientious and keen he was. As for his energy, it was boundless. Once, on the set, Danny Lockin, who played Barnaby, and who for some reason, always felt the need to compete with Gene, decided to show off and do four "butterflies" – a sort of cartwheel without hands. Gene just looked at him, and when he was finished, said: "Your legs should be a bit higher." Then he took off his peaked cap – always a sign that he meant business – and proceeded to do six perfect butterflies in a row. Well, the whole studio applauded. And for the next three days, there wasn't a murmur out of Danny Lockin!'

Apart from the numerous personality conflicts Gene had to contend with, his main problem in directing *Hello Dolly!* was how to 'blow up' its basically slender story to fit the big screen as well as make it consistently entertaining. Ideally, he would have preferred the film as an intimate musical, rather than a multi-million dollar road-show. But this was not to be. The studio was convinced that road-shows would be the saviour of Hollywood, and were gambling everything on the success of *Hello Dolly!* as well as on two other major musicals being shot at the same time, *Dr Dolittle* with Rex Harrison, and *Star!* with Julie Andrews.

As for superstar Streisand, there can be no doubt that she was far too young for the role. Her return to the Harmonia Gardens after an absence of fourteen years ('it's so nice to be back home where I belong'), would have meant that she had been ten years old when she had her last meal there! – and made no dramatic sense at all. Yet her performance is astonishingly effective – timeless, almost; so that her age is never really a serious obstacle and we suspend belief willingly in surrendering to her personality. And whatever her off-screen difficulties with Matthau may have been, their scenes together are delightful. Both performers radiate star quality and both compel attention. In fact, it is difficult to know at which one to look when they are on-screen together.

Whatever differences Gene and Michael Kidd may have had, the choreography is stunning and the dancers seem to be in a permanent state of levitation, nowhere more so than in the famous waiters' gavotte at the Harmonia Gardens – a routine of immense athletic agility in which the waiters leap about in a series of steps each more dizzying than the last.

But credit for the overall conception of the film must go to Gene, who with the assistance of Harry Stradling's photography brought to life something of the enchantment and the innocence of a world long since departed. And if the 'look and feel' of the film harks back to the golden years at MGM, this is deliberate. Harry Stradling had worked with Gene on *The Pirate*, and with Astaire on *The Barkleys of Broadway*, Roger Edens, the associate producer was a founder member, almost, of the Arthur Freed unit – as indeed were both Gene and Lennie Hayton. Michael Kidd received his early training under Freed's guidance as well, and Irene Sharaff, the costume designer was a fixture at MGM for years. Nor is it chance that much of *Hello Dolly!* has the joyous appeal of Vincente Minnelli's *Meet Me in St Louis*, which Gene still regards as his favourite musical.

Hello Dolly! combines all the best elements of the Metro musical and Gene, who contributed immeasurably to giving the genre its particular personality, turned out to be the perfect man for the job. Having been handed an established Broadway hit which could not be dissected and reworked in the manner of *On the Town*, he made a contribution to the film whose excellence cannot be over-estimated.

As the original production of *Hello Dolly!* was still running on Broadway (with Pearl Bailey) Fox was contractually obliged to sit on the picture until the New York run ended. But as it had cost so much by the time it was completed, Zanuck was anxious to release it as soon as possible, so he made a deal with David Merrick guaranteeing to meet his losses if the Broadway gross of the show dropped below a certain level. Satisfied with the arrangement, Merrick lifted his embargo on the film's release, and with much trumpeting and fanfares, *Hello Dolly!* opened at the Rivoli Theatre in New York on December 16th, 1969, to generally enthusiastic reviews.

For a while, the advance sales were encouraging. But five dollars, which was the top price, was more than most people were prepared to pay – especially as parents were bringing their children to see it, thus making it a most expensive family outing. Even the cheaper seats were slow to move, and a few weeks after the film had opened, the box-office returns dropped dramatically, and 20th

Century Fox found itself fighting for its life. The days of the road-show were over. Had *Hello Dolly!* been made in 1964, when the rights were first acquired, it might have made money. But by 1969, the cinema had undergone a revolution, and audiences wanted something meatier than *Hello Dolly!*. And it wasn't only *Hello Dolly!* that became a victim of the new permissiveness in the cinema: *Dr Dolittle* failed, so did *Star!*, *Paint Your Wagon* and *Darling Lili*, all expensive musicals the public did not want to see.

Despite the traumas, the personality clashes and the pressures Gene encountered during the making of *Hello Dolly!*, he emerged from it all unscathed and with his admiration for Barbra Streisand still intact. For, apart from her inability to arrive on time, a 'disease' he first encountered with Judy Garland, Gene found her no more difficult to work with than several of his other leading ladies. He does not and never did regard the experience with the same distaste as Walter Matthau, and his only regret is that he was not able to be more helpful to Streisand in her search for a convincing character-isation. For the rest, he is happy with what appears on the screen, and with good reason. *Hello Dolly!* – weighing in at $24,000,000, more than the total cost of *On the Town*, *Singin' in the Rain*, *Invitation to the Dance*, *An American in Paris* and *It's Always Fair Weather* put together – is the best film musical of the sixties.

As Zanuck had promised, Gene and Frank McCarthy were re-assigned to *Tom Swift*. Two giant dirigibles were built in Wichita, Kansas, a story-line was agreed onto everyone's satisfaction, and Gene and McCarthy went to look for locations in Dubrovnik, London, Monaco and New Jersey. But after the initial excitement of *Hello Dolly!* was over and the frenzy of ticket buying reduced to a trickle, Richard Zanuck was forced to concede that audiences no longer responded to this sort of family entertainment at five dollars a seat, and to continue making road-shows would be tantamount to garrotting the studio.

Thus the inevitable happened. After spending a couple of million dollars on *Tom Swift*, the project was abandoned before a single frame of film was shot and, like so many other projects in Gene's career, was shelved indefinitely.

Early in 1970, Gene made a TV special called *Gene Kelly and 50 Girls 50*, and was invited to revamp the show as an attraction for the International Hotel in Las Vegas. It was not an engagement he particularly wanted, and he refused at first, because ever since his cloop days in Pittsburgh and Chicago, he vowed never again to work in night-clubs, regardless of their status, because he objected to the customers eating and drinking while he performed. But the International Hotel persisted, and finally Gene agreed, on two conditions: that he was paid more money than any other artist had hitherto been paid there, and that he could do the show over the Easter vacation so that his wife and children could be with him. To his surprise, both conditions were met.

The show was called *Gene Kelly and 30 Girls 30* (fifty girls would have made it too expensive) and in April 1970 he began a four-week engagement, which was extended to eight – it was the only show in town that catered for children and was proving quite popular for that reason. There were two performances nightly – the first being patronised by the entire family, the second less well patronised by an audience comprising heavy drinkers and hard gamblers.

The show itself was pleasant enough and Gene's reputation was sufficient to silence the talkers, and his fears that he would be performing to unappreciative audiences were unfounded. He was quick to establish personal contact and a friendly rapport with them at the beginning of the act, flirting with the older women in the late show, and playing with the children in the earlier one. It was extremely corny, but it worked, even though it was hardly typical Las Vegas fare.

During the engagement, Jeannie went down with pneumonia and returned to Los Angeles with her children. A hotel strike, during which time the show laid off for a week, enabled Gene to be with her, but when he returned to finish his commitment, he found himself alone and rather miserable. He was worried about Jeannie, missed his children, and, as he didn't gamble, began to grow weary of the place. Whenever he got too depressed, however, he thought about the money he was being paid, which made it all a bit more palatable. But the best thing about those seven weeks, was that during them Gene overcame his distaste for night-club audiences; and would even return to Vegas, he said, but in a more sophisticated show.

Later that year, James Stewart approached Gene with an offer to direct a Western. Stewart was, of course, aware that Gene had never, in any capacity, been connected with one before, but anyone, he felt, who was capable of making *A Guide for the Married Man* and *Hello Dolly!*, not to mention *Singin' in the Rain*, could cope with the simple story he had in mind – one about an itinerant cowboy who discovers that the 'social club' he has been left in his brother's will is, in fact, a brothel.

The screenplay, an original by James Lee Barrett, was called *The Cheyenne Social Club*. Stewart wanted to play the cowboy, and he wanted Henry Fonda as the cowboy's best friend and travelling companion.

For Gene the thought of working with these two men was incentive enough to accept without qualms. Fonda, however, read the script and thought his part too 'uninteresting' to make it worth his while.

Undeterred, Gene called him and asked him not to commit himself to any other project for one week, during which time he and the author, he said, would try and inject some vitality into the part.

A week later Fonda received the rewrites and called Gene to tell him he'd do it. Gene was delighted for, as he put it, 'If you can't work with the people you most admire in the industry, why work at all?' Besides, Messrs Stewart and Fonda were hardly newcomers to Westerns, and he relied on them to give him all the help and advice that they could.

Early in 1970, Gene and his secretary Lois temporarily moved out of their luxurious suite of offices on the Fox lot and took up residence with National General, who were producing the film in the old David Selznick Studios in Culver City, where nearly thirty years earlier Gene had made his unsuccessful screen test to appear in A. J. Cronin's *The Keys of the Kingdom*. But Gene was destined never to work at the Selznick Studios – not in 1942 and not in 1970, for shortly after he and Lois moved in, National General sold their premises and they were transferred to the Samuel Goldwyn Studios.

That summer the entire *Cheyenne Social Club* unit flew to Santa Fé, New Mexico, where most of the film was shot. And, faithful to his decision never to leave home for any length of time without taking his family along, Gene brought his wife and children for moral support and peace of mind. They, in turn, had a wonderful holiday.

Initially, Gene's only concern about the picture was that Stewart and Fonda might treat it all as a light-hearted romp. 'So, before we began,' he said, 'I got them together and had a few words with them. "I know you guys," I said. "I know you've been friends for forty years, that you know each other's work backwards, and that all you have to do is give each other private little signals on the set, and I'm dead. I know that, because I've done it myself with directors I didn't trust." Well, they knew exactly what I was talking about, and assured me they wanted and needed direction. And once shooting began, they behaved like the professionals they are. After the problems of *Hello Dolly!* believe me, working with Jimmy and Hank was like paradise. It was a lovely picture to do.'

It was not a particularly easy film for Stewart – as it turned out. His stepson had recently been killed in Vietnam and there were, Gene recalled, many nights when he was unable to sleep because of his grief, with the result that in the morning he would be too tired to work. 'I knew what he was suffering,' Gene said, 'and whenever it happened, I'd either shoot around him or cancel work for that day, depending on the schedule. And we'd all go fishing.'

Henry Fonda enjoyed fishing as well, but preferred dabbling with a paintbrush. And when Gene suggested to him that he should try having a go at whittling wood in between takes, he did, and produced several pieces of sculpture Gene assured him were good enough to sell.

Gene, on the other hand, spent much of his free time questioning local cowboys about the correct way to do certain things, from branding cows to saddling horses; he also read as much about the period and its history as he could. 'He may not have known a damn thing about Westerns or the West when the picture started,' Paul Helmick the assistant director said, 'but when he finished it he was very knowledgeable about the subject, and there wasn't much you could tell him he didn't already know – just as there wasn't much you could tell him about the technical side of film-making, from editing to special effects. He never did things by halves. His undertaking something was guarantee enough he would do it to the best of his ability. And he expected the same from others. The only time I ever saw him lose his Irish temper was when other people "goofed off". That he couldn't stand.'

There was very little "goofing off" on the set of *The Cheyenne Social Club*. The hot, sunny New Mexican weather seemed to burn any displays of temperament out of the leading players, and filming progressed without setbacks or problems. The sun, however, also burned out the energy necessary to give the story momentum, and the finished film, though inoffensive, has a somewhat enervating effect on the senses, hardly helped by Stewart's drawl, unhurried at the best of times, but which here, as one reviewer noted, 'sounds like a 78 rpm recording played at $33\frac{1}{3}$.'

However, the film was popular with audiences, and grossed several million dollars.

After a brief promotional tour to London, climaxed by his appearance at a film exhibition, which took place at the Roundhouse Theatre, where he was invited to appear as guest of honour at the end of a day devoted entirely to the screening of several of his films, Gene returned to California and to a project he had wanted to do for some time.

Early in 1971, Harry Lishinsky and Franklin Roberts, a producer and theatrical investor, approached Gene with the idea of doing a mammoth mobile family show along the lines of *Disney on Parade*, called *Clownaround*. The *pièce de résistance* of the show was to be a giant 'clown machine' designed by Sean Kenny, the British set designer and architect, in, on and around which the entire entertainment would take place. To Gene the idea was utterly irresistible: not only did he approve of family entertainment of this sort, but the show had a circus feeling to it which he relished, and was quite unlike anything he had ever done before. It appealed to his sense of fantasy and wonderment, and was as exciting and original a project as had come his way in years.

305

Auditions for the seventy players the show would require began in October 1971, and rehearsals the week after Christmas at the MGM studios, on lot 27, where seventeen years earlier the whole of *Brigadoon* had been filmed. It was the first time Gene had returned to MGM since 1957, and although the studio had by then changed managements and was barely recognisable, he felt nostalgic and sentimental for the 'good old days' when he stepped on to stage 27.

The composer of *Clownaround* was Moose Charlap, the author–lyricist Alvin Cooperman, and the choreographer Howard Jeffrey – an up-and-coming young man who had once been Jerome Robbins' assistant and who, more recently, had staged the numbers in *On a Clear Day You Can See Forever* for Paramount.

The two principals chosen to give the show 'marquee value', apart from Gene himself, were Ruth Buzzi and humorist Dennis Allen, both late of Rowan and Martin's *Laugh-In*.

But the real 'star' of the show was Sean Kenny's set. Rising fifty-two feet above the arena, a hundred and thirty-four feet long and fifty feet wide, it dominated the whole production. More than twelve weeks were spent in its construction; the finished structure weighed forty-four thousand pounds, and took twenty hours to erect. It was designed by Kenny as a whirling series of stainless steel and aluminium multi-levelled ramps and rings, and operated on twelve separate levels, each served by an elevator. An all-purpose set, it was expected with the minimum of effort to be transformed into a jungle, a ship, a fairground or whatever else the script required.

One of the main considerations in casting *Clownaround* was to use dancers who were also gymnasts and who could negotiate Kenny's behemoth without endangering life and limb; another was to find acts as original as the set that was to house them, for there would be little point in showing off the great centrepiece with trite and tired old acts. Gene, therefore, spent whatever time he could searching for outstanding new talent.

One Saturday afternoon, on March 11th, 1972, while Gene was in the mid-West with Ruth Buzzi, looking at some speciality acts, Jeannie called Lois into the lounge at North Rodeo and confided to her that she was rather worried about something. Then she undid the dressing-gown she was wearing and displayed some bruise marks which had appeared on her body, and asked Lois what she thought they were. 'I thought she'd fallen and bumped herself,' Lois said, 'but she assured me she hadn't. Well, I had no idea what they could be and suggested she call the doctor, which she did. But the doctor was equally baffled and said maybe it had something to do with her "change of life". Obviously he couldn't diagnose what was wrong with her on the 'phone, without seeing the marks for himself, and Jeannie made an appointment with him for Monday morning. In the meantime, she had decided not to say anything to Gene about it, in case it turned out to be nothing at all. The following morning Gene arrived back from the mid-West and nothing was mentioned about the bruises. Then on Monday he and I drove off to the studios as usual, and Jeannie went to see her doctor. I expected to get a call from her at MGM a couple of hours later to tell me what it was all about, and when she still hadn't called by lunchtime, I began to get worried. And I wasn't able to mention anything to Gene, because he still didn't know. Well, finally, at two-thirty the 'phone rang on stage 27. It was Jeannie. All she said was would I please call Gene to the 'phone. There was something in her tone which told me I shouldn't ask any questions, and I called him. A few minutes later he disappeared into a dark corner of the stage and just wandered up and down. Jeannie had leukaemia and could be dead in three weeks.'

She was, in fact, to live for another fifteen months – in and out of hospitals, sometimes being allowed to return home after her regular check-ups; at other times, depending on how well she felt, she would have to remain in the hospital for four or five days.

From March to Christmas that year, Jeannie kept her illness as quiet as possible and did not even tell her family. But there came a point when it was no longer possible to keep it a secret, and just after Christmas she told her sister what was wrong. After that she was far less guarded.

'One day,' Lois said, 'Timothy was rummaging through some magazines and he came across a big feature article on leukaemia and asked Gene if that was what his mother had. He'd obviously heard the word in the house and was old enough to put two and two together. It was then that Jeannie decided to be perfectly frank about it and tell her children the truth – which she did. She saw no point in pretending otherwise. Timothy asked her whether leukaemia was fatal, and she said yes, it was. And once, I remember, Timothy saw her surrounded by lots of bottles of medicines and he asked her whether they were going to make her better. And very matter-of-factly she said: "No, nothing's going to make me better. They'll just help keep me around a bit longer." There was only one occasion in all the time she was ill that I saw her with her guard down – and that was a few days before she died. I went into her bedroom and she was looking out of the window with tears pouring down her cheeks. For the rest she was quite remarkable, and any visitors coming to cheer her up would leave the house far more cheered as a result of her conversation, than the other way round. She even joked about it. Once when Gene told her he was being honoured by the Thalians at a special banquet in Beverly Hills, as well as at the Arthur Freed Memorial Dinner – and that someone was coming from London to write his biography, she said to him: "One would think it was *you* who were dying of leukaemia, not me!" '

But Jeannie knew only too well how difficult a time it was for Gene, and how his heart could not possibly be in *Clownaround* any longer, and she determined to live as normal a life as possible until the end. 'Her spirit,' said Frank McCarthy, 'was incredible. There were times when, if you didn't know how ill she was, you would never have guessed. I never saw her with sadness in her eyes, and I never heard her complain. She was an unbelievable girl whom all her friends loved dearly.'

As soon as Jeannie knew she did not have long to live, she remained confined to her house as her doctor had told her to avoid crowds in case she caught an infection. She was also to avoid draughts. As a result, the little social life she and Gene had before her illness was reduced still further. The only occasion on which she socialised during the fifteen months, was when she accepted an invitation to a private screening of *Butterflies Are Free* which the producer, Mike Frankovich, arranged for her and Gene on the understanding that there were to be no more than a half a dozen people present. Another time she went to a department store to choose a communion dress for Bridget and to stock up on some clothes for Timothy. Even then she telephoned the store in advance, asked for a certain sales clerk whom she knew by name, and when she arrived immediately disappeared into a remote corner of the shop to avoid being near other people.

Right until the end, Jeannie continued to be as practical as she always had been, and discussed such things with Gene as whether her children should be allowed to see her when the end came, and the sort of services she wanted held. She did not, she said, want an open casket, and everything was to be as simple as possible. In truth, she really did not want a service of any kind, but because her children went to a Catholic school, she felt she would have to have one 'as a gesture'.

At one stage Gene suggested that if she would prefer not to discuss such matters, she should write her instructions on a piece of paper. She said she would, but ultimately became too weak to do so.

'In the last three weeks of her life,' said Lois, 'she told Thea, the housekeeper, and myself a number of things about the way she wanted the house run after she was gone. She showed us how to put the little corrections in her children's shoes, which no one but she had ever done before. She told us which of her friends would be the most suitable to take Bridget shopping, and even lectured us on such details as what place-mats were to be used for what meals. Just because she wasn't going to be around, there was no reason why the house should not continue to be run as it always had been.'

In the last couple of days of her life she was too weak to talk very much, and on May 10th, 1973, she died.

News of her death was not released to the Press until after the funeral, in accordance with her wishes to keep the service as simple and small as possible, and only a handful of her best friends, such as the writer Leonard Gershe, Frank McCarthy, Jean Simmons and Richard Brooks, Jack Haley, jun. and Natalie Wood and Bob Wagner, attended.

Jeannie's death was the sad climax to the unhappiest year of Gene's life, a year in which his mother died, as well as his friend and business manager, Noel Singer. Added to this, *Clownaround* closed a few weeks after it opened in Oakland, near San Francisco, when, during a week's lay-off prior to coming into Los Angeles, the producers ran out of money. Also, two of the dancers in the show fell from a height of eighty feet one night and were badly injured. Shortly after *Clownaround* closed, Gene had a cataract removed from his eye. And in June 1973 he learned of the death of Sean Kenny, who died at St Bartholomew's Hospital, London, from a kidney complaint.

After the failure of *Clownaround* and during Jeannie's illness, Gene refused work that took him more than a half an hour away from his home – no matter how attractive the offer, as there was no chance of Jeannie and the children accompanying him this time. As a consequence, he turned down several propositions – one of which was the chance to direct the film version of *Cabaret*. Cy Feuer, the producer, begged him to reconsider, but Gene had made up his mind and would not be swayed. 'I loved the idea of the whole show,' he said, 'and quite independent of Cy thought that Liza Minnelli was the only person who could play it – so at least our thinking was in harmony. But as wonderful as it would have been to do a picture with Liza, it would have meant my being in Munich for a year, and under the circumstances that was out of the question. I just couldn't do it.'

He did, however, recommend Bob Fosse and that story, at least, has a happier ending.

At Jeannie's insistence, he accepted six days' work in a comedy with Liv Ullman, Edward Albert and Binnie Barnes called *Forty Carats*, based on the long-running Broadway play about a New York socialite's infatuation with a boy eighteen years younger than herself. The producer was Mike Frankovich, and the director Milton Katselas – the same team that made *Butterflies Are Free*. Frankovich assured Gene there was no one else who could play the role of Billy, Miss Ullman's ex-husband, as well as he could, and promised to co-operate fully with him at such times as he might be needed at home or at hospital.

As Gene had not appeared in a film since 1966, and as Columbia Studios, the site of the filming, was no more than twenty minutes away from his home, he allowed himself to be persuaded. At least he would not have to worry about the numerous problems of pre-

and post-production, which had been his lot for the last five years, and the change he felt would do him good.

It did and he, in turn, did the film good by giving in it a light comedy performance of immense charm.

Two months after Jeannie's death, Gene took his family to Ireland for a month's holiday, stopping off in London to see his daughter Kerry, who had recently presented him with his first granddaughter. He returned to California in August with no fixed plans about anything, preferring to let life ride and see what happened. Since then he has appeared as one of the narrators of the highly successful film *That's Entertainment*; and in the summer of 1974 starred in a production of the stage musical *Take Me Along* in Dallas and St Louis. He was also invited by Frank Sinatra to be the only guest star on his 'unretirement' TV Special, *Ol' Blue Eyes is Back*.

In a number called, 'We Can't Do That Anymore', Gene and Sinatra, aided by the appropriate film clips, traded on audience nostalgia as they attempted to recreate a few merry moments from their early days at MGM.

As Gene evoked the past in a routine carefully choreographed to give the impression that he has lost little of his past vigour, the point forcefully driven home was, that regardless of what he has achieved, or might continue to achieve as a director, it is as a song-and-dance man by which he will, and is, remembered. Whatever his future ambitions, Gene has become part of entertainment history by arguing with his 'alter ego', teaching a reluctant Jerry Mouse to tap and a group of French kids to sing Gershwin, making heavenly music out of a piece of newspaper and a squeaky board, dancing from the Brooklyn docks to the top of the Empire State Building, splashing his way through a Californian rainstorm, and hoofing down a New York street attached to the lid of a dustbin.

Gene liberated the Hollywood musical and infused it with an infectious *joie de vivre*. He combined tap and ballet in a uniquely masculine way, and used the cinema's infinite potential with vigour and flair. He is one of the rare handful of originals who brought to the American cinema individuality and style. As Astaire dominated the thirties, so Gene monopolised the forties and fifties, in the process of which he irrevocably changed the face of the musical film and infused it with an exuberance it rarely achieves.

As the wound of Jeannie's death begins to heal, there is no doubt that Gene will continue to direct his attention to projects as challenging as *Clownaround*. It is simply not in his nature to do otherwise.

He claims he is a nicer, mellower person today than he was as a younger man, and one whose priorities have changed from making the world happy, to making his young family happy. One does not doubt him. But there is still too much energy in his body, too many ideas playing leapfrog in his imagination, for us to believe we have heard the last of him.

In a world starved of the special brand of innocence and joy with which he invested Harry the Hoofer in *The Time of Your Life* way back in 1939, Gene Kelly is more cherished than he realises.

Gene Kelly Filmography

(All dates refer to the year the film was released)

1 *For Me and My Gal* (1942) MGM.
   Produced by Arthur Freed, directed by Busby Berkeley.
   Judy Garland, Gene Kelly, George Murphy, Marta Eggerth, Ben Blue,
   Lucille Norman, Richard Quine, Keenan Wynn, Horace McNally.

2 *Pilot No. 5* (1943) MGM.
   Produced by B. P. Fineman, directed by George Sidney.
   Franchot Tone, Marsha Hunt, Gene Kelly, Van Johnson, Dick Simmons,
   Steve Geray, Howard Freeman, Frank Puglia.

3 *Dubarry Was a Lady* (1943) MGM.
   Produced by Arthur Freed, directed by Roy del Ruth.
   Red Skelton, Lucille Ball, Gene Kelly, Virginia O'Brien, Rags Ragland,
   Zero Mostel, Donald Meek, Douglas Dumbrille.

4 *Thousands Cheer* (1943) MGM.
   Produced by Joe Pasternak, directed by George Sidney.
   Kathryn Grayson, Gene Kelly, Mary Astor, John Boles, Ben Blue,
   Frances Rafferty, Mary Elliott.
   GUEST STARS: Mickey Rooney, Judy Garland, Red Skelton, Eleanor
   Powell, Ann Sothern, Virginia O'Brien, Lucille Ball, Lena Horne,
   Marsha Hunt, Frank Morgan, Marilyn Maxwell, Donna Reed, June
   Allyson, Gloria de Haven, Margaret O'Brien, John Conte, Sara Haden,

313

José Iturbi, Don Loper and Maxine Barrat, Kay Kyser, Bob Crosby and Benny Carter and their bands.

5 *The Cross of Lorraine* (1943) MGM.
Produced by Edwin Knopf, directed by Tay Garnett.
Jean-Pierre Aumont, Gene Kelly, Sir Cedric Hardwicke, Richard Whorf, Joseph Calleia, Peter Lorre, Hume Cronyn, Billy Roy, Tonio Stewart, Jack Lambert, Wallace Ford, Donald Curtis, Jack Edwards, jun., Richard Ryen.

6 *Cover Girl* (1944) Columbia.
Produced by Arthur Schwartz, directed by Charles Vidor.
Rita Hayworth, Gene Kelly, Lee Bowman, Phil Silvers, Jinx Falkenburg, Leslie Brooks, Eve Arden, Otto Kruger, Jess Barker, Curt Bois, Ed Brophy, Thurston Hall.

7 *Christmas Holiday* (1944) Universal.
Produced by Felix Jackson, directed by Robert Siodmak.
Deanna Durbin, Gene Kelly, Richard Whorf, Dean Harens, Gale Sondergaard, Gladys George, David Bruce.

8 *Anchors Aweigh* (1945) MGM.
Produced by Joe Pasternak, directed by George Sidney.
Frank Sinatra, Kathryn Grayson, Gene Kelly, José Iturbi, Dean Stockwell, Pamela Britton, Rags Ragland, Billy Gilbert, Edgar Kennedy, Henry O'Neill, Carlos Ramirez, Grady Sutton, Leon Ames, Sharon McManus.

9 *Ziegfeld Follies* (1946) MGM.
Produced by Arthur Freed, directed by Vincente Minnelli.
Fred Astaire, Lucille Ball, Lucille Bremer, Fanny Brice, Judy Garland, Kathryn Grayson, Lena Horne, Gene Kelly, James Melton, Victor Moore, Red Skelton, Esther Williams, William Powell, Edward Arnold, Marion Bell, Cyd Charisse, Hume Cronyn, William Frawley, Robert Lewis, Virginia O'Brien, Keenan Wynn.

10 *Living in a Big Way* (1947) MGM.
Produced by Pandro S. Berman, directed by Gregory LaCava.
Gene Kelly, Marie McDonald, Charles Winniger, Phyllis Thaxter, Spring Byington, Jean Adair, Clinton Sundberg, John Warburton.

11 *The Pirate* (1948) MGM.
   Produced by Arthur Freed, directed by Vincente Minnelli.
   Judy Garland, Gene Kelly, Walter Slezak, Gladys Cooper, Reginald Owen, George Zucco, The Nicholas Brothers, Lester Allen, Lola Deem.

12 *The Three Musketeers* (1948) MGM.
   Produced by Pandro S. Berman, directed by George Sidney.
   Lana Turner, Gene Kelly, June Allyson, Angela Lansbury, Van Heflin, Frank Morgan, Vincent Price, Keenan Wynn, John Sutton, Gig Young, Robert Coote, Reginald Owen, Ian Keith, Patricia Medina, Richard Stapley.

13 *Words and Music* (1948) MGM.
   Produced by Arthur Freed, directed by Norman Taurog.
   Mickey Rooney, Tom Drake, Marshall Thompson, Janet Leigh, Betty Garrett, Ann Sothern, Perry Como, Jeanette Nolan, Clinton Sundberg, Harry Antrim, Richard Quine, Ilka Gruning, Emory Parnell.
   GUEST STARS: Gene Kelly, Vera-Ellen, Judy Garland, Lena Horne, Cyd Charisse, Mel Tormé, Dee Turnell, The Blackburn Twins, Allyn McLerie.

14 *Take Me Out to the Ball Game* (1949) MGM.
   Produced by Arthur Freed, directed by Busby Berkeley.
   Frank Sinatra, Esther Williams, Gene Kelly, Betty Garrett, Edward Arnold, Jules Munshin, Richard Lane, Tom Dugan, Saul Gorss, Douglas Fowley, Eddie Parkes, James Burke.

15 *On the Town* (1950) MGM.
   Produced by Arthur Freed, directed by Gene Kelly and Stanley Donen.
   Gene Kelly, Frank Sinatra, Betty Garrett, Ann Miller, Jules Munshin, Vera-Ellen, Florence Bates, Alice Pearce, George Meader.

16 *The Black Hand* (1950) MGM.
   Produced by William H. Wright, directed by Richard Thorpe.
   Gene Kelly, J. Carrol Naish, Teresa Celli, Marc Lawrence, Frank Puglia, Barry Kelly, Mario Siletti, Peter Brocco.

17 *Summer Stock* (1950) MGM.
   Produced by Joe Pasternak, directed by Charles Walters.
   Judy Garland, Gene Kelly, Eddie Bracken, Gloria de Haven, Marjorie

Main, Phil Silvers, Ray Collins, Nita Bieber, Carleton Carpenter, Hans Conreid.

18 *An American in Paris* (1951) MGM.
Produced by Arthur Freed, directed by Vincente Minnelli.
Gene Kelly, Leslie Caron, Oscar Levant, Georges Guetary, Nina Foch, Martha Bamattre, Anna Q. Nilsson.

19 *It's a Big Country* (1952) MGM.
Produced by Robert Sisk, directed by Richard Thorpe, John Sturges, Charles Vidor, Don Weis, Clarence Brown, William Wellman, Don Hartman.
Ethel Barrymore, Gary Cooper, Van Johnson, Gene Kelly, Janet Leigh, Fredric March, William Powell, S. Z. Sakall, Marjorie Main, George Murphy, Keefe Brasselle, James Whitmore, Keenan Wynn, Nancy Davis, Lewis Stone, Leon Ames.

20 *Singin' in the Rain* (1952) MGM.
Produced by Arthur Freed, directed by Gene Kelly and Stanley Donen.
Gene Kelly, Donald O'Connor, Debbie Reynolds, Jean Hagen, Millard Mitchell, Rita Moreno, Douglas Fowley, Cyd Charisse, Madge Blake King Donovan, Kathleen Freeman, Bobby Watson, Tommy Farrell.

21 *The Devil Makes Three* (1952) MGM.
Produced by Richard Goldstone, directed by Andrew Marton.
Gene Kelly, Pier Angeli, Richard Rober, Richard Egan, Claus Clausen, Wilfred Seyferth, Margot Hielscher, Annie Rosar, Harold Benedict.

22 *Invitation to the Dance* (1956) MGM.
Produced by Arthur Freed, directed by Gene Kelly.
Igor Yousekevitch, Claire Sombert, Gene Kelly, Carol Haney, David Kasday, Irving Davies, Tamara Toumanova, Tommy Rall, Claude Bessy, Bellita, Dian Adams, Daphne Dalle, David Paltenghi.

23 *Crest of the Wave (Seagulls Over Sorrento)* (1954) MGM.
Produced and directed by John and Roy Boulting.
Gene Kelly, John Justin, Bernard Lee, Jeff Richards, Sidney James, Patrick Doonan, Ray Jackson, Fred Wayne, Patrick Barr, David Orr.

24 *Brigadoon* (1954) MGM.
Produced by Arthur Freed, directed by Vincente Minnelli.
Gene Kelly, Van Johnson, Cyd Charisse, Elaine Stewart, Barry Jones, Hugh Laing, Albert Sharpe, Virginia Bosier, Jimmy Thompson.

25 *Deep in my Heart* (1955) MGM.
Produced by Roger Edens, directed by Stanley Donen.
José Ferrer, Merle Oberon, Helen Traubel, Doe Avedon, Walter Pidgeon, Paul Henreid, Tamara Toumanova, Paul Stewart, Isobel Elsom, Douglas Fowley, Russ Tamblyn.
GUEST STARS: Rosemary Clooney, Gene and Fred Kelly, Jane Powell, Vic Damone, Ann Miller, William Olvis, Cyd Charisse, James Mitchell, Howard Keel, Tony Martin, Joan Weldon.

26 *It's Always Fair Weather* (1955) MGM.
Produced by Arthur Freed, directed by Gene Kelly and Stanley Donen.
Gene Kelly, Dan Dailey, Dolores Gray, Michael Kidd, David Burns, Jay C. Flippen, Hal March.

27 *The Happy Road* (1957) Released by MGM.
Produced and directed by Gene Kelly.
Gene Kelly, Barbara Laage, Bobby Clark, Brigitte Fossey, Roger Treville, Jess Hahn, Maryse Martin, Michael Redgrave, Van Doude.

28 *Les Girls* (1957) MGM.
Produced by Sol C. Siegel, directed by George Cukor.
Gene Kelly, Mitzi Gaynor, Kay Kendall, Taina Elg, Jacques Bergerac, Leslie Phillips, Henry Daniell, Patrick MacNee, Stephen Vercoe.

29 *The Tunnel of Love* (1958) MGM.
Produced by Joseph Fields and Martin Melcher, directed by Gene Kelly.
Doris Day, Richard Widmark, Gig Young, Gia Scala, Elizabeth Fraser, Elizabeth Wilson, Vikki Doughan, Doodles Weaver.

30 *Marjorie Morningstar* (1958) Warner Brothers.
Produced by Milton Sperling, directed by Irving Rapper.
Gene Kelly, Natalie Wood, Claire Trevor, Ed Wynn, Everett Sloane, Marty Milner, Carolyn Jones, Martin Balsam, Jesse White, Edward Byrnes.

31 *Inherit the Wind* (1960) United Artists.
Produced and directed by Stanley Kramer.
Spencer Tracy, Fredric March, Gene Kelly, Florence Eldridge, Dick

York, Donna Anderson, Harry Morgan, Elliott Reid, Philip Coolidge, Claude Akins, Paul Hartman, Jimmy Boyd.

32 *Let's Make Love* (1960) 20th Century Fox.
Produced by Jerry Wald, directed by George Cukor.
Marilyn Monroe, Yves Montand, Tony Randall, Frankie Vaughan, Wilfred Hyde White, David Burns, Michael David.
GUEST STARS: Milton Berle, Bing Crosby, Gene Kelly.

33 *Gigot* (1962) Seven Arts Production released by 20th Century Fox.
Produced by Kenneth Hyman, directed by Gene Kelly.
Jackie Gleason, Katherine Kath, Gabrielle Dorziat, Jean Lefebvre, Jacques Marin, Albert Remy, Yvonne Constant, Germaine Delbat.

34 *What a Way to Go!* (1964) Released by 20th Century Fox.
Produced by Arthur P. Jacobs, directed by J. Lee Thompson.
Shirley MacLaine, Paul Newman, Robert Mitchum, Dean Martin, Gene Kelly, Bob Cummings, Dick van Dyke, Reginald Gardiner, Margaret Dumont, Lou Nova, Fifi D'Orsay, Maurice Marsac, Wally Vernon, Jane Wald, Lenny Kent.

35 *The Young Girls of Rochefort* (1968) Warner Brothers Release.
Produced by Mag Bodard, directed by Jacques Demy.
Catherine Deneuve, François Dorleac, George Chakiris, Grover Dale, Gene Kelly, Danielle Darrieux, Jacques Perrin, Michel Piccoli.

36 *A Guide for the Married Man* (1967) 20th Century Fox.
Produced by Frank McCarthy, directed by Gene Kelly.
Walter Matthau, Robert Morse, Inger Stevens, Sue Ann Langdon, Claire Kelly, Linda Harrison, Elaine Devry.
GUEST STARS: Lucille Ball, Jack Benny, Polly Bergen, Joey Bishop, Ben Blue, Sid Caesar, Art Carney, Wally Cox, Marty Ingels, Ann Morgan Guilbert, Jeffrey Hunter, Sam Jaffe, Jayne Mansfield, Hal March, Louis Nye, Carl Reiner, Phil Silvers, Terry-Thomas.

37 *Hello Dolly!* (1969) 20th Century Fox.
Produced by Ernest Lehman, directed by Gene Kelly.
Barbra Streisand, Walter Matthau, Michael Crawford, Louis Armstrong, Marianne McAndrew, E. J. Peaker, Danny Lockin, Joyce Ames. Tommy Tune, Judy Knaiz.

38 *The Cheyenne Social Club* (1970) A National General Production.
Produced and directed by Gene Kelly.
James Stewart, Henry Fonda, Shirley Jones, Sue Ann Langdon, Dabbs Greer, Elaine Devry, Robert Middleston, Arc Johnson, Jackie Russell.

39 *Forty Carats* (1973) Columbia.
Produced by Mike Frankovich, directed by Milton Katselas.
Liv Ullman, Edward Albert, Gene Kelly, Binnie Barnes, Deborah Raffin, Billy Green Bush, Nancy Walker, Don Porter, Rosemary Murphy.

Index

325

328

330